BASIC
Computer Programming

BASIC Computer Programming

THOMAS C. BARTEE
Harvard University

1817

HARPER & ROW, PUBLISHERS, New York
Cambridge, Hagerstown, Philadelphia, San Francisco,
London, Mexico City, São Paulo, Sydney

Project Editor: Pamela Landau
Production Manager: Marion A. Palen
Compositor: Science Typographers
Printer and Binder: The Maple Press Company
Art Studio: Vantage Art Inc.

BASIC Computer Programming

Library of Congress Cataloging in Publication Data

Bartee, Thomas C
Basic computer programming.

Bibliography: p.
Includes index.
1. Basic (Computer program language)
2. Electronic digital computers—Programming.
I. Title.
QA76.73.B3B37   001.64′24   80-27357
ISBN 0-06-040517-1

Contents

Preface

The purpose of this book is to introduce computer programming using the BASIC language. Many programming examples are included to clarify explanations; and tables are included to make coverage of the language more complete. There are questions at the end of each chapter and answers to selected questions at the end of the book.

Good programming requires more than a knowledge of how to write individual program statements. Techniques that make program writing better organized and less prone to error have now been developed and are widely used by competent programmers. The techniques that are explained include structured programming, top-down design, and modular program organization. These techniques result in making programs more readable and aid in program debugging. This material is very important and should be learned and used as early as possible.

The fundamental materials needed to use a computer system are also presented; these include saving programs and files, correcting errors, logging on and off the computer, the concept of work space, and so on. Some concepts concerning different types of computer systems and their characteristics are also included.

The intent of this book, therefore, is to introduce computer programming using the BASIC programming language in as clear and understandable a manner as is possible and also to include enough material so that useful, substantial programs can be written. In order to reach this goal, each chapter includes an introduction giving objectives for the chapter, a summary including appropriate tables of material for future reference, and enough programming examples to reinforce each principle introduced.

The first two chapters of the book introduce such computer concepts as hardware, software, memories, time-sharing, programming languages, and so on. In addition, operational data on computer usage including getting on and off the computer and correcting errors in programs are also presented. This information is necessary for successful computer system usage.

Chapters 3 through 6 serve as the introduction to the BASIC language, presenting the fundamental BASIC statements and illustrating their usage. Flowcharts are also introduced along with control statements and their usage.

Chapter 7 explains some of the techniques used in modern programming practice, focusing on the ideas of structured and modular programs, program readability, and program documentation. These concepts are illustrated in the text examples so as to reinforce the underlying principles previously put forth.

Chapters 8 and 9 present additional features of BASIC and present examples of programs written for business, science, economics, the social sciences, mathematics, and other areas. These chapters also include examples of computer graphics, instructional programs, and the use of arrays.

The final chapter gives an idea of the way data are organized in a computer. It includes the concepts of files, records, and sorting, searching, and merging operations.

The BASIC programming language was developed by J. Kemeny and T. Kurtz at Dartmouth College in the 1960s. Since that time BASIC has become one of the most widely used programming languages and the best known language for interactive systems. Most computer manufacturers now have BASIC systems programs for their computers and the language is also very popular on microcomputers and small "personal" computers. The American National Standards Institute (ANSI) has developed a BASIC language standard (refer to the References at the end of the book) to help standardize details of the language. The ANSI standard is used as a point of reference in this book. At the same time the variations in language detail for the major computer systems are pointed out when appropriate.

The author would like to thank Professors J. E. Castek, F. A. Ciccarelli, J. K. Mullin, and A. Weinstein of the University of Wisconsin, Niagara College, the University of Western Ontario, and Nassau Community College, respectively, for acting as advisors on this book. Their comments and suggestions were greatly appreciated.

Thomas Quentin Bartee contributed significantly to this book during its preparation and the book owes a great deal to his efforts.

THOMAS C. BARTEE

Chapter 1
Computer Systems

The subject of this book is a computer programming language called BASIC. After learning this language it is possible to use a computer to process data and to solve problems in many areas including business, mathematics, the social sciences, engineering, chemistry, physics, and other "hard" sciences. Before using this language, however, certain facts about computer systems and procedures for computer usage should be learned.

Chapters 1 and 2 present background information about computer systems which needs to be understood before a user can successfully use a computer. Also, because the computer user will be faced with interacting with a specific computer system, some preliminary data about that system must be acquired before it can be used. For example, in order to give the computer instructions, the user must first get its attention, and, for many systems, this involves establishing the user's identity and right to use the computer. This is called *logging in*. After using the computer the user must tell the computer system he or she is finished by *logging out*.

Logging in and logging out require learning some specific procedures for the computer system being used; Chapter 2 deals with this subject.

In addition, certain facts and some computer terminology need to be understood in order to use a computer effectively and to better comprehend why computer systems are organized the way they are.

Chapter 1 presents some background material on computer systems, providing a general introduction in this area. Chapter 2 is primarily concerned with the operational procedures for using a computer.

1-1 OBJECTIVES

Hardware, Software, Programming, and Coding

The concepts of hardware and software are introduced. Programs, programming, and coding are then defined so that the programmer's role in using a computer can be understood.

General-Purpose and Special-Purpose Computers

The two types of computers, general-purpose and special-purpose computers, are discussed; their similarities, differences, purposes, and uses are given.

Computer Organization

Some information concerning the physical organization of computers is presented and the role of the devices used in computers is discussed.

Types of Computer Operation

Computers can be used in several different modes of operation. Several of these are explained, with particular emphasis on the interactive usage of computers generally found in BASIC systems.

Programming Languages

The BASIC language is one of several widely used computer languages. The reasons for having different programming languages are discussed along with some details concerning the BASIC language.

1-2 HARDWARE, SOFTWARE, PROGRAMMING, AND CODING

There are two fundamental aspects of a digital computer. First, there is the physical computer itself, which consists of the metal boxes, semiconductor devices, printed circuit boards, printer(s), lights, and so on, which have been assembled to make the computer. This assembly of physical devices is called the *hardware*. Computer designers have seen to it that these pieces interact in a logical manner so that a computer results.

A program, or list of instructions to the computer, is an example of *software*. In most cases, the program is first written (on paper) and is then read into the computer memory from a keyboard, punched cards, or some other input device. Then the list of instructions is performed by the computer. This is called *running* the program.

The process of preparing the instructions for the computer is called *programming*. In general, the entire activity of formulating the approach to solving a problem and preparing the instructions to the computer is called *programming*. The final step of writing the specific instructions to the computer is often called *coding*.

This book will primarily be concerned with software. Some facts about computer organization and functioning are useful in order to use a computer effectively, however, and these are discussed in the following sections of this chapter. Then programming languages and modes of operation will be discussed.

1-3 GENERAL-PURPOSE AND SPECIAL-PURPOSE COMPUTERS

A *general-purpose digital computer* is designed to solve a wide variety of problems. An important characteristic of a general-purpose computer is that it has a memory which stores the set of instructions, or program, that has been prepared. The general-purpose ability of the computer comes because after one program has been read in and executed, another different program can be read into the same memory and executed.

The remarkable thing about a general-purpose computer is that programs designed to solve problems in different areas can be executed one right after the other. For instance, a program to prepare a payroll can be run followed by a chemistry problem, followed by a test evaluation program for a psychology course.

The *special-purpose computer* is designed to handle only a restricted class of problems. A given special-purpose computer might control the lights in a theater, for example, or sequence traffic lights, but it could not perform other functions. A general-purpose computer can generally be programmed to perform the same functions as a special-purpose computer, but the special-purpose computer may be simpler to construct. This book will only be concerned with general-purpose computers.

1-4 COMPUTER ORGANIZATION—HARDWARE

A modern digital computer can be divided into four major sections. In using a computer it is useful to know what these sections are and the general functions of each section. Figure 1-1 shows a block design of a computer with these sections outlined.

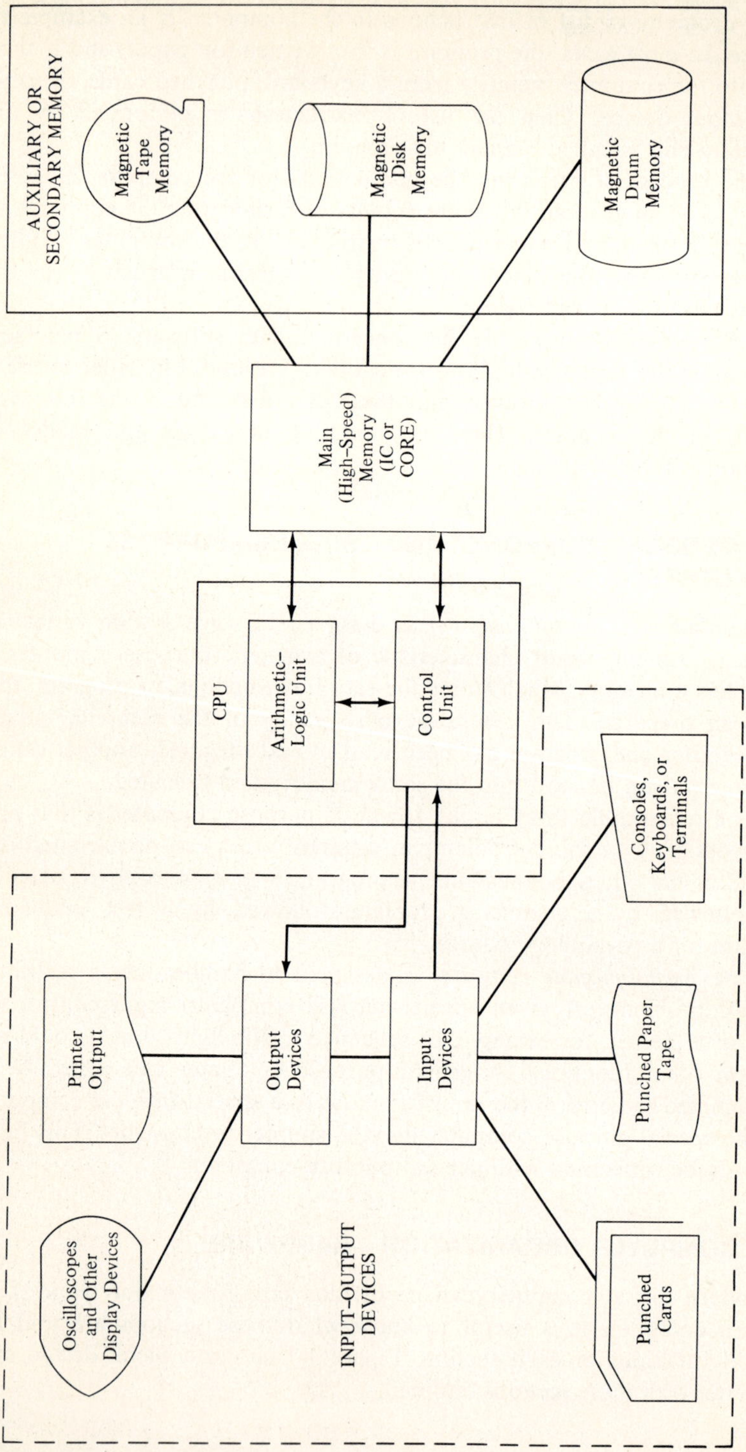

Fig. 1-1 Block Diagram of a Computer

Input-Output Devices

In order to use a computer, both the program to be executed and the data must be entered into the computer. For BASIC users, the input device will generally be a keyboard as shown in Figure 1-2. The output device will be a printer or a cathode-ray tube (CRT) display as shown in Figure 1-3. A keyboard-printer or keyboard-CRT display combination is called a *terminal*. Computers use many other input-output devices, including punched card readers, punched tape readers, optical devices to read bar codes (on grocery items, for instance), large high-speed printers, and so forth.

When a terminal is located some distance from a computer, telephone lines are sometimes used to make a connection. In this case an *acoustic*

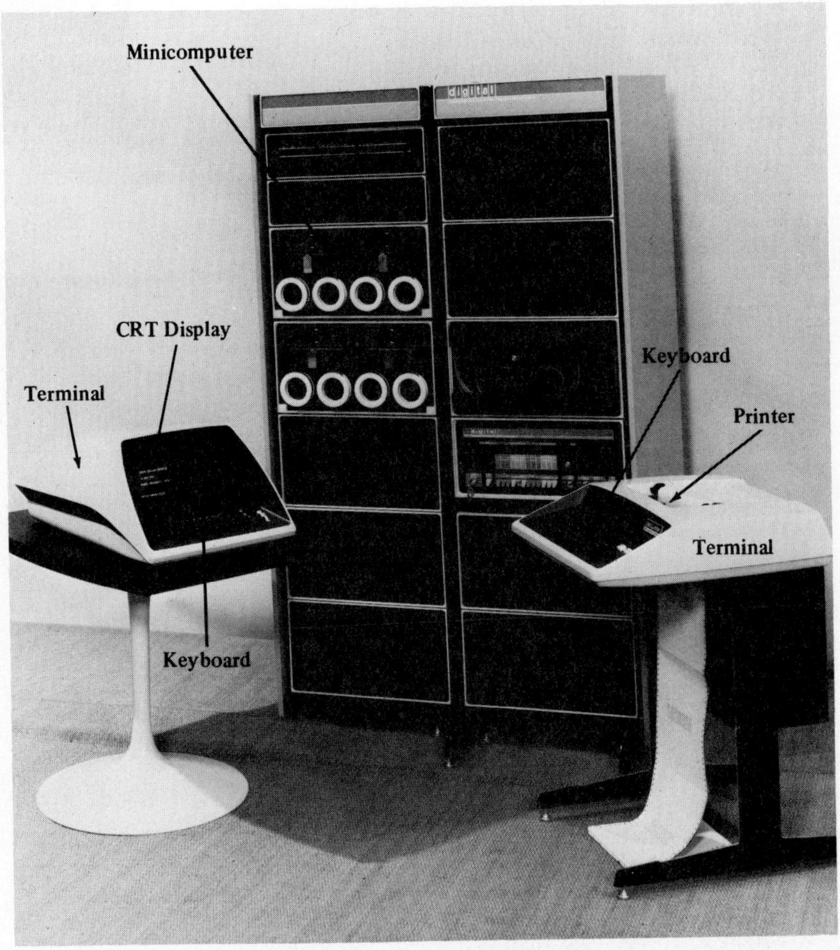

Fig. 1-2 Two Terminals and a Minicomputer (Courtesy DEC Corp.)

Fig. 1-3 Terminal with CRT Display (Courtesy Honeywell Corp.)

coupler is used which converts electrical signals from the keyboard to audio. These signals are then transmitted through the telephone system and a device at the other end of the line converts these audio signals back to electrical signals which are read and interpreted by the computer. The coupler also converts signals from the computer to the terminal to a form suitable for displaying or printing.

When an acoustic coupler is used, it is necessary to dial the computer's phone number and then place the telephone headset in the coupler before the terminal can be used. (More information on terminal usage will be found in later sections.)

Some terminals contain a *modem* which connects to telephone lines and generates electrical signals to the computer. Modums are generally permanently fastened to a telephone line and a disc is provided for dialing a computer number.

The Central Processing Unit (CPU)

The CPU includes an *Arithmetic-Logic-Unit* (ALU) which does the actual calculations—including arithmetic and logical operations—and a *control unit* which interprets the instructions in the program, directing the arithmetic-logic-unit, memories, and other computer sections.

The Main Memory (or Inner Memory)

The main memory is generally a *high-speed* semiconductor memory. This memory holds the data and instructions that are to be immediately used by the arithmetic-logic-unit and control unit. The important thing about this memory is that anything stored there can be accessed or replaced at a high speed. Often, a memory access requires less than one millionth of a second.

Auxiliary or Secondary Memory

The integrated circuit (or sometimes core) memory used in the CPU is fast but is also so expensive that less expensive secondary or auxiliary memory devices are required to supplement the main memory. These devices provide inexpensive bulk storage. The auxiliary memory, however, has a much slower access time than does the main memory. Data and programs are moved from the auxiliary memory into the main memory when needed and transferred from the main memory to the auxiliary memory when necessary or convenient.

Popular auxiliary memory devices are: floppy disk drives (Figure 1-4), fixed disk drives and removable disk packs (Figure 1-5), large magnetic tape drives (Figure 1-6), small cassette tape drives, and so on.

Fig. 1-4 Floppy Disk drive (Courtesy DEC Corp.)

Fig. 1-5 Disk Drive (Courtesy DEC Corp.)

Fig. 1-6 3470 Magnetic Tape Drive (Courtesy IBM Corp.)

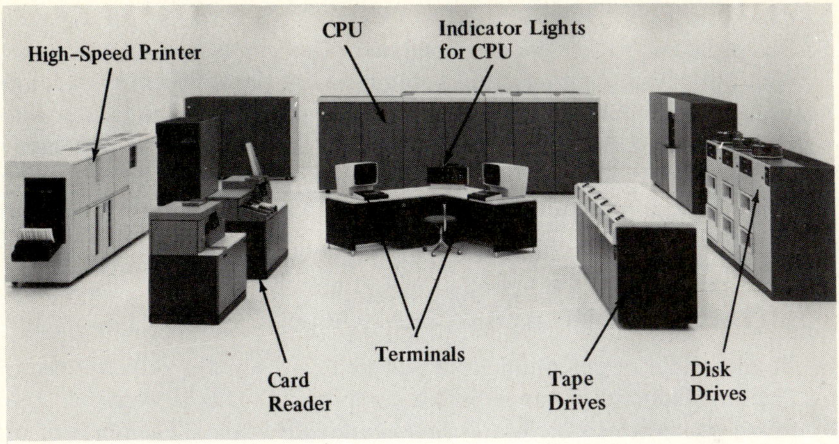

Fig. 1-7 3033 Computer System (Courtesy IBM Corp.)

In large computers such as that in Figure 1-7, the CPU and auxiliary memories are generally in separate cabinets and spread over a considerable area. In minicomputers and microcomputers the CPU can be on one or more printed circuit boards or "chips" and the auxiliary memories can be anything from conventional "audio" tape cassettes to inexpensive floppy disks.

1-5 SOFTWARE: APPLICATION PROGRAMS AND SYSTEMS PROGRAMS

There are two general categories of programs: *applications programs* and *systems programs*.

The programs written by computer users to solve problems, process data, and so on, are examples of applications programs. These programs are generally written in an *application language* such as BASIC, FORTRAN, or COBOL. The programs shown in this book and written by the book's readers will be applications programs.

Systems programs are programs prepared to aid the applications programmer and to coordinate use of the computer facilities. As examples: (1) the BASIC programs that are written must be translated by a computer program into the actual language of the computer before operation. This is done by a systems program called a *BASIC Interpreter* or *BASIC Compiler*. (2) When several terminals are connected to the same computer and systems resources must be shared, a program called an *operating system* (or, sometimes, a *monitor*) is used. An operating system calls the BASIC system when required, logs you on and off the computer, manages the memories, and so on. The operating system programs direct the operation of other programs and coordinate the use of main memory and auxiliary memory.

It should be made clear that the computer user interacts with the hardware through the systems programs and not directly. As a result, BASIC programs written for one computer often can be run on a different computer because the translator accommodates the differences in hardware. A program that can be moved from computer to computer is said to be *transportable*. One of the reasons BASIC is so popular is that many different computer manufacturers provide BASIC translators and therefore BASIC programs (except for some variations, which will be discussed) are transportable.

1-6 TYPES OF COMPUTER OPERATION

In the early days of computing, the punched card was the primary means for entering data and programs into a computer. The cards were prepared by a card punch which perforates cards with coded holes. The operator of a card punch has a keyboard resembling a typewriter keyboard and simply "types" the program and data, thus entering them into cards. This is called *keypunching* a program or data.

The punched cards were then gathered into decks which were generally kept together using elastic bands for small operations, or card files for large users. A deck of cards containing a program and data was submitted to an operator who placed the cards in a card reader attached to the computer. The computer then read the cards, executed the program, and printed output results on a high-speed printer.

In order to use the computer facilities more efficiently, operating system programs were developed which controlled computer operations and could read in several applications programs, one right after the other, the operating system then alternating operation of the programs. The reason for this is that peripheral devices (such as the auxiliary memory disks, tape drives, and input-output devices such as card readers, printers, and so on) all operate slowly compared to the high speeds attainable by the CPU. The operating system would therefore place one program (or a part thereof) in high-speed memory, start the program, and when a peripheral device was called for, another program would be started and operated until it called for a peripheral, at which time the first program might be restarted or a third program might be started.

In this way, by interleaving the operation of the programs, the CPU and peripherals were more fully used, thereby increasing the *throughput* or total work performed by the computer.

The above interleaving of program operation by an operating system is called *multiprogramming* the computer. After the great success of multiprogramming systems, operating systems were expanded so that a terminal connected to the computer could also be used at the same time that other programs were being run. Finally, as terminal usage became more popular, the *time sharing* of several terminals on a computer became a widely used computer practice. Time sharing refers to the interleaved use of time on a computing system which enables two or more users to execute programs concurrently.

Further, in computer jargon, if you are using a terminal connected to a computer, and the computer responds directly to your actions, the computer system is said to be an *interactive* system.

A BASIC programmer using a terminal connected to a time-shared system may find that the system reacts so quickly that the time sharing does not bother him or her. In times of heavy activity, however, the system's responses to the user may include noticeable delays. For instance, in most systems, when a key is depressed on the keyboard, the printer or CRT response of a character being printed may actually involve the computer. In these systems electrical signals are generated (when the key is depressed) which are read by the computer. The computer then prints this character on the printer or CRT. This is called *echoing* the character and ensures the terminal user that the computer has successfully read the character. Hopefully, this echoing will occur so quickly it will not affect keyboard operation, but if the computer is very busy, delays may occur and it may be necessary to slow down typing. For computer systems with only a few users this is rarely a problem.

1-7 PROGRAMMING LANGUAGES

One of the most important steps forward in computer usage came when users discovered that it was possible to have a computer translate strings of characters in one language into another language. The earliest translations were from relatively simple languages called *assembly languages* into the computer's actual language, which is generally called *machine language*.

The next step came when programmers decided more ambitious translations were possible. A language called FORTRAN (for Formula Translation) was invented which was specifically intended for scientific and engineering purposes. This language was designed so that it was reasonably easy to write scientific formulas and to solve scientific and engineering problems using it, but also so that it was possible for a computer to translate it without great effort (unlike natural languages such as English, French, and so on, which are difficult to translate).

FORTRAN became, and still is, a great success. Another language, COBOL (for Common Business Oriented Language) was invented for business users and it is a considerable success in commercial circles.

As time passed more and more languages have been invented that are intended to improve or enlarge on earlier language capabilities.

The BASIC language is the most used of the newer languages. Its popularity is attested to in studies run by professional societies concerning language usage. The advant of low-priced minicomputers and microcomputer systems has further increased BASIC's popularity because it is particularly well adapted for use on small computers.

BASIC has a characteristic that makes it particularly attractive for use in interactive systems. BASIC programs consist of a sequence of statements, each statement giving the computer a specific order to execute. It is possible to translate and then execute these statements one at a time. Thus a computer can translate and then run one or more statements from one user's program, skip to another user's program and run a few statements, and so on. This makes the time sharing of several terminals connected to the same computer easier to implement.

A systems program which translates and then executes each statement of an applications program before proceeding to the next statement is called an *interpreter*. A *compiler*, on the other hand, is a translator which translates an entire program as a unit. FORTRAN and COBOL are normally compiled, and in their design little or no consideration is given to making the statements independently translatable. On the other hand, BASIC can be conveniently operated in an interpretive mode, by design.

An interpreter translates a program a statement at a time. This means the interpreter can interpret one or two statements, execute them, and then do one or two more. This facilitates time sharing because the main memory is generally limited in size and pieces of programs can be read back and forth between auxiliary memory and main memory while the program is being translated and run. A compiler translates an entire program and the machine code thus generated is run as a unit (although sections can be read back and forth between secondary and main memory in a time-shared mode.)

It should be noted that the BASIC system is a set of programs that not only provides for translation from a program written in BASIC into machine language but also provides several other services to the computer user. These services will be discussed in the next chapter and include running a program, editing a program, saving a program on a secondary memory device, and so on.

1-8 SUMMARY

This chapter has introduced several important concepts. The terms *hardware* and *software* were defined as were *programmer* and *program*.

The organization of computers centers around four sections: (1) input-output; (2) The Central Processing Unit (CPU); (3) main (high-speed) memory; (4) secondary or auxiliary memory. The CPU controls operation of the computer, reading and interpreting the program which is stored in memory. The reasons for having both a main memory, which is generally Integrated Circuit, and an auxiliary memory concern cost. The main memory is high speed (all sections of the memory can be quickly accessed) but is expensive; the auxiliary memory uses devices (disks and tapes, for example) that are slower but cost far less per character stored.

Applications programs are those written by computer users to solve problems and process data; systems programs provide services to applications programmers, including translation from such applications oriented languages as BASIC and FORTRAN into machine (computer) language. Systems programs also control computer resources so they are effectively used and the principal types of programs for this are called monitors or operating systems.

Systems programs also make it possible for several jobs or users to run on a computer concurrently. This makes it possible to operate a computer in a time-shared mode where several users with terminals use the computer at the same time. When the user and the computer interact on a second-by-second basis (the user inputs something and the computer responds at once) the mode of operations is said to be *interactive*. BASIC systems generally operate in an interactive mode. Unlike FORTRAN and COBOL, BASIC is specifically designed to be translated by an interpreter, a program which translates an applications program a statement at a time. FORTRAN and COBOL are generally translated into machine language by a compiler.

Questions

1. Why are there two categories of memory: high-speed main memory and auxiliary memory?
2. What is an acoustic coupler?
3. Which of these programs are applications program and which are systems programs?
   (a) a payroll program
   (b) a FORTRAN compiler
   (c) a program to process data from an interferometer
   (d) an operating system
4. Why does interleaving the operation of several programs by an operating system increase the throughput of a computer system?
5. Define time sharing.
6. What is the difference between an interpreter and a compiler?
7. Categorize each of the following items as either hardware or software:
   (a) payroll program
   (b) CPU
   (c) BASIC compiler
   (d) FORTRAN compiler
   (e) terminal

Chapter 2
Programming Interactive Computer Systems

In order to use an interactive computer system it is necessary to learn the operational procedures for that system. For instance, there will generally be a procedure to log in, to log out, and to ask for the BASIC system. There are other less obvious aspects of computer usage that also must be learned, however, For example, it is inevitable that typing errors will occur in using the computer and these must somehow be corrected using a procedure that has been established and that must be understood by the user.

This chapter discusses those procedures that must be learned to interact with a computer.

2-1 OBJECTIVES

Terminal Usage

The keyboard on the computer terminal, which is used to communicate with the computer, will generally have some special keys and functions. These need to be understood before the terminal can be used, and are discussed in this section.

Logging In and Out

The procedure for logging in the computer and for logging out at the end of a session must be learned and are discussed here.

Operating a Program—Work Space

In order to run a program on a computer the program must first be entered into the computer; the computer must then be ordered to execute (run) the program. The procedures for this are discussed. The important concept of *work space* and its assignment to a user by the computer system is also discussed.

Correcting Errors and Listing

The procedures for correcting typing and other errors that may occur in program preparation must be learned. Also, often after a program has been read into the computer it is desirable to *list* the program on the user's terminal. This subject is also discussed in this chapter.

2-2 TERMINALS

As has been discussed, a keyboard plus either a CRT display or printer which can be connected to a computer is called a terminal. It would be nice to report that the keyboards in general usage all have the same format and characters but this is not the case. Fortunately, the differences between keyboards are not overwhelming (all have letters and numbers plus most punctuation marks). Generally the differences concern several control or special facility characters.

For many years the Teletype series of keyboards were pretty much unofficial standards in the industry because of their wide usage. Some of the newer keyboards have what their manufacturers consider to be improved layouts and often additional keys which provide extra facilities. In order to introduce keyboard operation we will use the Teletype keyboard as an example. Differences between these keyboards and others can then be learned quickly. It is primarily a question of finding how certain functions have been implemented on a particular keyboard.

Figure 2-1 shows a Teletype keyboard layout. The principal difference between this and conventional typewriter keyboards lies in the CTRL (Control) key and the presence of several other special keys.

In general, if the SHIFT key is depressed and another key with two single characters on it is then depressed, the upper character will be printed. For example, if the key labeled

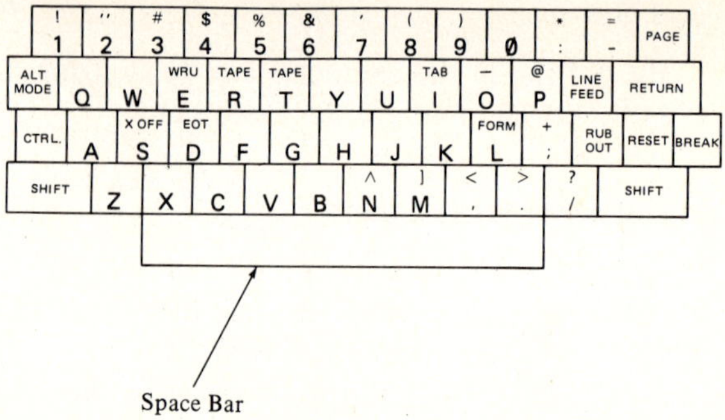

Fig. 2-1 Teletype Keyboard Layout

is depressed while the SHIFT key is held down, the # will be printed, not the 3.

If, however, you press the SHIFT key and then a letter key with several letters at the top, for example,

then nothing will be typed. These keys are to be used with the CTRL key which selects the upper characters when depressed.

Some of these special keys on the teletype are listed in Table 2-1 along with their functions. More details of their operation will be given as the functions are introduced.

Table 2-1 TELETYPE KEY FUNCTIONS

RETURN	Returns the typing head to the beginning of the next line, signaling the computer that you have finished typing a line. We use ⟨CR⟩ to denote this key.
LINE FEED	Advances the paper in the teletypewriter one line.
RUB OUT	In some systems, if this key is depressed before RETURN, it deletes the line just typed so that the line is not recorded by the computer.
BREAK	This key is used on some systems to stop a program (or the automatic retyping of a program). ⟨CTRL C⟩ is also often used.
ALT MODE or ESC	In some systems, if this key is depressed before RETURN, it deletes the line just typed.
REPT	This key, when depressed simultaneously with another key, causes a repeat of the key depressed.
HERE IS	This key is used in punching a paper tape to produce holes in the tape for a leader or trailer.

It is a good idea to inquire as to whether there are special features of the keyboard you are using. An important consideration is the carriage return—line feed functions(s). A *carriage return*, technically speaking, simply returns the print positioning mechanism so the next character printed will be at the beginning of the line. A *line feed* advances the roller so that the next character will be printed on the next line. In most systems, however, these functions are combined in a RETURN key, which causes both the carriage to return and the roller position to advance when depressed. You should find out if this is the case for your system. In this book, a carriage return, which will often be designated ⟨CR⟩,[1] will stand for both a carriage return and a line feed.

There is a substantial chance that the computer system to be used will require you to *log in* (sign on) the computer before you can use it and to *log out* when you have completed your work.[2] The procedures for logging in and out a computer may differ significantly from system to system.

For most systems, certain information must be given to the computer before it will allow you to use it. This information often includes (1) your name; (2) your account or identification number, and; (3) a password. Which of these must be given to the computer and the exact procedure for entering them depends on your computer system. In some time-shared systems and in personal or single user computers, no log on is required or a very minimal procedure (such as simply typing BASIC) is required.

Some computer systems offer *prompting* during log in, spelling out what information you are to provide. For example, after the user types "log in," such a system might print (on your terminal)

```
NAME
```

You are then to type your name followed by a carriage return ⟨CR⟩. This is an important point; information given to the computer is generally entered by pressing the ⟨CR⟩ key on the terminal; the computer will wait for this signal before proceeding.

In a prompting system, the computer might then print

```
ACCOUNT NUMBER
```

after which you would type your account number followed by a carriage return ⟨CR⟩.

Finally, the password would be asked for by the computer, printing

```
PASSWORD
```

You then enter your password followed by the carriage return.

[1] This is often simply a RETURN key and most keyboards have a RETURN key which causes both a carriage return and line feed.

[2] This is sometimes called *logging on* and *logging off*.

In some systems little prompting is used. For instance, in the ARPANET system, which is a nationwide network of computers interconnected by telephone lines, to log in you simply type

```
LOGIN JONES      C7A4B
```

(*Your name*) ((*Your password*)

As can be seen, to log in you type LOGIN followed by your name and then the password and a carriage return. The system then prints

```
ACCOUNT NUMBER
```

You are then to type your account number followed by a ⟨CR⟩.

In some systems it is only necessary to type LOGIN (or sometimes HELLO or some other phrase).

Logging out, or signing off, is a similar process. This is accomplished by typing a BYE (or perhaps LOGOFF, EXIT, FIN, or LOGOUT) in some systems or a control C (hold the control key (CTRL) down and then press C) in other systems. You will have to find out whether you must sign off to both the BASIC system and the operating system or if a single BYE will do.

When you log in or log out, the computer is liable to print some information it feels is relevant; for instance, the time when you log in or out, notices of when the system will be closed down, new program releases, and so on.

Clearly, local operating procedures must be obtained before a terminal can be used. One other important point arises here. What has been accessed is often the operating system. If you want to operate BASIC programs, you must ask the operating system to put you in the BASIC system. Generally, this is accomplished by simply typing BASIC followed by a carriage return ⟨CR⟩ but this should be checked because it may vary from computer system to system.

Comment

In some systems it is necessary to name programs before they can be run. For instance, when the BASIC system is entered, several BASIC systems will immediately type

```
OLD OR NEW
```

You must then type NEW (and then a "carriage return") if you have a new program. The computer will then type

```
NEW PROGRAM NAME
```

You then type some name you wish to give the program (JACK, for example).

This will give the program you type the name JACK. Generally numbers can be placed in the program name (although not as the first character). Thus you can have a JACK1 or JACK2, and so on.

A later section will deal with saving programs and recalling them; for now we consider only entering and running new programs without saving them.

If the above seems overly complex, it really is not. Some computers must service many different users and may provide many other program systems than BASIC. Also, the need to identify users for bookkeeping and security purposes seems evident in large systems.

2-3 RUNNING A PROGRAM AND THE CONCEPT OF WORK SPACE

So far, procedures for logging in the computer and then calling the BASIC system have been discussed. In order to actually enter and run a program a little more information is required.

Once the computer has been logged in and the BASIC system called for, the computer will type "READY." Now, in order to enter a program we simply type the program on the keyboard. In order to illustrate this a short, very simple, program is as follows:

```
10 PRINT "ALLS WELL"
20 END
```

This program consists of two *statements*, a PRINT statement and an END statement. In BASIC, each statement is numbered using what is called a *line number*. The above program has the line numbers 10 and 20. Line numbers always occur at the beginning of a statement and each statement must have a line number. Line numbers can have up to four digits in most systems so 0 to 9999 can be used in line numbers.

When a program is run, the statements are translated and executed by the computer in the order of their line numbers. Thus, for the above program the PRINT statement is executed before the END statement.

This simple program does only one thing; it causes the computer to print ALLS WELL. Details of how this program operates will be given in the next chapter. The END statement marks the end of the program; every program must have an END statement with the highest line number in the program.

Figure 2-2 shows an entire session on a terminal in which the above program is run. The material printed by the computer is underlined, the material entered by the terminal user is not underlined.

PRINTOUT FROM TERMINAL	COMMENTS
@LOGIN BARTEE AX43B	User types this to log in
JOB 13 ON TTY23 26-Apr-80 08:40	
PREVIOUS LOGIN: 26-APR-80 07:43	Computer types some information for the user
@BASIC	User asks for BASIC system
READY, FOR HELP TYPE HELP.	Computer says BASIC is ready
10 PRINT "ALLS WELL"	User enters the BASIC program
20 END	
RUN	User types "RUN" causing program to be run
NONAME 08:41 26-APR-80	Computer gives name to program and lists time program was run
ALLS WELL	BASIC program prints "ALLS WELL"
TIME: 0.10 SECS.	Computer then prints amount of time used
READY	Computer says it is ready for more instructions
BYE	User signs off
KILLED JOB 13, USER BARTEE	Computer gives summary information

Fig. 2.2 A complete terminal session

In this example the user first logged in, and then called for the BASIC system by typing BASIC. The BASIC system program typed back READY and the user then entered his program.

The program was run by the user simply typing the word RUN. An important point occurs here: the word RUN is a *systems command*. The BASIC program system provides a language translation and operation facility for BASIC and also several other facilities to the user. These include the ability to run programs, list programs, renumber the line numbers, and so on. Each of these services is provided when the user simply types a systems command such as RUN, LIST, RESEQUENCE, and so on. These commands are *not* BASIC language statements or parts of a program, they are *systems commands*. The BASIC system distinguishes systems commands from BASIC program statements by the presence or absence of the line numbers. Systems commands do not begin with line numbers and BASIC program statements each begin with a line number.

As can be seen, typing RUN caused the program to be translated and operated, resulting in the words ALLS WELL being typed by the computer.

Having completed the program run, the terminal user then exits from BASIC and the operating system by typing BYE, after which the computer types some data concerning the computing session.

The above session was on a computer at the University of Southern California which was a PDP-10 with a TENEX operating system and a DEC (Digital Equipment Corporation) BASIC system.

An important concept arises here. When each user logs on the computer, the BASIC system allocates a section of memory to the user. This is called the user's *work space*. When the user types in a program, the program goes into the user's work space. Then, if a RUN command is given, it is the program currently in the user's work space that is operated.

If a line is added to a program or a line is replaced, it is to the program currently in the work space. As mentioned earlier, sometimes BASIC systems require that the program in the work space be named. These systems generally ask for a name by typing NEW OR OLD (for new program or old program) on the user's terminal. The user then types NEW (followed by a ⟨CR⟩); the system asks for the name of the new program and the user then types this name (followed by a ⟨CR⟩).

In any case, the concept of work space is important. If a certain amount of memory has been allocated to a user and this space is exceeded, the BASIC system will complain by printing a message indicating the user's work space is full on the user's terminal.

When a program is run, intermediate and final results are all kept in the user's work space.

As may be seen, in order to successfully run a program, you must have the following information on your system's procedures.

1. How to log in.
2. How to enter BASIC.
3. How to re-enter the operating system.
4. How to log out.

(Items 2 and 3:) These are not required in some systems.

The above may seem like unnecessary work for someone eager to write and run a first program, but the hard reality is that these procedures are necessary to successful terminal usage.

2-4 CORRECTING ERRORS AND LISTING A PROGRAM

It is inevitable that typing errors will occur when a terminal is used. Almost all BASIC systems provide two techniques to enable terminal users to correct such errors.

The first technique concerns correction of a single typing error. If such an error is caught before the next character is typed, there is generally a "delete" character that can be used to delete the preceding character. For the teletype the ← character is most often used.[3]

As an example, suppose we wish to enter

```
20 END
```

In the process of typing we enter

```
20 EM
```

Noting this error we type a ←, thereby deleting the preceding character. Please note that the character will not be deleted on the user's terminal printout (unless a cathode ray tube (CRT) display is used; it may or may not be deleted in this case, depending on the system). What happens is that when it reads the ← the computer simply discards the preceding character (and the ←). If the following is typed

```
20 EM←ND
```

what the computer will store is

```
20 END
```

This can be repeated for several characters. If this is typed

```
20 FND←←←END
```

the computer will enter

```
20 END
```

Note that the delete key was depressed three times and three characters were deleted.

The delete character will probably be the same for the operating system as for BASIC and can be used in logging in or out if you make a typing error.

Not all systems use the ← symbol to delete a character. For some systems, including the PDP-10 system (when used with a TI "Silent 70" terminal) a "control A" character (press the CTRL key down and push A key) is used to delete the preceding character. Further, when "control A" is given a / is printed and the character deleted is printed immediately to the

[3] On many keyboards the key that generates the delete character is marked DEL or DELETE.

right of this. If we type[4]

```
20 EM&lt;CTRL A&gt;ND
```

the terminal will print

```
20 EM/MND
```

and the computer will store

```
20 END
```

You must find out what will work for your terminal since you are certain to make typing errors. The RUBOUT or DELETE keys are also often used, and on some Hewlett Packard Systems a control H is used. If the above seems complicated now, it will soon become very natural.

The BASIC system also provides an easy way to correct an entire line in a program. If we type

```
10 PRIMT "ALLS WELL"
20 END
```

and then notice "print" has been misspelled, it is only necessary to retype the line correctly at the end of the program. Thus if we type

```
10 PRIMT "ALLS WELL"
20 END
10 PRINT "ALLS WELL"
```

the computer will store

```
10 PRINT "ALLS WELL"
20 END
```

Here the BASIC system has discarded the original statement with line number 10 and replaced it with the later entry.

An important fact is: *BASIC systems list and execute statements in order of their line numbers. Also, if line numbers are duplicated, only the last line typed is kept.*

Therefore, if we type

```
10 PRINT "ALLS NOT WELL"
20 EMT
10 PRINT "ALLS WELL"
20 PND
20 END
```

[4]The ⟨CTRL A⟩ here means depress the CTRL key and then the A key.

the computer will store

```
10 PRINT "ALLS WELL"
20 END
```

Another error correcting facility is generally provided: the ability to delete an entire line when too many errors have been made. Quite often this is done by depressing the ESC (for "escape") key:

```
10 CRINT "ALLS⟨ESC⟩
                ↗
      A single push
```

Then this entire line will be discarded by the computer.

You should find what character will delete lines in your system. It is sometimes the "ALTMODE" or "RUBOUT" key instead of the "ESC" key. In other systems it is ⟨CTRL U⟩ and also ⟨CTRL X⟩. You must find this specific procedure for your system. (If it is one of those listed you might underline it.)

The line deleting procedure will also erase systems commands which need to be deleted before the ⟨CR⟩ is given. A way to erase an entire line in BASIC is to simply type the line number followed by a ⟨CR⟩. If we type

```
10 PRINT "ALLS WELL"
15 REM WHO
20 END
15
```

all that will be stored is line 10 and 20. Typing 15 followed by a ⟨CR⟩ will eliminate line 15.

If a program has been typed and errors have been, hopefully, corrected it is a good idea to examine the corrected program before attempting to run it. This is done by typing LIST at the beginning of a new line. The word LIST, when typed in a line by itself, is a BASIC systems command and the computer will immediately list the current program on the terminal. Thus, if we type

```
10 PRIM←NT "ALLP←S WELL"
20 EMD
20 END
LIST
```

the computer will print on the terminal[5]

```
10 PRINT "ALLS WELL"
20 END
```

This is most useful and it is a good idea to list a program before running it. Also, notice the word LIST is a systems command and contains no line number.

Another useful BASIC systems command is SCRATCH which will delete all program statements that have been entered up to that time. The word SCRATCH (or sometimes simply SCR) is simply typed at the beginning of a line (no line number; it is a systems command). When the "carriage return" ⟨CR⟩ key is hit all program statements that have been entered will be erased from the computer's memory. You should check to make sure SCRATCH is the word used in your system; in some systems it is NEW and in others it is CLEAR.

2-5 SUMMARY

In order to use a computer successfully, it is necessary to learn the *local* systems procedures. Before attempting to use a terminal the following information should be obtained.

1. How to log on.
2. How to log off.
3. How to call the BASIC system, if necessary.
4. How to correct single character typing errors. (What is the single character delete procedure.)
5. How entire lines can be deleted.
6. How to erase (scratch) all programs statements in a user's work space.

A BASIC program consists of a list of statements to the computer. Each statement begins with a line number. The computer executes the statements in the order of the line numbers. The order in which the statements are typed does not affect order of execution, unless two statements are typed with the same line number. In this case only the last statement typed is kept.

The procedure for changing statements is to simply type in a new (correct) statement in its entirety. If two statements with the same line number are typed into the BASIC system, the first statement typed is disregarded and only the last statement typed is kept.

[5]The word LIST must be followed by a ⟨CR⟩; it is a systems command.

Table 2-2 HOW TO DELETE A CHARACTER WHEN TYPING

TYPICAL SYSTEMS
Press ← key
Press DELETE or RUBOUT key
Press CTRL and A keys simultaneously, ⟨CTRL A⟩
Press CTRL and H keys simultaneously, ⟨CTRL H⟩
Your System ____________

Table 2-3 HOW TO DELETE A LINE WHEN TYPING

TYPICAL SYSTEMS
Press ESCAPE key
Press CTRL and H simultaneously, ⟨CTRL H⟩
Press CTRL and U simultaneously, ⟨CTRL U⟩
Press SHIFT and L simultaneously
Press RUBOUT or DELETE key
Your System ____________

Table 2-4 HOW TO GENERATE A COMPUTER LISTING OF PROGRAM IN WORK SPACE

Type Systems Command LIST

Your System ____________

Table 2-5 HOW TO HAVE COMPUTER EXECUTE YOUR PROGRAM

Type Systems Command RUN

Your System ____________

Table 2-6 HOW TO CLEAR WORK SPACE

TYPICAL SYSTEMS
Type Systems Command SCR
Type Systems Command SCRATCH
Type Systems Command CLEAR
Your System ____________

Table 2-7 HOW TO SIGN OFF COMPUTER

TYPICAL SYSTEMS
Type Systems Command BYE
Type Systems Command LOGOUT
Type Systems Command LOGOFF
Type Systems Command EXIT then BYE
Type Systems Command FIN
Your System ________________

A procedure for eliminating a statement from a program is to type the statement line number immediately followed by a ⟨CR⟩.

Tables 2-2 through 2-8 show typical systems procedures. At this point you should make sure you know your system's characteristics relating to each of these tables.

Table 2-8 HOW TO SIGN ON COMPUTER (LOGIN)

There are no typical systems.
Your System

____

____

____

____

Questions

1. What is *work space*?
2. What are *systems commands* in BASIC?
3. How do you log on your computer?
4. How do you log off your computer?
5. When the systems command RUN is typed, what happens?
6. In a BASIC program, what are the *line numbers*?
7. In what order are the statements in a BASIC program executed?
8. Suppose you are typing a line into the computer and make a mistake. How do you:
   (a) Correct a single character.
   (b) Delete the current line.
   (c) Delete everything typed in so far.
9. How do you list a program in work space on your computer's BASIC system?

Chapter 3
BASIC Programs—An Introduction

This chapter begins the study of BASIC programs. The approach is based on the fact that a BASIC program consists of a sequence of statements, each statement giving a specific type of instruction to the computer.

There are several different types of BASIC statements. Each statement in a program begins with a line number and the word following the line number tells the translator the kind of statement in that line.

For example, consider this BASIC statement:

```
10 LET A = B + C
```

This is a LET statement.

The statement

```
20 PRINT "JOHN JONES"
```

is a PRINT statement, and so is

```
30 PRINT A, B, A + B
```

Similarly,

```
50 GO TO 150
60 END
```

are examples of GO TO and END statements.

In this and following chapters the various types of BASIC statements will be described and examples of usage presented. The statements will be presented in a logical order beginning with the LET, PRINT, and REM statements in this chapter.

3-1 OBJECTIVES

The LET Statement

The LET statement is the most used BASIC statement. The arithmetic LET statement is presented here and examples of its usage are given so that it can be used in constructing programs.

The PRINT Statement

The PRINT statement is used to output data on a terminal. Some details of PRINT statement usage which permit formatting the material printed are presented. Both variable values and character string printing is introduced.

The REM Statement

The REM statement enables the programmer to document programs (REM is a contraction of REMARK). It is a valuable and important feature of BASIC and should be used by all programmers.

3-2 A SAMPLE PROGRAM

It is instructive to examine a BASIC program to see how programs are constructed. Here is a short program.

```
10 LET A = 2.5
20 LET B = 3
30 LET C = A + B
40 PRINT "A", "B", "A + B"
50 PRINT A, B, C
60 END
```

This program contains six statements. The program's first statement is a LET statement which assigns the value 2.5 to a variable A. The second LET statement assigns the value 3 to B, and the third LET statement adds these values, assigning the sum 5.5 to the variable C. The PRINT statement with line number 40 causes the terminal printer to print the line

```
A                    B                    A+B
```

Finally, the statement with line number 50 causes the values of A, B, and C (which has the value A + B) to be printed under the above line as follows:

```
A                    B                    A+B
2.5                  3                    5.5
```

Notice that each PRINT statement generates a new line of print.

The program then has the necessary END statement to mark the end of the program. The PRINT and LET statements will be studied in the next two sections.

This is a complete program. It performs a simple calculation and then prints the result.

A note concerning statement numbers is in order here. So far we have incremented the statement numbers of succeeding statements by 10 but this is not necessary. A program is performed starting with the statement with the lowest line number. The statement with the next lowest line number is then performed and this process continues until the statement with the highest line number, which must be an END statement, is performed.

This program performs the same calculation and prints the same result as the preceding program.

```
 1 LET A=2.5
 2 LET B=3
 3 LET C=A+B
 5 PRINT "A", "B", "A+B"
 6 PRINT A, B, C
14 END
```

The advantage of incrementing the line numbers by 10 is that a statement can be added at any time between the existing statements by simply adding the statement with a number in the interval skipped.

For instance, we could type

```
1 LET A=2.5
2 LET B=3
```

```
3 LET C = A + B
4 PRINT A, B, C
5 END
```

If this program is run, it will print the following line:

```
2.5                3                5.5
```

Having seen this, we decide that the numbers need labeling. The PRINT "A", "B", "C" statement will accomplish this but there is no place to insert it.

If instead we had typed

```
10 LET A = 2.5
20 LET B = 3
30 LET C = A + B
40 PRINT A, B, C
50 END
```

we could insert the desired PRINT statement by simply typing

```
35 PRINT "A", "B", "A + B"
```

If the system command LIST is now given, the listing will be as follows:

```
10 LET A = 2.5
20 LET B = 3
30 LET C = A + B
35 PRINT "A", "B", "A + B"
40 PRINT A, B, C
50 END
```

If the RUN command is now given, the above program will be executed.

Notice that a line can be added (or changed) at any time, even after the program has been run or listed, by simply typing the new line. Also, a line can be deleted by simply typing the line number followed by a carriage return ⟨CR⟩. If after the above sequence we type

```
40     (This is a "40" followed by a carriage return)
```

the statement with line number 40 will be eliminated.

One other facility is generally offered by the BASIC program system. If we wish to renumber our statements, the system will renumber them for us if the systems command RESEQUENCE is given.[1] For most systems the renumbering will be in increments of 10.

If we type

```
1 LET A = 3
2 LET B = 6
3 PRINT A, B
5 END
```

This program, when run, will simply print values for A and B. If we now type the systems command

```
RESEQUENCE
```

followed by this systems command

```
LIST
```

the computer will print

```
10 LET A = 3
20 LET B = 6
30 PRINT A, B
40 END
```

This is the program that will now be stored by the computer. (The other has been discarded.) To add or modify statements it is this program which must be used, not the original.

It is also possible, for most systems, to resequence (renumber) by increments of other than 10. As an example, if we type RENUMBER 25, 5 for the DEC PDP 10 BASIC, the line numbers will proceed as follows: 25, 30, 35, 40, ... Just typing RENUMBER will give the "default" numbers 10, 20, 30, ...

3-3 THE LET STATEMENT

The preceding programs each used a type of statement called a LET statement. LET statements require the use of a variable; the first type of variable to be described is called a *numeric variable*.

A numeric variable is so called because the variable can only take numeric values. Numeric variables consist of a single letter (A, B, . . . , Z) or a single letter followed by a single decimal digit (0, 1, . . . , 9). Therefore A is

[1] In some systems this command is called RENUMBER.

a numeric variable; B is a numeric variable; M is a numeric variable; A1, A2, and A3 are numeric variables as are X3, B6, and C7. On the other hand, AB, A21, 2A, ABLE, and 24A are *not* numeric variables.

Any of the numeric variables can take numeric values such as 5, 17, 23.5, −16.3, −2579.3, and so on. Also, the value associated with a numeric variable can change as the program is executed.

In an arithmetic LET statement, a single numeric variable occurs to the left of the = symbol. For instance,

```
10 LET A = 2 + 3
```

is a LET statement. This statement, when executed, will give the numeric variable A the value 5.

LET statements are executed by calculating the value of the expression to the right of the = symbol and assigning this value to the numeric variable to the left of the = symbol.[2] What the = symbol means here is "takes the value of" and not "is equal to." So LET A = 5 is read "Let A take the value of 5."

As an example consider

```
10 LET A = 5
20 LET B = 6.1
30 LET C1 = 3
40 LET D2 = A + B + C1
```

Execution of the above by the computer proceeds as follows: Statement 10 causes A to be given the value of 5; the statement 20 causes B to be given the value of 6.1, after which statement 30 gives value 3 to the numeric variable C1. Finally, statement 40 assigns the value 5 + 6.1 + 3 to D2, giving D2 the value of 14.1.

It is important to understand that only a single variable can appear to the left of the equals sign.

It is also important to understand that the same numeric variable can have different values at different stages of program operation.

Consider, for example,

```
10 LET A = 5
20 LET B = 6
30 LET C = 4
40 LET A = B + C
50 PRINT A
60 END
```

[2] The = symbol is called an assignment operator. Because the = symbol is also used to indicate equality, in mathematics, to avoid confusion some other programming languages use symbols such as := or ← instead of the = symbol. The most used languages, FORTRAN, COBOL, and BASIC, all use the = symbol, however. A great advantage is its presence on keyboards.

When this program is run, A is first given value 5, then B gets value 6, and C gets value 4. After this, A is given the value 6 + 4, or 10, and the PRINT statement will cause this value, 10, to be printed. The previous value of A, which was 5, is simply discarded when statement 40 is executed. (The computer stores values for A at a location in memory and replaces the original value with the new value when statement 40 is executed. It is a good idea to think of the variable A as being associated with a location in memory in the user's work space.)

The same numeric variable can even occur on both sides of a LET statement = symbol. Consider the program

```
10 LET A = 3
20 LET A = A + 1
30 PRINT A
40 END
```

This program gives A the value 3 in statement 10 but then gives A the value 3 + 1, or 4, in statement 20, and it is this value that will be printed.

3-4 THE PRINT STATEMENT

Several PRINT statements have been used in the programs so far displayed. In general, use of a PRINT statement is quite straightforward. However, there are a number of rules concerning positioning the printed material on a page which makes it possible to format printouts attractively, but which complicate the PRINT statement's usage. These rules will be presented here and in later sections.

Consider the following program:

```
10 LET A = 15
20 LET B = 25
30 PRINT A, B
40 END
```

This will cause the printing of this line:

```
15                    25
```

When used in this way, the PRINT statement simply causes the printing of the values of the variables in the statement in the order they occur. As an example consider the program

```
10 LET A = 20
20 LET B = 25
30 LET C = A + B
40 PRINT C, A, B
50 END
```

This will cause the print of the following line:

```
45              20              25
```

Notice that the numbers printed are not placed closely together. A printed line in BASIC consists of a number of *zones* and each variable value is printed in a separate zone, if a comma is placed between the variables (A comma or a semicolon must be placed between each pair of variables.)

Unfortunately, there is no standard for the number of zones on a line or the number of print positions in each zone. Fortunately, most systems have either 5 zones of 15 characters each or 5 zones of 16 characters each.

For a system with 15 print positions per zone and 5 zone positions, the line from the preceding example is spaced as follows[3]:

ZONE 1	ZONE 2	ZONE 3
15 POSITIONS	15 POSITIONS	15 POSITIONS
45	20	25

If a semicolon is placed between variables, the printed values will be placed close together; as shown in the following:

```
10 LET A = 15
20 LET B = 20
30 PRINT A; B; B; A
40 END
```

This will generate the line

```
15  20  20  15
```

Normally, each new PRINT statement generates a new line.

```
10 LET A = 15
20 LET B = 20
30 PRINT A, B
40 PRINT B, A
50 END
```

When run, this program generates these lines:

```
15              20
20              15
```

[3]Space is left for a sign to the left of each number in some systems.

Placing a comma at the end of a PRINT statement will cause the next PRINT statement's output to continue on the same line.

```
10 LET A = 15
20 LET B = 20
30 PRINT A, B,
40 PRINT B, A
50 END
```

This will generate the line

```
15                   20                   20                   15
```

A semicolon at the end of a PRINT also causes a continuation of the line, but with a close spacing:

```
10 LET A = 15
20 LET B = 20
30 PRINT A; B;
40 PRINT B; A
50 END
```

This causes the line

```
15  20  20  15
```

It is also possible to print *character strings*[4] using a PRINT statement. The character string is simply enclosed in quotation marks. The characters within the quotation marks will be printed *exactly as they appear*. For example, consider the following program:

```
10 PRINT "WHY NOT"
20 END
```

This short program will cause the printing of

```
WHY NOT
```

The same spacing rules for commas or semicolons as were explained for variables apply to character strings, and for mixed cases. For example,

[4]The character string WHY NOT in the following program is also called a *character constant* in the ANSI Standard.

consider this program:

```
10 LET A = 10
20 PRINT "A = ", A
30 END
```

This will cause the printing of the line

```
A =                 10
```

To make this printout more attractive, we change the comma in the printout to a semicolon:

```
10 LET A = 10
20 PRINT "A = "; 10
30 END
```

This will cause the printing of the line

```
A = 10
```

Since character string printing uses the same rules as number printing, it is easy to format displays. For example, consider this program:

```
10 LET A = 10
20 LET B = 25
30 LET C = 35
40 PRINT "VALUES ARE PRINTED UNDER VARIABLE NAMES"
50 PRINT "A", "B", "C"
60 PRINT A, B, C
70 END
```

This program causes the following printout:

```
VALUES ARE PRINTED UNDER VARIABLE NAMES
A                   B                   C
10                  25                  35
```

The commas cause each character "A", "B", and "C" to be printed at the beginning of a new zone and also the values for A, B, and C to each begin in a new zone.

3-5 THE REM STATEMENT

A most important statement is the REM statement ("REM" is a contraction of "REMARK") because this statement allows programs to be made understandable. When a program is first written, the programmer is invariably eager to run it and not to document the program for other users (and for himself or herself at a later time). This tendency must be overcome when writing programs of any size or complexity.

The REM statement function is quite simple: anything written after the REM is ignored by the translator during program operation. This enables the programmer to include comments, titles, name, dates, and so on in the program and to keep this information with the program.

Consider this program:

```
10 REM A PROGRAM TO PRINT A SUM
20 REM JACK JONES, 5/15/80
30 LET A = 10
40 LET B = 20
50 REM NOW WE ADD A AND B
60 LET C = A + B
70 PRINT "THE VALUE OF"; A; "+"; B; "= "; C
80 END
```

The BASIC translator will operate this program as if the statements with line numbers 10, 20, and 50 did not exist. It will assign values, add, and print while ignoring all REM statements. However, a LIST command will cause a print of the program with the REM statements intact.

The important thing here is that programs can be titled, their operation explained, the author listed, and so on, with no effect on program operation.

Programs of any size and value should certainly be adequately documented and in the major programs in this book we will adhere to this policy. In order to save space, however, many very short, self-explanatory programs will not be titled and REM statements will be used sparingly because the book's text will explain operation. In the author's opinion, however, the beginning programmer should use REM statements liberally. Certainly programs submitted in assignments should be readily understandable and titled. Also, programs saved for future use should contain enough REM statements and comments so they can be understood at a later date.

3-6 SUMMARY

The LET, PRINT, and REM statements have been presented and examples given of their usage. After this chapter has been studied, the computer user should be able to write programs which assign values to variables,

Table 3-1 LET STATEMENTS

The LET Statement has the form

line number LET *variable* = *expression*

The *expression* is evaluated and its value assigned to the variable to the left of the = sign.

Example:

```
20 LET A = 5 + B
```

Here 20 is the line number, A is the (numeric) *variable*, and 5 + B is the (numeric) *expression*.

---

print variable values and character strings, format output lines using commas and semicolons to control spacing, and add comments to a program to aid in documentation.

The important idea that a BASIC program consists of a sequence of statements of various types has been presented and will be used to introduce future BASIC statements.

Some facts about LET, PRINT, and REM statements are given in Tables 3-1, 3-2, and 3-3.

Table 3-2 THE PRINT STATEMENT

The general form of the PRINT statement is

line number PRINT *item p item p . . . p item*

p is either a semicolon or a comma.

An *item* can be a numeric variable, a character string variable (to be discussed in the next chapter), a numeric expression (discussed in the next chapter), a TAB call (in Chapter 8), or a null.

The value of numeric expressions can be output; therefore the statement

```
20 PRINT 20 * 5
```

will result in the printing of the value 100, and

```
30 PRINT 5 + 5, A + 5, A, A + 6
```

will result in the printing of the following line if A has value 7.

```
10              12              7               13
```

A comma, when used in a PRINT statement, causes the next character to be printed at the beginning of the next zone. Each print line is separated into zones with a fixed number of characters (generally 15 or 16). The semicolon, when used

Table 3-2 Continued

to separate print items, causes the next item printed to follow closely the preceding item.

Unless the preceding PRINT statement ended with a semicolon or comma, each PRINT statement generates a new line of print.

When a comma or semicolon is at the end of a PRINT statement, the first item in the next print statement is printed as if it followed in the preceding PRINT statement.

Example:

```
10 PRINT 5, 6;
20 PRINT 7, 8
```

causes the printing of

```
5              6    7              8
```

Table 3-3 THE REMARK STATEMENT

The general form of the REMARK statement is

line number REM *remark string*

The *remark string* can be any string of characters.

When the BASIC system translator encounters a REM statement, it proceeds to the next line with no other effect.

Example:

```
20 REM THIS PROGRAM LISTS COURSES
30 REM JOHN JONES, 8/12/82
```

Questions

1. What is the systems command which will resequence the line numbers in a BASIC program for your BASIC computer system?
2. What is a numeric variable? How many different numeric variables can be formed in BASIC? Explain your answer.
3. What happens when this short program is executed?

```
10 LET A = 5
20 PRINT A
30 LET A = A + 2
40 PRINT A
50 END
```

4. How many print positions and how many print positions per zone are in your BASIC system?

5. What will the printouts be for these programs?

(a)

```
10 PRINT "JACK"
20 PRINT
30 PRINT "BILL"
40 END
```

(b)

```
10 PRINT "JAMES",
20 PRINT
30 PRINT "SUE"
40 END
```

6. What is the purpose of the REM statement?
7. In a PRINT statement, what is a collection of characters between quotation marks called?
8. In the programs below X = 3, Y = 2, Z = 7, and W = 9. Give the printouts.

(a)

```
15 PRINT X;
20 PRINT Y; W
30 PRINT Z
40 END
```

(b)

```
15 PRINT Y
20 PRINT X;
35 PRINT Z; W
40 END
```

(c)

```
10 PRINT W; Y
20 PRINT X; W
30 END
```

9. If the following program is executed, what will be printed?

```
10 LET A = 2
20 LET B = 4
30 PRINT A, B
40 PRINT A; B
50 END
```

10. What will happen if the following program is executed?

```
10 LET X = 1
20 LET Y = 2
30 PRINT "Y = "; X
40 END
```

11. What will be printed if this is run?

```
10 LET X = 5
20 PRINT 20 * X, X
30 END
```

12. What will be printed if this is run?

```
10 PRINT 5, 10, "5 PLUS 10 = "; 5 + 10
20 END
```

13. Run this program on your computer.

```
10 A=5
20 B=6
30 PRINT A; "PLUS"; B; "EQUALS"; A+B
40 END
```

14. Run this program on your computer.

```
10 A=4
20 B=9.3
30 PRINT A; "TIMES"; B; EQUALS; A*B
40 END
```

15. What will be printed on the terminal when each of the following BASIC statements is performed? If nothing, say so. Assume X = 5 and Y = 4.

```
10 PRINT X
10 PRINT X+Y
10 PRINT "X=", X
10 PRINT "X="; X
10 PRINT "X+Y"; "="; X+Y
10 REM PRINT "X+Y"; "="; X+Y
10 PRINT
```

16. Write a program that will print out two copies of your mailing address so that there is a blank line separating each copy.
17. What will the printout be?

```
10 PRINT "JOHN"; "SMITH"
20 PRINT "JOHN", "SMITH"
20 END
```

18. What will the printout be?

```
10 PRINT "ZONE ONE", "ZONE TWO", "ZONE THREE"
20 PRINT "ZONE ONE", "IS THIS STILL IN ZONE TWO?", "IS THIS IN
   ZONE THREE?"
30 END
```

Chapter 4
The INPUT Statement, String Variables, and Numeric Expressions

In order to perform arithmetic using a programming language, it is necessary to write expressions involving arithmetic operations such as addition, subtraction, multiplication, and so on. There must be rules for forming and interpreting these expressions so the programmer can be certain how a program will be interpreted by the translator. There must also be rules for writing numbers, particularly very large and small numbers. This chapter first presents the rules for forming numeric expressions and for writing numbers in BASIC.

Chapter 3 introduced numeric variables and the LET statement; the first sections of this chapter show how to perform arithmetic operations. BASIC also provides the ability to compute using alphanumeric character strings. Special *character string variables* are used for this purpose and these are introduced in this chapter.

Several applications areas of interest are in this chapter, including automated form letter writing and a compound interest problem.

4-1 OBJECTIVES

Numeric Constants and Numeric Expressions

In order to calculate using numbers it is generally necessary to have different ways to represent the numbers. The BASIC rules for writing integers, numbers with decimal points, and exponential notation numbers are presented here. Then the rules for forming the arithmetic or numeric expressions used in calculations are presented.

The INPUT Statement

There are several ways to introduce data into a BASIC program, but one of the most useful is the INPUT statement. This statement allows the inputting of data during program operation from the user's terminal. The rules for using INPUT statements are introduced in this chapter.

String Variables and Constants

BASIC allows for strings of alphanumeric characters to be used in calculations. These strings can be input using the INPUT statement and used in LET statements. Rules for using character strings in BASIC programs are introduced in a following section along with some examples of the rules for program usage.

4-2 NUMERIC CONSTANTS

In BASIC, numbers can be input in several different forms and printed in several different forms. The simplest format is for a number which is an integer (a number with no decimal point or fraction part),[1] but with a sign perhaps preceding the first digit. Here are several examples:

```
12    124    -16    +16    -132
```

Notice there are no decimal points or fractions in these written numbers. (The ANSI standard calls this *implicit point representation*. The term *integer constant* is also widely used.)

A second form for numbers uses a decimal point and perhaps a preceding sign. Here are several numbers in this form:

```
12.5    24.0    -36.4    -37.    +124.63    124.63
```

[1]The integers are 0, +1, −1, +2, −2, +3, −3, ... Numbers such as 2.5, $3\frac{1}{2}$, 14.63, are not integers.

(In the ANSI specification, the above numbers are said to be in *explicit point unscaled representation*. The term *real constant* is often used in BASIC manuals, also.)

Another form for writing numeric constants involves the use of exponential notation. Commonly, a small number such as 0.00024 is written 24×10^{-5} and a large number such as 24,900,000 is written 249×10^{5}. BASIC makes use of exponential notation without use of superscripts because superscripts cannot be easily accommodated on many computer input or output devices. In BASIC, an E is used instead to indicate the use of exponential notation. The format of a number in this form consists of a real number or integer constant followed by an E, followed by an integer constant. For instance,

59 E 2 means 59×10^{2}

Integer constant | Indicates use of exponential form | Integer constant

Another example is:

– 59.4 E-4 means -59.4×10^{-4}

Real constant | Integer constant

In the ANSI standard, the above examples are said to be in *implicit form scaled representation* (the first) or *explicit form scaled representation* (the second). Here are more examples:

– 0.5E0	means	$-0.5 \times 10^{0} = -0.5$
8.0E4	means	$8 \times 10^{4} = 80{,}000$
8E4	means	$8 \times 10^{4} = 80{,}000$
7.4E6	means	$7.4 \times 10^{6} = 7{,}400{,}000$
– 8.69E – 4	means	$-8.69 \times 10^{-4} = -8.69/10000$
– 8.69E + 5	means	$-8.69 \times 10^{5} = -869{,}000$

Notice that an integer (no decimal point) must follow the E. As a result 7E6.4 is not legal, nor is 8E6. because there is a decimal point after the 6. (The 6 is an integer but is not in integer form. Some BASIC systems will accept this, however.)

The computer you are using has some limit on how many digits it uses in every number it represents. You can find the number of digits by testing, reading a manual, or by asking. To test, try this program.

```
10 PRINT 123456789123
20 END
```

The computer will then print a number such as

```
1.23457E + 11
```

By counting the number of digits in the left part (to the left of E) of the number you can find how many digits are carried in your computer. (The above print showed six digits in each number.)

What the above means to the computer user is that numbers with many digits are truncated[2] by the computer and stored in exponential form. This can become a problem only if care is not taken with long sets of calculations or if numbers with many significant digits are used. The number of digits carried in BASIC will be adequate for most calculations, however, and there are ways around this problem if numbers with many significant digits must be used.

4-3 NUMERIC EXPRESSIONS

In the LET statement

```
20 LET A = B + C
```

The B + C to the right of the = symbol is called a *numeric expression*. So far, the numeric expressions have used only addition symbols but they can also contain multiplication, division, and subtraction, symbols.

Except for multiplication (and exponentiation) the symbols used in numeric expressions are those in common usage. Parentheses are used just as in conventional mathematics. The arithmetic operation symbols used in BASIC are

+	for addition
−	for subtraction (also for negative numbers)
*	for multiplication
/	for division

[2] They are generally rounded, also. Notice the rounding of a 6 to a 7 in the immediately preceding example.

Here are several numeric expressions:

```
A*B          A*(B + C)        6*A
A*(B/C1)     A/(A1 - B1)      5.5/6.6
A*(B/C - D)  A1(B1*C1/D1)     18.4/B*A1
```

It is important to note that spaces do not affect numeric expressions in BASIC. As a result, A+B+C is treated the same as A + B + C and A*B/C is treated the same as A * B/C. However, you cannot put spaces in numbers or variable names; thus 2 5.2 is *not* the same as 25.2 nor is B 1 the same as B1.

Assume A = 5, B = 2, and C = 3 when the following LET statement is executed:

```
40 LET D = A - (B*C)
```

After this statement is executed D will have value −1.

Some numeric expressions cannot be evaluated by the computer without assumptions as to which operations should be performed first.

For instance, what does this statement mean?

```
30 LET A = B*C + A
```

Does it mean (B*C) + A or B*(C + A)?

If A = 1, B = 2, and C = 3, the first expression gives A the value of 7 and the second 8 because (2*3) + 1 equals 7 while 2*(3 + 1) equals 8. Using parentheses would make this question unnecessary but sometimes too many parentheses are inconvenient.

The programming language rule for ordering execution of arithmetic operations in a section of a numeric expression without parentheses is:

RULE

Multiplication and division are performed first, followed by addition and subtraction.

As a result of this rule, A + B * C means A + (B * C). Because multiplication is performed first, B is multiplied by C and then A is added to this sum. A/B + C means (A/B) + C because the division of A by B is performed and then C is added. Here are four more examples:

A + B*C − D	means	A + (B*C) − D
A/B − C	means	(A/B) − C
A + B/C − D/E	means	A + (B/C) − (D/E)
A − B1*C1 − D1	means	A − (B1*C1) − D1

As a final rule, expressions are evaluated from left to right, after the above precedence rule has been applied. As a result A/B*C means (A/B)*C and A*B + C/D*E means (A*B) + (C/D)*E. Also A*B/C + E means ((A*B)/C) + E.

The *exponentiation* operator varies from terminal to terminal. The ↑ is sometimes used, however, so A↑2 means A^2 and B1↑3 means $B1^3$. We call this operation *exponentiation* or *raising to a power*.

In many systems a ˆ symbol is used, so Aˆ2 means A^2 and Bˆ3 means B^3. (The ˆ symbol is called a *circumflex* and is specified by the ANSI standard.) Other systems use two asterisks as follows: A**5 means A^5, 2**4 means 2^4, A**B means A^B, and so forth.

With regard to the ordering of operations, *exponentiation is always performed first*. As a result,

Aˆ5 − B

or

A↑5 − B means $A^5 - B$ (in some other systems this could be A**5 − B)

and

Bˆ3*Cˆ5/D

or

B↑3*C↑5/D means $\dfrac{(B^3)*(C^5)}{D}$

The left to right rule for ordering execution of arithmetic operations also applies so that

AˆBˆC

or

A↑B↑C means $(A^B)^C$

Here is a program using the rules for numeric expressions.

```
10 LET A = 2
20 LET B = 3
30 LET C = 4
40 LET D = A/(B − C)
50 LET E = A − Bˆ2 + C
60 PRINT D, E
70 END
```

This program will cause the final values for D and E to be printed. D will have the value 2/(3 − 4), or −2, and E will have the value $2 - 3^2 + 4$, or −3.

4-4 THE INPUT STATEMENT

Values have so far been assigned to variables using LET statements. It is also possible to input values from the user's terminal during program operation; this greatly increases what can be accomplished using BASIC. This is done by using a BASIC statement called an INPUT statement. The INPUT statement allows the introduction of data while a program is in operation. A ? typed by the computer on the terminal indicates an input statement is being executed and data is to be input from the user's terminal.

Here is a sample program using an input statement:

```
10 PRINT "WHAT IS YOUR NUMBER"
20 INPUT A
30 LET B = A*5
40 PRINT A; "TIMES 5 = "; B
50 END
```

When the program is run, the first statement (10) causes the terminal to print WHAT IS YOUR NUMBER. Then statement 20 is executed. At this point the computer prints a question mark; then the computer waits for a number to be typed on the terminal keyboard. Nothing more will happen until this number is input. *When the number is typed it must be followed by a carriage return ⟨CR⟩* because the computer has no way of knowing when the last digit of a number has been entered. Some sign must be given and the sign used is a carriage return.[3]

After this, the value typed is assigned to A, multiplied by 5, and the PRINT statement then prints the results.

If the above program has been entered at the keyboard and RUN is typed, the computer will print

```
WHAT IS YOUR NUMBER
?
```

If this number is typed on the keyboard

```
55.5
```

the computer will generate the line

```
55.5 TIMES 5 = 277.5
```

[3]A comma or semicolon will work in some systems but the ⟨CR⟩ will always work.

A single INPUT statement can be used to read in several values.

```
 5 PRINT "WHAT ARE A, B, AND C"
10 INPUT A, B, C
20 LET D = A + B + C
30 PRINT "A + B + C = "; D
40 END
```

If the above program is typed on the terminal and then the RUN command is typed, the terminal will print WHAT ARE A, B, AND C. Then a question mark will appear, below this line. The terminal operator must then type the input values for A, B, and C *separated by commas*[4] and at the end a carriage return (⟨CR⟩) must be typed.

For example, if we type

```
12.5, 5, −15
```

the following will be printed on the terminal:

```
A + B + C = 2.5
```

To further illustrate this, Figure 4-1 shows an entire session at a terminal where this program was run. The underlined characters are those generated by the computer.

If not enough input values are keyboarded. The computer will print a statement requesting more data. For example, if for the above INPUT we type

```
14, 5
```

with a carriage return at the end, the computer will respond by printing some statement such as

```
NOT ENOUGH DATA, TYPE IN MORE
```

An additional number must then be typed followed by a carriage return.

If data in an incorrect form are introduced, for instance, if we type BOB, 5, 10 when three numbers are expected, the computer will respond with some printed statement on the terminal saying an error has been made. The statement printed varies according to the system being used. (A similar comment will be generated if too many values are input.)

[4] Other punctuation marks such as the ; or − may work in some systems but the comma works in all systems and is recommended.

Terminal Print Out	**Comments**
@LOGIN WHARTON AXQ5	User logs in
JOB 72 ON TTY155 29-APR-80 13:57:30	System prints job number and time
@BASIC	User asks for BASIC
READY BASIC	System says it is ready
10 PRINT "WHAT ARE A, B, AND C"	
20 INPUT A, B, C	User types program
30 LET D = A + B + C	
40 PRINT "A + B + C="; D	
50 END	
RUN	User asks for a program run
NONAME.B20	System gives program a name and gives the date
TUESDAY, APRIL 29, 1980 14:00:34	
WHAT ARE A, B, AND C	Computer prints line from program
? 24, 35, 45	Input is asked for. User types 3 numbers
A + B + C = 104	Program prints sum
COMPILE TIME: 0.103 SECS	
RUN TIME: 0.139 SECS ELAPSED TIME: 0:00:18	
BYE	User logs out
KILLED JOB 72, USER WHARTON	

Note: The underlined characters are those generated by the computer. Characters not underlined were entered by the terminal user.

Fig. 4-1 Session at Terminal Using Input Statement

4-5 A PROGRAM FOR TEMPERATURE CONVERSION

A government program has been initiated to cause Americans to use Centigrade (Celsius) temperatures instead of Fahrenheit temperatures. The conversion of Fahrenheit to Centigrade and from Centigrade to Fahrenheit involves a straightforward calculation which can be readily programmed in BASIC. We will now develop a program to convert Centigrade to Fahrenheit and also to print the temperatures involved. (The questions at the end of the chapter will develop a Fahrenheit to Centigrade program.)

Let us divide the program to be developed into three sections: (1) An input section which reads from the user's terminal the Centigrade temperature to be converted, (2) the conversion of the temperature from Centigrade to Fahrenheit, and (3) the printing of the result.

Because the program we will develop converts a Centigrade temperature to Fahrenheit, to begin we first write a section which prints

```
INPUT A CENTIGRADE TEMPERATURE
```

on the terminal and then assigns the temperature the user types into a variable C. This requires the following statements:

```
10 PRINT "INPUT A CENTIGRADE TEMPERATURE"
20 INPUT C
```

Now, if C is the Centigrade temperature and F the Fahrenheit temperature, the formula for converting Centigrade to Fahrenheit is

$$F = \frac{9C + 160}{5}$$

This requires one BASIC statement, which is

```
30 LET F = (9*C + 160)/5
```

Now, we wish to print the converted temperature in Fahrenheit along with the original Centigrade temperature. These statements will accomplish this:

```
40 PRINT C; "DEGREES CENTIGRADE EQUALS"; F; "DEGREES";
50 PRINT "FAHRENHEIT"
```

This statement prints (1) the temperature C, immediately followed by (2) the characters DEGREES CENTIGRADE EQUALS, followed by (3) the Fahrenheit temperature, followed by (4) the statement "DEGREES FAHRENHEIT."

A typical printed line from this statement would read

```
0 DEGREES CENTIGRADE EQUALS 32 DEGREES FAHRENHEIT
```

An END statement must also be added, as follows:

```
60 END
```

The complete program ready to be typed in on a terminal is:

```
10 PRINT "INPUT A CENTIGRADE TEMPERATURE"
20 INPUT C
30 LET F = (9*C + 160)/5
40 PRINT C; "DEGREES CENTIGRADE EQUALS"; F; "DEGREES";
50 PRINT "FAHRENHEIT"
60 END
```

Here are three typical runs of the program.

```
RUN

INPUT A CENTIGRADE TEMPERATURE
?0
0 DEGREES CENTIGRADE EQUALS 32 DEGREES FAHRENHEIT

READY
RUN

INPUT A CENTIGRADE TEMPERATURE
?50
50 DEGREES CENTIGRADE EQUALS 122 DEGREES FAHRENHEIT

READY
RUN

INPUT A CENTIGRADE TEMPERATURE
?100
100 DEGREES CENTIGRADE EQUALS 212 DEGREES FAHRENHEIT
```

In order to make this into an acceptable program for future use, documentation is required so that future users and the original author can understand it at a later date. Here are some possible REM statements.

```
1 REM PROGRAM TO CONVERT CENTIGRADE TO FAHRENHEIT
2 REM C. JOHNSON, 2/15/81
3 REM C IS THE TEMPERATURE IN CENTIGRADE
4 REM AND F THE SAME TEMPERATURE IN FAHRENHEIT
```

These statements can be typed in after the above program has been run. If this is done and we then type the systems command

```
LIST
```

the following printout on the terminal will result:

```
 1 REM PROGRAM TO CONVERT CENTIGRADE TO FAHRENHEIT
 2 REM C. JOHNSON, 2/15/81
 3 REM C IS THE TEMPERATURE IN CENTIGRADE
 4 REM AND F THE SAME TEMPERATURE IN FAHRENHEIT
10 PRINT "INPUT A CENTIGRADE TEMPERATURE"
20 INPUT C
30 LET F = (9*C + 160)/5
40 PRINT C; "DEGREES CENTIGRADE EQUALS"; F; "DEGREES";
50 PRINT "FAHRENHEIT"
60 END
```

In order to improve the program numbering we now type the systems command

```
RESEQUENCE
```

(This may be RENUMBER in your system.)
If we then type the following command

```
LIST
```

the computer will then print on the terminal:

```
 10 REM PROGRAM TO CONVERT CENTIGRADE TO FAHRENHEIT
 20 REM C. JOHNSON, 2/15/81
 30 REM C IS THE TEMPERATURE IN CENTIGRADE
 40 REM AND F THE SAME TEMPERATURE IN FAHRENHEIT
 50 PRINT "INPUT A CENTIGRADE TEMPERATURE"
 60 INPUT C
 70 LET F = (9*C + 160)/5
 80 PRINT C; "DEGREES CENTIGRADE EQUALS"; F; "DEGREES";
 90 PRINT "FAHRENHEIT"
100 END
```

It is generally better to write REM statements as a program is developed instead of afterward as was done here. Because the text discusses the programs as they are developed, REM statements are not used to the extent they might be in actual programming. Also, adding the REM statements after this program was developed shows the value of the spacing by 10 of statement numbers which leaves room for additional statements and illustrates use of the RENUMBER (RESEQUENCE) systems command.

4-6 STRING VARIABLES

The variables that have been used so far have all been numeric variables. The capabilities of BASIC are greatly expanded by variables that can have values consisting of character strings.

A *character string variable* in BASIC is represented by a letter followed by a $ sign. Therefore, A$, B$, C$, . . . , Z$ are the 26 possible character string variables in BASIC. These variables can have values which are strings of characters. Here is an example program containing a character string variable B$.

```
10 LET B$ = "GO AHEAD"
20 PRINT B$
30 END
```

This program assigns the value GO AHEAD to the variable B$ and then prints B$, which will result in the terminal printing GO AHEAD.

When a character string is assigned to a string variable in a LET statement, it is enclosed in quotation marks. A sequence of characters enclosed in quotation marks is called a *character string constant*.

Character string constants can have from 0 to any number of characters according to the ANSI specification, but if you are going to use long strings, you had better check you own system to see how many characters strings can have.[5]

Character strings can be input from a terminal into a character string variable using an INPUT statement. Here is an example program and a sample run.

Program

```
10 PRINT "TYPE YOUR FIRST NAME"
20 INPUT N$
30 PRINT "TYPE THE DATE"
40 INPUT D$
50 PRINT "ON"; D$; "YOU GAVE YOUR NAME AS "; N$
60 END
```

Systems Command

```
RUN
```

Program run

```
TYPE YOUR FIRST NAME
  ?JOHN
TYPE THE DATE
  ?JAN 4 1981
ON JAN 4 1981 YOU GAVE YOUR NAME AS JOHN
```

After this program is typed in and the systems command RUN is given, statement 10 causes the line "TYPE YOUR FIRST NAME" to be printed. The INPUT N$ is then executed. This causes a question mark to be printed on the user's terminal and the computer then waits for a string of characters to be input, followed by a ⟨CR⟩. In the example the terminal

[5] By using long strings of characters for inputs to a test program such as the above, when it is run you can determine how many characters can be in a character string in your system. Often up to an entire printed line can be used in a string variable.

NOTE: On Hewlitt-Packard computers the first occurrence of a character string variable which is to contain more than a single character must be preceded by a DIM statement telling the maximum number of characters to be used. For example, if the string variable A$ will contain at most 20 characters, it is necessary to insert this statement in the program.

```
10 DIM A$(20)
```

The line number can be any line number less than the line number of the first statement containing A$.

Two or more character variables can be placed in the same DIM statement using commas. For example,

```
5 DIM A$(20), B$(15)
```

operator input

```
JOHN
```

The computer reads this into the variable N$ and then executes the next statement which causes the printing of

```
TYPE THE DATE
```

The INPUT statement at line number 40 is now executed, which caused the terminal to print a question mark and then wait for a character string from the terminal. In the example the terminal operator input JAN 4 1981. This value is then assigned to variable D$ by the computer.

Finally, the computer executed statement 50 causing the printing of

```
ON JAN 4 1981 YOU GAVE YOUR NAME AS JOHN
```

The above example shows how character strings can be both input and printed in BASIC and opens up a whole area of applications in both science and business. This example should be carefully studied and the program shown operated on a terminal.

4-7 PRINT STATEMENT FORMATTING

The use of character string variables makes it possible to produce letter writing programs and many business form generating programs. Also, attractive printouts are made possible by using character string constants, and adjusting the spacing by use of the comma and semicolon rule for PRINT statements given in Chapter 3. An important PRINT rule used in programs which print forms and letters is as follows:

PRINT RULE
Each new PRINT statement generates a new line of print, except if a comma or semicolon are used at the end of the statement. A comma moves the print position to the beginning of the next zone and a semicolon continues the line with a close spacing.

Here is an example:

```
10 PRINT "NOW IS THE TIME";
20 PRINT "FOR ALL GOOD MEN";
30 PRINT "TO COME TO THE AID"
40 PRINT "OF THEIR COUNTRY"
50 END
```

This causes a print as follows:

```
NOW IS THE TIME FOR ALL GOOD MEN TO COME TO THE AID
OF THEIR COUNTRY
```

Here is another example:

```
10 PRINT "NAME", "RANK", "SERIAL NUMBER"
20 PRINT "JOHN JAY", "PRIVATE", "6943200"
30 END
```

This prints

```
NAME                RANK                SERIAL NUMBER
JOHN JAY            PRIVATE             6943200
```

Now consider this program:

```
10 LET A = 10
20 LET B = 20
30 PRINT "A", "B"
40 PRINT A,
50 PRINT B
60 END
```

This causes the printing of

```
A                   B
10                  20
```

4-8 FORM LETTER WRITING USING A COMPUTER

The following example of the use of character strings shows how form letters are generated using a computer. We often receive a letter in the mail with our name and address in the heading and a salutation followed by a standard form letter's text. These are used to sell subscriptions to magazines, for contest entries, and so on. The company wishing to send the form letters has a list of names and addresses of prospects. The company prepares a form letter program and then hires someone to enter names and addresses using a keyboard. For each name and address entered a letter is typed by the computer.

Figure 4.2(a) is a letter writing program which will type a letter and Figure 4.2(b) is a sample run.

The first statements ask the terminal operator to input the name and address, city, state, and zip code of the recipient for the letter. The

```
LIST

 10 REM LETTER WRITING PROGRAM
 20 REM C. JOHNSON, 9/2/81
 30 PRINT "ENTER FIRST NAME"
 40 INPUT N$
 50 PRINT "ENTER LAST NAME"
 60 INPUT X$
 70 PRINT "ENTER STREET ADDRESS"
 80 INPUT S$
 90 PRINT "ENTER CITY, STATE, AND ZIP CODE"
100 INPUT C$
110 PRINT "ENTER THE DATE"
120 INPUT D$
130 PRINT
140 PRINT
150 PRINT
160 PRINT
170 PRINT
180 PRINT "                              JAKE'S PUBLISHING CO."
190 PRINT "                              43 SAMPSON BLVD."
200 PRINT "                              CULVER, CA. 93342"
210 PRINT "                             "; D$
220 PRINT
230 PRINT N$; "   ";
240 PRINT X$
250 PRINT S$
260 PRINT C$
270 PRINT
280 PRINT "DEAR"; N$; ":"
290 PRINT
300 PRINT "CONGRATULATIONS; YOU HAVE BEEN SELECTED TO"
310 PRINT "RECEIVE A COMPLIMENTARY SUBSCRIPTION TO"
320 PRINT "TECHNOLOGY MAGAZINE PROVIDED YOU SUBSCRIBE"
330 PRINT "TO SCIENCE NEWS MAGAZINE AT THE ASTONISHINGLY"
340 PRINT "LOW PRICE OF $15.15 PER YEAR."
350 PRINT
360 PRINT "RUSH US YOUR $15.15 NOW USING THE CONVENIENT"
370 PRINT "ENCLOSED BLANK AND ENVELOPE AND BEGIN YOUR"
380 PRINT "SUBSCRIPTION TO BOTH SCIENCE NEWS AND TECH-"
390 PRINT "NOLOGY MAGAZINES AT ONCE."
400 PRINT
410 PRINT "                               SINCERELY,"
420 PRINT
430 PRINT
440 PRINT
450 PRINT "                               JAKE SKENIAN"
460 PRINT "                               PRESIDENT,"
470 PRINT "                               JAKE'S  PUBLISHING  CO."
480 END
```

Fig. 4-2 Computer Generated Form Letters. (a) Letter Writing Program

```
RUN

ENTER FIRST NAME
 ?"JOSEPH"
ENTER LAST NAME
 ?"SMITH"
ENTER STREET ADDRESS
 ?"101 JOHNSON LANE"
ENTER CITY, STATE, AND ZIP CODE
 ?"BOSTON, MA 02215"
ENTER THE DATE
 ?"MARCH 3, 1981"

                                        JAKE'S PUBLISHING CO.
                                        43 SAMPSON BLVD.
                                        CULVER, CA. 93342
                                        MARCH 3, 1981

JOSEPH SMITH
101 JOHNSON LANE
BOSTON, MA 02215

DEAR JOSEPH:

CONGRATULATIONS; YOU HAVE BEEN SELECTED TO
RECEIVE A COMPLIMENTARY SUBSCRIPTION TO
TECHNOLOGY MAGAZINE PROVIDED YOU SUBSCRIBE
TO SCIENCE NEWS MAGAZINE AT THE ASTONISHINGLY
LOW PRICE OF $15.15 PER YEAR.

RUSH US YOUR $15.15 NOW USING THE CONVENIENT
ENCLOSED BLANK AND ENVELOPE AND BEGIN YOUR
SUBSCRIPTION TO BOTH SCIENCE NEWS AND TECH-
NOLOGY MAGAZINES AT ONCE.

                                        SINCERELY,

                                        JAKE SKENIAN
                                        PRESIDENT,
                                        JAKE'S PUBLISHING CO.
```

Fig. 4-2 (Continued). (b) Sample Run of Letter Writing Program

remaining statements print the body of the text. Statements such as 130 through 170 cause lines to be skipped in printing. Statements 180 through 210 cause the address to be centered on the page because of the spaces after the quotation marks.

Here are some important facts concerning the inputting of strings from a terminal when an INPUT statement is used to read into a character string variable.

1. Most systems will input any string typed up to a ⟨CR⟩ even if quotation marks are not used around the string. Here is an example input statement:

   ```
   20 INPUT S$
   ```

   If we now type

   ```
   JOHN ⟨CR⟩
   ```

   or

   ```
   "JOHN" ⟨CR⟩
   ```

   most systems will simply input JOHN into S$ because they have been programmed to be "tolerant" of strings without quotation marks.
2. If two character string variables are used in the same INPUT statement, the strings input from the terminal can be separated by either commas or ;s. Here is an example:

   ```
   30 INPUT A$, B$
   ```

   If we type

   ```
   ARIZONA, MEXICO ⟨CR⟩
   ```

   or

   ```
   ARIZONA; MEXICO ⟨CR⟩
   ```

   A$ will have value ARIZONA and B$ will have value MEXICO.
3. Since commas, and sometimes semicolons, or even colons, can be used to terminate strings there can be a problem inputting a string containing commas. Suppose we have the statement

   ```
   40 INPUT N$
   ```

Now suppose we wish to input the string BOSTON, MA. 02138. If this is simply typed, the system will probably drop the ,MA. 02138 because it thinks the comma ends the input. (Remember that to input two numbers 14 and 15 we would simply type 14, 15.) To get around this problem we simply type

```
"BOSTON, MA. 02138"
```

The BASIC translator now knows that what is in quotation marks[6] is the string and will input the entire BOSTON, MA. 02138 into N$.

4-9 COMPOUND INTEREST PROGRAM

There is a famous example of the benefits of compound interest in savings first originated by Ben Franklin. This example shows how money grows when interest on the money is compounded. (Franklin was trying to point out why saving was a good idea.) We now develop a program which performs a typical business calculation, that of figuring compound interest and which also demonstrates Franklin's ideas. We assume an initial deposit of $100.00 and an interest rate of 6 percent (which is more than Franklin's rate). The initial deposit is to have been made in 1800. The variable A will be the initial amount deposited. Y will be the present year, which is input, and D will be the year the money was originally deposited (1800).

The formula which gives the value of the final principal P is $P = A \times (1 + I)^N$ where N is the number of years the interest is compounded, I is the interest, and A is the original amount deposited.

First we will use REM statements to list the program name, the programmer's name and date, and the variables used.

```
 10 REM FRANKLIN'S PROBLEM
 20 REM T. JEFFERSON, 2/15/1779
 30 REM THIS PROGRAM CALCULATES THE VALUE
 40 REM OF $100.00 COMPOUNDED YEARLY FROM
 50 REM 1800 TO THE PRESENT DATE
 60 REM THE VARIABLES USED ARE
 70 REM P IS THE FINAL PRINCIPAL
 80 REM A IS THE ORIGINAL DEPOSIT
 90 REM I IS THE INTEREST
100 REM Y IS THE PRESENT DATE
110 REM D IS THE YEAR OF ORIGINAL DEPOSIT
```

[6]To input a string containing quotation marks, type quotation marks around the string and then type two quotation marks for each occurrence of one quotation mark in the string.

Now, we wish to ask for and input the present year. These two statements will print WHAT YEAR IS IT and then input the year from the terminal. (The year should be greater than 1800 and remember a carriage return must follow the number input.)

```
120 PRINT "WHAT YEAR IS IT"
130 INPUT Y
```

Now, we assign values to A, the original deposit, I, the interest, and D, the year of original deposit.

```
140 LET A = 100
150 LET I = 0.06
160 LET D = 1800
```

We now calculate the number, N, of years the interest is to be compounded:

```
170 LET N = Y - D
```

The next step is to calculate the principal using our formula.[7]

```
180 LET P = A*(1 + I)^N
```

We now wish to print the final principal along with an appropriate statement and end. Here are the necessary statements:

```
190 PRINT "THE PRINCIPAL IS NOW"; P
200 END
```

The complete program is shown in Figure 4-3 along with several runs and results.[8]

Several comments should be made here. The assignment of values to variables in statements 140, 150, and 160 was not necessary if we only

[7] This could also be

```
180 LET P = A*(1 + I)↑N
```

or

```
180 LET P = A*(1 + I)**N
```

depending on your system.

[8] Franklin actually set up a savings account of this kind which continued after his death but it finally became so large the government closed it down.

```
10 REM FRANKLIN'S PROBLEM
20 REM T. JEFFERSON, 2/15/1779
30 REM THIS PROGRAM CALCULATES THE VALUE
40 REM ON $100.00 COMPOUNDED YEARLY FROM
50 REM 1800 TO THE PRESENT DATE
60 REM THE VARIABLES USED ARE
70 REM P IS THE FINAL PRINCIPAL
80 REM A IS THE ORIGINAL DEPOSIT
90 REM I IS THE INTEREST
100 REM Y IS THE PRESENT DATE
110 REM D IS THE YEAR OF ORIGINAL DEPOSIT
120 PRINT "WHAT YEAR IS IT"
130 INPUT Y
140 LET A = 100
150 LET I = 0.06
160 LET D = 1800
170 LET N = Y - D
180 LET P = A*(1 + I)^N
190 PRINT "THE PRINCIPAL IS NOW"; P
200 END

READY
RUN

WHAT YEAR IS IT
 ?1850
THE PRINCIPAL IS NOW 1842.01

READY
RUN

WHAT YEAR IS IT
 ?1900
THE PRINCIPAL IS NOW 33930.2

READY
RUN

WHAT YEAR IS IT
 ?1980
THE PRINCIPAL IS NOW 3.58968E + 6
```

Fig. 4-3 Compound Interest Program

Table 4-1 NUMERIC CONSTANTS

Written numbers are called *numeric constants* in the ANSI standard for BASIC. They can have these forms:

(a) $sd \cdots d$
(b) $sd \cdots drd \cdots d$
(c) $sd \cdots drd \cdots \mathrm{E}sd \cdots d$
(d) $sd \cdots d\mathrm{E}sd \cdots d$

In the above s is an optional sign, d is a decimal digit, and r is a period.

"E" stands for "times 10 to the power"; if no sign follows E a plus sign is understood.

In the ANSI standard (a) above is called *implicit point representation*
Examples:

55 −32 +42 −39640

Form (b) above is called *explicit point unscaled representation*.
Examples:

39.4 −369.05 +64.75 +32

Form (c) above is called *explicit point scaled representation*.
Examples:

3.2E2	means	$+3.2 \times 10^2$
−6.15E3	means	-6.15×10^3
−2.5E−6	means	-2.5×10^{-6}

Form (d) above is called *implicit point scaled representation*.
Examples:

53E−5	means	53×10^{-5}
64E5	means	64×10^5
79E+72	means	79×10^{72}

want to run this problem for one value of interest, for one value of date of deposit, and for one value or original deposit. Statement 180 would then input specific values. If we eliminate statements 140, 150, and 160, then statement 180 can be made to read as follows:

```
180 LET P = 100*(1 + 0.06)^N
```

Notice, however, that the program in Figure 4-3 allows for a change in any value by simply retyping a LET statement. For example, to change the interest rate to 0.08 in the original program in Figure 4-3 we simply type on our terminal this line:

```
150 LET I = 0.08
```

As programs become more complicated the value of this policy of assigning values to variables so they can be changed will increase. So will the benefits gained from declaring the variables in REM statements and using REM's to document the program.

Table 4-2 INPUT STATEMENTS

The general form of an INPUT statement is

line number INPUT *variable*, . . . , *variable*

Example:

```
30 INPUT A, B, C1
40 INPUT A$, B
50 INPUT A$
```

The variables can be either numeric variables or character string variables.

An INPUT statement causes a question mark to be printed on the user's terminal. The values then typed from the terminal are assigned, in order, to the variables listed in the INPUT statement. Numeric variables must be assigned number values and string variables are assigned string values.

Execution of the program is suspended until all values for variables in the INPUT statement have been assigned.

Numeric values typed in from the terminal should be separated by commas. A ⟨CR⟩ denotes the values have all been input.

If several character string variables occur in single INPUT statements the character strings input from the terminal should be typed in, if needed, separated by commas using quotation marks.

Example:

```
30 INPUT A$, B$
```

To assign BILL to A$ and CARL to B$ the terminal user types

```
"BILL", "CARL" ⟨CR⟩
```

Using quotation marks around character strings permits the inputting of commas in character strings. To input GO ON, CONTINUE to A$, and BILLY to B$ the terminal user types

```
"GO ON, CONTINUE", "BILLY" ⟨CR⟩
```

Most systems will tolerate character strings input without quotation marks but using them is a safe practice.

4-10 SUMMARY

The rules for forming arithmetic expressions and for writing BASIC numbers were explained and examples given. Tables 4-1 and 4-3 show the rules introduced in summary form.

The INPUT statement was introduced and rules for its usage given. Table 4-2 summarizes these rules. Both numbers (number constants) and strings (string constants) can be input into programs using these statements.

Character string variables and character string constants play an important role in BASIC programming. An example of a letter writing program which used both INPUT and PRINT statements to generate a form letter was shown as an example of the power of these statements.

Table 4-3 NUMERIC EXPRESSIONS

Numeric expressions consist of numbers (numeric constants), operation symbols, numeric variables, and parentheses. The operation symbols used are

+	addition
−	subtraction
*	multiplication
/	division
↑, ^, **	exponentiation (Different systems use different symbols, ANSI uses ^.)

Order of evaluation of operation symbols:

(1) exponentiation

(2) multiplication and division

(3) addition and subtraction

After the above ordering of operations, evaluation proceeds from left to right.
Examples:

```
32
A + 324
(B*64) + 18.5
63^2 + 18 or 63↑2 + 18 or 63**2 + 18
(A*3.2)/18
A
B1 + A
32*A1/43
```

A temperature conversion program was used to demonstrate use of the statements in this chapter and to illustrate the process of developing and running a program.

Questions

1. What are the four forms in which number constants (numbers) can be written in BASIC?
2. Show how the following numbers would be written using BASIC "E notation."
   (a) 1050000
   (b) -0.00056
   (c) 2.5×10^6
   (d) -379.4×10^{-5}
   (e) 295/100
   (f) 247/100000
   (g) 29567000
3. Write three numeric expressions in BASIC.
4. Is A a numeric expression in BASIC? Is 6.3? Is A + 6.3? Explain.
5. Prepare a letter writing program to input a name and address and then ask the letter addressee for a campaign contribution for Senator Johnson.
6. Prepare a letter writing program to input a name and address and output a letter trying to sell the "Le Grand Cuisine," a book of cooking recipes.
7. In BASIC, what is a string variable?
8. How many different string variables can be used?
9. How can you input character strings (string constants) into a string variable in BASIC?
10. Write a program to add 1E7 and 1E − 4.
11. You are to develop a BASIC program which will calculate simple interest on short-term loans. The simple interest, I, on a loan of D dollars at a rate of P percent for a period of T days is given by the formula:

    I = D * P * (T/365)

    In the above, P is the annual interest rate. You are to develop a BASIC program which will input D, P, and T for a loan and calculate and print the simple interest.
12. Write a program to calculate W according to the following formula. Assign numeric variable values as follows: Let A = 5, B = 9, X = 6, Y = 4, and D = 3.

    $$W = (A + B)^2 - [(X + Y)/D]^3(A^2) + (1/A)^2$$
13. Have the computer multiply 4E3 by 1E − 4.
14. Have the computer print a decimal value for $\frac{2}{4}$ and $\frac{2}{3}$.
15. Write equivalent algebraic expressions for each of the following BASIC expressions:
    (a) X = A/B*C + D
    (b) X = A*B/D
    (c) X = B**3/4
    (d) D = A/B/C
    (e) K = (A − B)*(C − D)
    (f) H = (A*B)*C + D

16. Write algebraic expressions for these BASIC expressions.
    (a) Y = A/(B + C)
    (b) Y = (A/(B + C))
    (c) P = X/Y + X*2/Y + (X/Y)*2
    (d) Y = 7 *[A/5 + 3]
17. Are the following all valid names for numeric variables in BASIC: A, B, Z2, T6, J8, AB?
18. Are the following two statements equivalent?

```
45 LET A = B + (X*Y)
45 LET A = B + X*Y
```

19. In BASIC arithmetic expressions is exponentiation always performed before subtraction? (Assume no parenthesis in the expression.)
20. Miles can be converted to kilometers by multiplying the number of miles by 1.609. Write a program to convert an input number in miles into kilometers.
21. Each of these BASIC expressions contains at least one error. Find the errors and write a correct statement.

```
(a)    X = (A + B)(C + D)
(b)    X = (A - B)*(CD)
(c)    X = B*2 - 4*AC/2*A
(d)    X = (A + B)*(C + D) + E)
(e)    X = Z/(B + C)*2
(f)    Y = 6.46*X + 44, 497*Z
(g)    Y = A + C23
```

22. Write these numbers in BASIC using the special exponential notation:
    (a) 53,000,000,000 (b) 894,000,000
    (c) 0.00000000135 (d) 0.0000769
23. What is the value of these BASIC numeric expressions?
    (a) 2*3 + 4 + 5 (b) 5 + 1/2*6
    (c) 12*2 + 3*30 (d) 4*3*2 + 4
    (e) 4 + 3*4 + 2 (f) (2 + 1)/30
    (g) 3/4*9 (h) 2/4/2*(4 + 1)
24. Write in BASIC the following expressions:
    (a) $\frac{A+2}{X}$ (b) $12X^2 + 1.3A$
25. Write a program to input a weight in pounds and output that same weight in grams.
26. Prepare BASIC statements for each of the following algebraic expressions:

    (a) $y = -\frac{p+q}{x}$

    (b) $a = (b^2 + c^2)^3$

    (c) $y = \frac{x^3}{80}$

    (d) $y + 2.4x^3 + 16x^2 + 1.2x$

(e) $x = \dfrac{a+b}{c} \cdot \dfrac{d}{e} + \dfrac{x}{y^3}$

(f) $x = 1 + \dfrac{1}{a + \dfrac{1}{b}}$

27. Prepare a program which converts yards to feet. The printout should output, for example,

    3 YARDS EQUALS 9 FEET

28. Prepare a program which converts hours and minutes into minutes only. A typical printout should be

    3 HOURS AND 10 MINUTES EQUALS 190 MINUTES

29. To convert Fahrenheit into Centigrade the formula is

    $C = (5/9)(F - 32)$

    Write a program to input a Fahrenheit temperature and perform the conversion.

30. Write a program to print your initials in magnified form. For example:

```
TTTTT      C C    B  B  B
  T       C       B     B
  T      C        B   B
  T      C        B B
  T      C        B   B
  T       C       B     B
  T         C C   B  B  B
```

Chapter 5 Control Statements—Flow Charts

An important point in the study of BASIC has now been reached. Control statements which make decisions will be introduced in this chapter. Control statements form the basis of the decision-making capability which give the BASIC language a considerable amount of its power.

In order to utilize the full power of control statements, it is useful to learn certain procedures and programming aids which programmers use to formulate and prepare programs. The best-known programming aid, the flow chart, will be studied in this chapter.

5-1 OBJECTIVES

GO TO Statements

The most straightforward control statement in BASIC is the GO TO statement. It must be carefully used because in complicated programs the use of many GO TO's can present a considerable problem in developing a BASIC language program. The GO TO statement is described and explained along with examples of its usage.

IF THEN Statements

The most used BASIC decision-making statement is the IF THEN statement. The IF THEN statement enables the programmer to control the flow of program execution, permitting alternative paths through a program to be taken depending on the values of variables used in the program. IF THEN statements use relational operators and expressions, which will be explained.

Algorithms and Procedures

An algorithm is a procedure with some special characteristics. A great deal of the research work in computer science is concerned with developing and analyzing algorithms. Algorithms are important because they can be implemented by programs. The basic idea of an algorithm and some examples of its usage are given here. The idea of *efficiency* of an algorithm is also explained, and several examples of algorithms and more efficient algorithms are presented.

Flow Charts

In order to develop a program effectively, it is sometimes a good idea to first represent the program using some technique other than the written program itself. The flow chart is a means for representing an algorithm which can then be programmed using the flow chart as a basis. Also the flow chart provides a straightforward means of transmitting to others the operating details of a program. The flow chart provides a convenient, illustrative method for conveying information about the structure of the program in visual form. Examples of algorithms and their flow chart are given along with the corresponding programs.

5-2 GO TO STATEMENTS

The BASIC language has a class of statements called *control statements* which provide control over the sequencing of the statements as they are executed by the computer. The most readily understood of these control statements is the GO TO statement.

Here is an example of a GO TO statement:

```
30 GO TO 60
```

This statement is at line number 30 in the program. It directs the computer to "go to line number 60 next." Or, in other words, "execute the statement at line number 60 next."

The following is a short program with a GO TO statement:

```
10 LET N=0
20 LET N=N+1
30 PRINT N
40 GO TO 20
50 END
```

In this program, the numeric variable N is set to 0 by statement 10 and then incremented to 1 by statement 20. This value, 1, is then printed. The GO TO statement at line 40 then causes the statement with line number 20 to be executed next. Statement 20 increments N from 1 to 2 this time, and 2 is then printed and the GO TO again causes a jump back to statement 20, which causes N to be incremented from 2 to 3, and the 3 is then printed.

How long will this continue? N will become 4, 5, 6, 7, and so on, indefinitely; there is nothing to stop the program. This is called an *infinite loop* and you have just been introduced to one of the great pitfalls in programming. This particular loop is easy to find, but in more complicated programs finding infinite loops can be a genuine problem.

Since none of us is perfect, *if you are going to write programs containing control statements, you should at once find out how to stop a program that is being operated from your terminal.*

A common way to stop a program is to depress the BREAK key on the terminal. Some systems require a CONTROL C, some a CONTROL S, and others use the ESC key, however. In any case, it is important that you understand exactly how to stop a program that is running (and will not stop) from your terminal.

The format of the GO TO statement is quite simple; it is

line number GO TO *line number*

Here is a program with two GO TO's.

```
 10 LET A=0
 20 LET B=3
 30 GO TO 70
 40 LET C=A+B
 50 LET D=C*2
 60 GO TO 90
 70 LET C=15
 80 LET D=C*3
 90 PRINT D
100 END
```

What is the value of D printed by the program? It is 45. The sequence of line numbers in the statements executed in this program is 10, 20, 30, 70, 80, 90, 100.

5-3 IF THEN STATEMENTS

A very important statement in BASIC is the IF THEN statement. A typical IF THEN statement is

```
20 IF A = 5 THEN 60
```

This statement says "if A is equal to 5 then execute the statement with line number 60 next (otherwise take the next statement in order)." Here is this statement in a program.

```
10 LET B = 2.5
20 LET A = 2*B
30 IF A = 5 THEN 60
40 PRINT "THE IF THEN CAUSED NO JUMP"
50 GO TO 70
60 PRINT "THE IF THEN CAUSED A JUMP"
70 END
```

In this program, B is given value 2.5, then A is given value 5. When the IF THEN statement is reached the *relational expression* A = 5 is satisfied (because 5 = 5) and therefore a jump is taken to statement 60, which prints the fact that the jump was taken.

If B is made any number but 2.5, for instance 3, the program will print "THE IF THEN CAUSED NO JUMP" because when statement 30 is reached A will not equal 5, and the jump to 60 will not be taken, but statement 40 will instead be executed.

Here is a short program that asks the terminal operator to pick a digit. If the digit agrees with that in the program, which is 6 for our example, the program prints RIGHT.BYE and ends. If the digit input from the keyboard is not 6, the program prints NO and asks for another digit; this continues until the value 6 is given and the program prints RIGHT.BYE.

```
10 PRINT "INPUT A DIGIT"
20 INPUT X
30 IF X = 6 THEN 60
40 PRINT "NO"
50 GO TO 10
60 PRINT "RIGHT.BYE"
70 END
```

The X = 6 in statement 30 above is an example of a *relational expression* in BASIC. The *relation* in this relational expression is the equals (=) relation. This relational expression is true when X has the value 6.

Here is another relational expression:

```
A > 7
```

In this expression *greater than* (>) is the relation, and this relation is said to be *satisfied* (the relational expression is *true*) if the value of A is greater than 7 when the statement containing the relational expression is reached.

For example, consider

```
20 LET X = 9
30 IF X > 1.5 THEN 90
```

In the above, the relational expression in the IF THEN statement is X > 1.5, and, since X has value 9 when this is reached, the relation is true and the next statement executed will be statement 90.

The relations allowed in BASIC are shown in Table 5-1. Notice that < = stands for "less than or equal to" instead of the more common $\leqslant$ because $\leqslant$ is not available on most keyboards. Similarly, A <> 5 means "A is not equal to 5," instead of the conventional "A ≠ 5" because ≠ is not available on most keyboards.

In an IF THEN statement a numeric expression is on each side of the relation symbol in a relational expression (or a *string expression*, to be discussed later). As in Chapter 4, numeric expressions can use combinations of variables, numeric constants, and arithmetic operations (+, −, /, and so on). Consider

```
30 IF A + B*2 > C - D/5 THEN 120
```

This says "if the value of $A + (B \times 2)$ is greater than $C - D/5$ when this statement is executed, execute the statement with line number 120 next, otherwise execute the next statement in order."

Table 5-1 RELATIONS FOR IF THEN STATEMENTS

SYMBOL	MEANING
=	equality
<	less than
>	greater than
> =	not less ("greater-than-or-equal-to")
< =	not greater ("less-than-or-equal-to")
# or <>	not equal

Table 5-2 IF THEN STATEMENTS

The basic form of an IF THEN statement is

line number IF *relational expression* THEN *line number*

A relational expression has form

numeric expression relation numeric expression

or

string expression relation string expression

Relations are >, <, =, <>, < =, > =
[NOTE: Some BASIC systems allow for IF THEN's with any complete statement at the end of the statement. Then an IF THEN might contain a PRINT statement, a LET statement, and so on.

A typical statement might be

```
30 IF A = 5 THEN LET B = 7
```

If A has value 5, then B would be given value 7, if A does not have value 5, B will be left as is. This is not ANSI standard BASIC. Other systems have an IF THEN ELSE statement to be discussed in Chapter 7.]

Consider

```
10 LET A = 5
20 LET B = 6
30 LET C = 3
40 IF A + B > C*6 THEN 140
50 PRINT "NO GO"
```

If this sequence of statements in a program is run, then the PRINT statement with line number 50 will be executed because $A + B > B \times C$ is not true since $5 + 6$ is not greater than 6×3.

Consider

```
10 LET A = 5
20 LET B = 6
30 IF A - 4 <> B - 7 THEN 120
40 PRINT "NO GO"
```

If these statements in a program are run, statement 120 will be executed (and not 40) since $+1$ is not equal to -1.

Table 5-2 shows the basic format for the IF THEN statement.[1]

[1]String expressions will be discussed in a later section.

A program that answers a business question is now presented. The problem is to develop a program to assist in the ordering of masking tape. The "Consolidated" company charges 75¢ for each roll of masking tape it sells. The "Acme" company charges 90¢ for a similar roll but gives your company a $5.00 discount on every reasonable order (this is for a company which only buys in quantity and would not buy less than ten rolls). You are to input the number of rolls of masking tape to be purchased and the program then chooses and prints the name of the company that will charge less for the order.

Here is the program.

```
 10 REM DECISION OF SUPPLIER PROGRAM
 20 REM S. H. BABEL, 4/5/81
 30 REM M IS NUMBER OF ROLLS, N IS CONSOLIDATED'S PRICE
 40 REM AND T IS ACME'S PRICE
 50 PRINT "INPUT NUMBER OF ROLLS"
 60 INPUT M
 70 LET N = 0.75 * M
 80 LET T = 0.90 * M - 5
 90 PRINT "CONSOLIDATED CHARGES"; N
100 PRINT "ACME CHARGES"; T
110 IF T = N THEN 150
120 IF T > N THEN 170
130 PRINT "BUY FROM ACME"
140 GO TO 180
150 PRINT "BOTH COMPANIES CHARGE THE SAME"
160 GO TO 180
170 PRINT "BUY FROM CONSOLIDATED"
180 END
```

Statement 110 determines if Acme's price is equal to Consolidated's and jumps to 150 if they are. Statement 120 determines if Acme's price is greater than Consolidated's and jumps to statement 170 if it is. The program prints the company's name with the lower price (or that they are equal).

5-4 A PAYROLL PROGRAM

In this section we develop a program to calculate the total pay and number of overtime hours for an employee in a business. The hourly rate for the employees is $6.50 per hour and overtime is paid for all hours in excess of 40 at a rate of 1.5 times the regular rate. The employee's name and the number of hours worked are to be input from the terminal and the program should print the employee's name, total pay, and number of overtime hours. (This might be on a check.)

First, we notice that the program can be prepared in three sections: (1) input employee's name and hours worked, (2) calculate total pay and overtime hours, and (3) print employee's name, total pay, and number of overtime hours.

Now, these statements will call for and then input the employee's name and number of hours worked into the variables E$ and H.

```
10 PRINT "TYPE EMPLOYEE'S NAME"
20 INPUT E$
30 PRINT "TYPE NUMBER OF HOURS WORKED"
40 INPUT H
```

It is now necessary to determine if the employee worked any overtime hours. If not, the total pay will simply be equal to 6.50 times the hours worked and the overtime hours will be 0.

If the employee worked more than 40 hours, however, total pay will be equal to 40×6.50 plus the number of overtime hours times (1.5×6.50). To make our calculations we will need several variables in addition to E$, the employee's name, and H, the number of hours worked. These are

B	the base or regular pay rate
T	the overtime hours
P	the total pay

We begin this section of program by establishing initial values for these variables.

```
50 LET B = 6.50
60 LET T = 0.0
70 LET P = 0
```

The following statements (1) test for overtime and (2) calculate base pay plus overtime, if any:

```
 80 IF H < = 40 THEN 120
 90 LET T = H - 40
100 LET P = (40*B) + (T*(1.5*B))
110 GO TO 130
120 LET P = H*B
```

The final section prints the employee's name, pay, and overtime hours. It is as follows:

```
130 PRINT "THE EMPLOYEE'S NAME IS"; E$
140 PRINT "HIS PAY IS $"; P
150 PRINT "HIS OVERTIME HOURS ARE"; T
160 END
```

```
 10 PRINT "TYPE EMPLOYEE'S NAME"
 20 INPUT E$
 30 PRINT "TYPE NUMBER OF HOURS WORKED"
 40 INPUT H
 50 LET B = 6.50
 60 LET T = 0.0
 70 LET P = 0
 80 IF H < = 40 THEN 120
 90 LET T = H - 40
100 LET P = (40*B) + (T*(1.5*B))
110 GO TO 130
120 LET P = H*B
130 PRINT "THE EMPLOYEE'S NAME IS"; E$
140 PRINT "HIS PAY IS $"; P
150 PRINT "HIS OVERTIME HOURS ARE"; T
160 END

READY
```

(a)

```
TYPE EMPLOYEE'S NAME
 ?JIM JACKSON
TYPE NUMBER OF HOURS WORKED
 ?40
THE EMPLOYEE'S NAME IS JIM JACKSON
HIS PAY IS $260
HIS OVERTIME HOURS ARE 0
READY
RUN
TYPE EMPLOYEE'S NAME
 ?ED JONES
TYPE NUMBER OF HOURS WORKED
 ?35
THE EMPLOYEE'S NAME IS ED JONES
HIS PAY IS $227.5
HIS OVERTIME HOURS ARE 0
READY
RUN
TYPE EMPLOYEE'S NAME
 ?GRANT DEVONS
TYPE NUMBER OF HOURS WORKED
 ?45
THE EMPLOYEE'S  NAME IS GRANT DEVONS
HIS PAY IS $308.75
HIS OVERTIME HOURS ARE 5
```

(b)

Fig. 5-1 Calculating a Payroll. (a) A Payroll Program; (b) Testing the Program

Our next step is to list the program using the LIST system command. The result is shown in Figure 5-1(a). We then test the program as shown in Figure 5-1(b). (More testing would be a good idea.)

Finally, in order to make this into a more attractive, better documented program we first add remarks and the program will then be renumbered using a systems command. (Programmers should write REM statements as they write the program. This is intended to show how REM's can be conveniently inserted if statement numbers are spaced by tens.)

Here are the remark statements. These are now typed at the console.

```
  1 REM PAYROLL PROGRAM
  2 REM J. MURPHY, 8/4/81
  3 REM PROGRAM CALCULATES TOTAL PAY AND OVERTIME
  4 REM VARIABLES USED ARE: E$ IS EMPLOYEE'S NAME
  5 REM H IS HOURS WORKED, B IS BASE PAY RATE
  6 REM T IS OVERTIME HOURS, P = TOTAL PAY
 75 REM TEST FOR OVERTIME GO TO 120 IF THERE IS NONE
 85 REM CALCULATE OVERTIME THEN TOTAL PAY
115 REM THERE IS NO OVERTIME CALCULATE TOTAL PAY
125 REM PRINT EMPLOYEE'S NAME, PAY AND OVERTIME
```

Having typed the above, the following system command is typed[2] (for some systems this will be RENUMBER):

```
RESEQUENCE
```

Now, we type

```
LIST
```

The result is shown in Figure 5.2.

This should again be tested with a few input values for which results are known. A complete program has now been developed.

5-5 CONTROLLING OPERATIONS USING IF THEN STATEMENTS

It is possible to use the IF THEN statement to control the number of times a certain set of BASIC statements is executed. Recall that this statement adds 1 to the current value of a variable N.

```
20 N = N + 1
```

[2] Notice even the line following the GO TO in the REM statement is resequenced. This may not be the case in some systems.

```
 10 REM PAYROLL PROGRAM
 20 REM J. MURPHY, 8/4/81
 30 REM PROGRAM CALCULATES TOTAL PAY AND OVERTIME
 40 REM VARIABLES USED ARE: E$ IS EMPLOYEE'S NAME
 50 REM H IS HOURS WORKED, B IS BASE PAY RATE
 60 REM T IS OVERTIME HOURS, P = TOTAL PAY
 70 PRINT "TYPE EMPLOYEE'S NAME"
 80 INPUT E$
 90 PRINT "TYPE NUMBER OF HOURS WORKED"
100 INPUT H
110 LET B = 6.50
120 LET T = 0.0
130 LET P = 0
140 REM TEST FOR OVERTIME GO TO 210 IF THERE IS NONE
150 IF H < = 40 THEN 210
160 REM CALCULATE OVERTIME THEN TOTAL PAY
170 LET T = H - 40
180 LET P = (40*B) + (T*(1.5*B))
190 GO TO 230
200 REM THERE IS NO OVERTIME CALCULATE TOTAL PAY
210 LET P = H*B
220 REM PRINT EMPLOYEE'S NAME, PAY AND OVERTIME
230 PRINT "THE EMPLOYEE'S NAME IS"; E$
240 PRINT "HIS PAY IS $"; P
250 PRINT "HIS OVERTIME HOURS ARE"; T
260 END
```

Fig. 5-2 Completed Payroll Program

If N is started at value 0, incremented by 1 each time a set of statements is executed, and then N is tested after it is incremented, a scheme can be derived for controlling statement execution. The set of statements which is repeatedly executed is called a *loop*.

Here is the scheme in outline form of a loop that is executed 6 times.

```
10 LET N = 1
20 --------        (Statements to be executed)
60 LET N = N + 1
70 IF N < = 6 THEN 20
80 --------
```

In the above, first N is set to 1 and then the statements to be executed are executed the first time. Then N is incremented to 2 and tested, and because it is less than 6 the program jumps back to statement 20, and the statements up to 60 are again executed. N is then incremented to the value 3, tested, and found to be less than 6 and the statements from 20 to 60 executed again. This continues until N is incremented to 7, at which time N is not less than or equal to 6 and so the jump to 20 is not taken but instead statement 80 is executed. Examination will show that statements 20 to 60 will be executed 6 times with this scheme.

Here is an example of using this technique in a simple program.

Suppose we wish to sum the integers from 1 to 7. There are 7 of these integers and we can make a program to add them as follows:

```
10 LET N = 1
20 LET S = 0
30 LET S = S + N
40 LET N = N + 1
50 IF N < = 7 THEN 30
60 PRINT S; "IS THE SUM OF THE INTEGERS FROM 1 TO 7"
90 END
```

The loop in this case consists of statements 30, 40, and 50.

As another example, here is a program to find the value of $1 \times 2 \times 3 \times 4 \times 5 \times 6 \times 7$ (called the "factorial of 7").

```
10 LET N = 1
20 LET F = 1
30 LET F = N*F
40 LET N = N + 1
50 IF N < = 7 THEN 30
60 PRINT "THE FACTORIAL OF 7 IS"; F
70 END
```

Notice that $N < = 7$ has exactly the same effect as $7 > N$ in an IF THEN statement.

The above program can be generalized so that the number for which the factorial is desired is input from the terminal. (The factorial of a number M is equal to $1 \times 2 \times \cdots \times M$.)

```
10 PRINT "INPUT AN INTEGER"
20 INPUT G
30 LET N = 1
40 LET F = 1
50 LET F = F*N
60 LET N = N + 1
```

```
70 IF N < = G THEN 50
80 PRINT "THE FACTORIAL OF": G; "IS"; F
90 END
```

5-6 EXAMPLES USING LOOPS AND IF THEN STATEMENTS

The number of times a loop is executed can be input when a program is run. Suppose the owner of a store wishes to do some calculations on his sales figures each day. He has a list of the sales price of each item sold and he wants a program to (1) find total sales and (2) find the average sale price. The inputs will then be the sales prices, and the outputs, the total sales and average price.

Here is a program with no comments since a description will follow.

```
 10 PRINT "INPUT NUMBER OF SALES"
 20 INPUT N
 30 PRINT "INPUT A SALES PRICE AFTER EACH QUESTION MARK"
 40 LET S = 0
 50 LET K = 1
 60 INPUT P
 70 LET S = S + P
 80 LET K = K + 1
 90 IF K < = N THEN 60
100 LET A = S/N
110 PRINT "THE TOTAL SALES ARE"; S; "AND THE AVERAGE IS"; A
120 END
```

In the above, the program asks for the number of sales made and inputs this number (from the terminal keyboard) in N. A statement asking for the sales price is then printed and initial values are given to S which will be used to sum the sales prices, and K, which will control the number of times the loop is executed. The loop, consisting of statements 60 through 90, is then entered. This loop is executed N times, each time it adds the sales price input to the current sum. Finally the total sales are divided by N giving the average sales; then the total sales and average sale are printed.

In the above program K < = N in statement 90 is called the *loop-terminating condition*.

In the programs so far each program has been arranged to go through each loop some predetermined number of times. The loop-terminating condition and its inputs can be arranged, however, so that the number of times through the loop can vary from one program run to the next.

For example, suppose the same store owner decides he wants to take money to the bank every time he sells $500.00 or more. He still wants to input sales prices continuously and still wants his average and total printed.

Here is a program to implement the merchant's request.

```
10 LET S = 0
20 LET K = 0
30 PRINT "INPUT A SALES PRICE AFTER EACH QUESTION MARK"
40 INPUT P
50 LET K = K + 1
60 LET S = S + P
70 IF S < 500 THEN 40
80 LET A = S/K
90 PRINT "THE LAST"; K; "SALES TOTAL"; S; "DOLLARS AND THE";
100 PRINT "AVERAGE IS"; A
110 END
```

The above program asks for sales prices until the sum of these prices is $500.00 or more. Then the sales total and average price is calculated. Notice the loop-continuing condition is IF $S < 500$ and also notice K counts the number of prices entered but is not used to terminate the loop. (The loop-terminating condition is $S >= 500$, incidentally.)

As a final example we consider a problem from biology with a mathematical flavor. The mathematician Fibonacci solved this problem; suppose we start with one pair of newly born rabbits. A pair of new rabbits gives birth to another pair of rabbits at the end of the third month and produces another pair of rabbits every month thereafter. How many pairs of rabbits will we have after 6 months? For 2 months we have 1 pair, in 3 months 2 pairs, after 4 months 3 pairs, after 5 months 5 pairs, and after 6 months 8 pairs. The rule which Fibonacci found is to form a sequence of numbers starting with 1, 1 and to then obtain each succeeding number by summing the preceding two numbers. Thus, to obtain the third number we add $1 + 1$ and this gives 2, then $1 + 2$ gives 3, then $2 + 3$ gives 5, and then $3 + 5$ gives 8. This gives the sequence of numbers $1, 1, 2, 3, 5, 8$. We can continue in the same manner: $1, 1, 2, 3, 5, 8, 13, 21, 34, 55, 89, \ldots$. As you can see the rabbits increase at a goodly pace. This sequence $1, 1, 2, 3, 5, 8, 13, 21, 34, 55, 89, \ldots$ is called a *Fibonacci sequence* with 11 terms and can be continued for as many terms (numbers) as desired.

A biologist buys a pair of rabbits and wants to know how long he must wait to start some experiments. He needs more than 600 rabbits. The program to solve this problem is as follows:

```
10 LET N = 2
20 LET A = 1
30 LET B = 1
40 LET C = A + B
50 LET N = N + 1
60 LET A = B
```

```
 70 LET B = C
 80 IF C < = 600 THEN 40
 90 PRINT "AFTER"; N; "MONTHS YOU WILL HAVE"; C; "RABBITS"
100 END
```

The loop-terminating condition here is: IF C < = 600. If you run this program from a terminal, it is instructive to add these statements which will print the Fibonacci sequence

```
 5 PRINT "1 1";
65 PRINT C;
```

Questions at the end of the chapter investigate how to change the loop-terminating conditions so that an arbitrary number of Fibonacci terms can be printed.

5-7 IF THEN STATEMENTS USING CHARACTER STRINGS

The relational expression in an IF THEN statement can contain character strings or character string variables as well as numeric expressions. An example of an IF THEN with two character strings is:

```
20 IF "A" = "B" THEN 50
```

The relational expression in this statement is "A" = "B". This expression is false because the letter A does not equal the letter B and so no jump to 50 is made.

Notice that this expression is not the same as that above:

```
20 IF A = B THEN 50
```

This statement asks whether the current value of the numeric variable A equals the current value of the numeric variable B and a jump is to be taken if they are equal. In the preceding IF THEN statement the A and B in "A" and "B" are *character constants* or *character strings* because they are enclosed in quotation marks.

String variables can also be used in IF THEN statements. Here is a short program.

```
READY
10 LET A$ = "ABLE"
20 LET B$ = "BAKER"
30 IF A$ = B$ THEN 60
40 PRINT "ABLE DOESN'T EQUAL BAKER"
```

```
50 GO TO 70
60 PRINT "ABLE EQUALS BAKER"
70 END
```

This program will print "ABLE DOESN'T EQUAL BAKER" because when statement 30 is executed A$ will have value ABLE and B$ will have value BAKER, and the relational expression A$ = B$ will be false. As a result, the jump from 30 to 60 will not be taken.

Here is a program that mixes a character string and a character variable in an IF THEN statement.

```
10 LET A$ = "GO"
20 IF A$ = "GOT" THEN 60
30 PRINT "CHARACTER STRINGS MUST HAVE THE SAME NUMBER";
40 PRINT "OF CHARACTERS TO BE EQUAL"
50 GO TO 70
60 PRINT "GO EQUALS GOT"
70 END
```

This program gives A$ the value GO and then compares GO with GOT in an IF THEN statement. GO does not have the same number of characters as GOT, however, so they are not equal and the jump is not taken. *For two character strings to be equal in BASIC they must each have the same number of characters and the characters in each position must be the same.*

Here is a program using character string variables and the equals relation to ask a simple question and to then respond.

```
10 PRINT "ANSWER YES OR NO"
20 PRINT "DID YOU VOTE IN THE ELECTION?"
30 INPUT A$
40 IF A$ = "YES" THEN 70
50 PRINT "THEN DON'T COMPLAIN"
60 GO TO 80
70 PRINT "GOOD"
80 END
```

The INPUT in line 30 will accept a character string from the terminal (a carriage return must follow the YES or NO) and places the string into variable A$. Then statement 40 tests if the character string is YES. If it is, then the program will go to statement 70 and print GOOD, otherwise it will print THEN DON'T COMPLAIN.

It should be noted here that the relational operators >, <, <=, >=, and <> can also be used in IF THEN statements containing character strings. The <> relational symbol is straightforward, two character strings are not equal when they have a different number of characters or when they differ in some character with the same position. For example, "A"<>"B" is true; "ABLE"<>"ABLE" is false, and "ABLE"<>"ABL" is true.

Relational symbols such as < and > are less straightforward and their usage is based on knowing how characters are ordered in your BASIC system. The ordering is based on the codes used to represent the characters in the computer but several principles always hold. Before discussing this, here is an example of a statement.

```
20 IF "ABLE"<"ABLF" THEN 60
```

In this statement "ABLE"<"ABLF" is a relational expression and the character string ABLE is compared with ABLF. ABLE is "less than" ABLF because E precedes (is less than) F in the alphabet; therefore the jump will be taken.

Here is a second example:

```
30 IF AB < ABA THEN 60
```

In this example AB is compared with ABA. It will be found "less than" because it agrees with every character which exists but has fewer characters and so the jump will be taken. (The rule that the shorter string is less if every character agrees is the same as saying that a "blank character" or "no character" precedes any actual character.)

Here are some further examples of relational expressions.

EXPRESSION	TRUE OR FALSE
"AB"<"ABC"	true
"AB"<"BC"	true
"BEGIN">"BEGAN"	true
ABLE < ABLEST	true
A123 < A223	true
14B < 18B	true
20A < 10A	false

When alphanumeric characters such as spaces, and punctuation marks are compared, the situation becomes more complicated and it is necessary to know how the characters are ordered in the computer's character set. For instance, does ";" come before ":"? This will be discussed in Chapter 10 (also see Question 34).

We will only use the = and <> relation in the programs until sorting is discussed in Chapter 10. Sorting is the organizing of a set of numbers or character strings into an ordered sequence and programs which sort use the >, <, <=, and >= relations in IF THEN statements. As an example, the names in a dictionary, telephone book, or library reference system are all sorted and programs containing IF THEN's can be used to sort lists of names (and numbers) as will be discussed.

5-8 PROCEDURES AND ALGORITHMS

In business, the term *procedure* is used to describe how situations which arise are to be handled. For instance, in banks there are well-established procedures for processing checks and deposits. Good business procedures are thought to be essential to success in modern commerce and businesses continually examine these procedures, hoping to make them more efficient or effective.

In the computer world, the word *algorithm* is used to describe what would generally be called a procedure in business.[3] The term "algorithm" describes one of the most important concepts in computer science. "Algorithm" has a long history: its origin can be traced to a medieval Arabic mathematician called Abu Ja 'Jar Mohanned ibn Mûsâ al-Khowârzmi who developed the procedures we commonly use when adding, subtracting, multiplying, or dividing two decimal numbers with pencil and paper. These procedures are good examples of what an algorithm is, for they are systematic, efficient, always applicable, and cover a large class of useful problems. Once learned, these procedures are easily followed; grade school students learn them and use them all their lives, often without further thought.

If we were asked to define the word "algorithm," common usage would lead us to consider it a synonym for such words as "rule," "procedure," "method," or "technique." In computer science, however, "algorithm" has come to have a special meaning.

The following are several characteristics a procedure or method must have in order to qualify as an algorithm.

1. An algorithm must always end after a finite number of steps. That is, if an algorithm is used to solve some problem, it must not require an infinite number of steps. (An algorithm may require an excruciatingly high number of computational steps, but it must finally terminate.)
2. An algorithm must be capable of being described by a finite list of steps (or instructions) which detail exactly what is to be done at all times. An algorithm must be able to handle *any* condition that may arise.
3. An algorithm must be capable of dealing with all members in some class of problems. For instance, the algorithm for multiplying can

[3]While all algorithms are procedures, not all procedures are algorithms. The word *procedure* is used loosely and for many less-than-completely-defined sets of steps to be performed, whereas an *algorithm* in computer science must be well-defined.

be used on any two decimal numbers we happen to write down; it does not exclude numbers with leading digit 7, for example, or negative integers, or integers greater than 45 and less than 98.

As may be seen, an algorithm is a particular kind of procedure which has special properties particularly useful to those using computers. The logical question is now, "What motivates this concern and the need for this special term?" The answer is that an algorithm is particularly suited to be programmed for a digital computer, and an important step in using a computer to solve a problem is to formulate the algorithm to be used. A program is then written which expresses this algorithm in the programming language that has been selected. The final program is then as good as, but no better than, the algorithm.

An important consideration is always the efficiency of an algorithm. Some algorithms are far more efficient than others in that, when programmed, one may require fewer steps (or perhaps less memory) than another and will therefore be more satisfactory or economical in actually solving problems on a computer. Considerations of this sort will arise in what is to follow. The development and analysis of the efficiency of algorithms is central to several areas of business, science, and mathematics, and the computational efficiency of an algorithm can be studied at various levels ranging from calculations of computer program running times for various inputs to very mathematically oriented and abstract comparisons with other algorithms concerning ultimate efficiency.

5-9 EXAMPLES OF ALGORITHMS

Algorithms are not limited to numerical procedures. We can write an algorithm for starting a car, making out a deposit slip in a bank, and so on. However, because numerical algorithms make good examples and are much used in computers we will start with them.

First, let us consider two problems and try to develop algorithms for solving them.

Problem 1

Given two numbers m and n, calculate a number x such that $m + x = n$.

ALGORITHM

Subtract m from n and then print this value, which is the correct value for x.

This procedure is simple, efficient, and yields an immediate solution to all problems in this class. The algorithm assumes that whoever or whatever performs the algorithm can subtract and print.

Problem 2

If we consider only integers[4] as candidates for x, m, n, and r, let us try to find and print a satisfactory integer value for x in the equation $m + nx = r$. We immediately use algebra to form $x = (r - m)/n$. Now, let us call an algorithm that works for only some (not necessarily all) possible sets of input values for r, m, and n, a *semialgorithm*.

SEMIALGORITHM

- *Step 1.* Subtract m from r. Call this value b (that is, $b = r - m$).

- *Step 2.* Divide b by n. Call this result x and print this value.

The above two steps are certainly efficient. As an example, let $m = 6$, $n = 3$, and $r = 12$, in which case we have $6 + 3x = 12$. Then in Step 1 we have $12 - 6 = b$, and so $b = 6$; in Step 2 we have $b/n = 6/3 = 2$, and so we print $x = 2$.

The two steps in the semialgorithm above have two fatal flaws, however. First, if n equals 0, then either $m = r$ and x can be anything, or $m \neq r$ and a solution is impossible. Second, if there is a nonzero remainder when b is divided by n, there is no *integer* x which satisfies the equation. Thus we must patch our rules so that when these cases arise, we can deal with them. Here is an algorithm with the necessary "patches."

- *Step 1.* If $n = 0$ and $m = r$, go to Step 6, otherwise go to Step 2.

- *Step 2.* If $n = 0$ and $m \neq r$, go to Step 5, otherwise go to Step 3.

- *Step 3.* Subtract m from r; call this b. (That is, $b = r - m$.)

- *Step 4.* Divide b by n; if there is a remainder, go to Step 5. If there is no remainder, print the value of b/n. Stop.

- *Step 5.* Print "No integer satisfies this equation." Stop.

- *Step 6.* Print "Any integer satisfies this equation." Stop.

The above algorithm contains several *decision steps*. In Step 4, for example, after b is divided by n, we must decide whether the remainder is nonzero: differing actions are taken for 0 and for nonzero remainders. Such decisions are common in algorithms, as are *loops* where the same

[4] The set of all integers is the set 0, +1, −1, +2, −2, +3, −3, ... That is, integers do not include fractions such as 0.25 or 0.33 or mixed numbers such as 1.25 or 2.36. Integers are sometimes called *whole numbers*.

sequence of steps is performed a number of times. In order to further investigate these and other aspects of algorithms, we shall introduce techniques for representing algorithms with flow charts in the following sections.

5-10 FLOW CHARTS

In order to prepare a problem or class of problems for computer solution, we must first decide what steps the computer is to take. This involves working out an algorithm for the problem. As the number of steps increases and as the number of decisions that must be made increases, the need for a good visual representation of the algorithm with strong intuitive appeal arises. The flow chart provides such a representation and is widely used.

When flow charts are used, the general procedure for preparing problems for computer solution is as follows. First, the general approach to the problem is considered, and the outlines of an algorithm for the problem are formulated. Second, a flow chart of the algorithm is drawn. Third, the flow chart is coded (translated) into a suitable computer programming language, read into the computer, and operated.

Flow charts provide a widely used method for representing algorithms diagrammatically and as a preparation for coding problems for computer solution. There are several sets of flow chart symbols; those of the American National Standards Institute (ANSI) and the International Organization for Standardization (IOS) are used here.

The basic symbols used in flow charts are shown in Figure 5-3 along with a brief description of the purposes of each symbol. The following sections tell what can be written in the symbols and give the uses of the symbols in describing algorithms.

5-11 ASSIGNMENT AND COMPARISON OPERATORS

The process blocks of flow charts often use an *assignment operation* (sometimes called a *replacement* or *substitution* operation). This operation consists of assigning some value to a variable and is indicated by means of the assignment operator symbol "= ". Thus, LET A = 5 means "Assign the value 5 to the variable A." Similarly, LET A = 5 + 6 − 3 means "Assign the value of 5 + 6 − 3, which is 8, to A."

The following sequence of assignment operations results in C having value 15 (and A having value 7 and B having value 8):

```
LET A = 7
LET B = 8
LET C = A + B
```

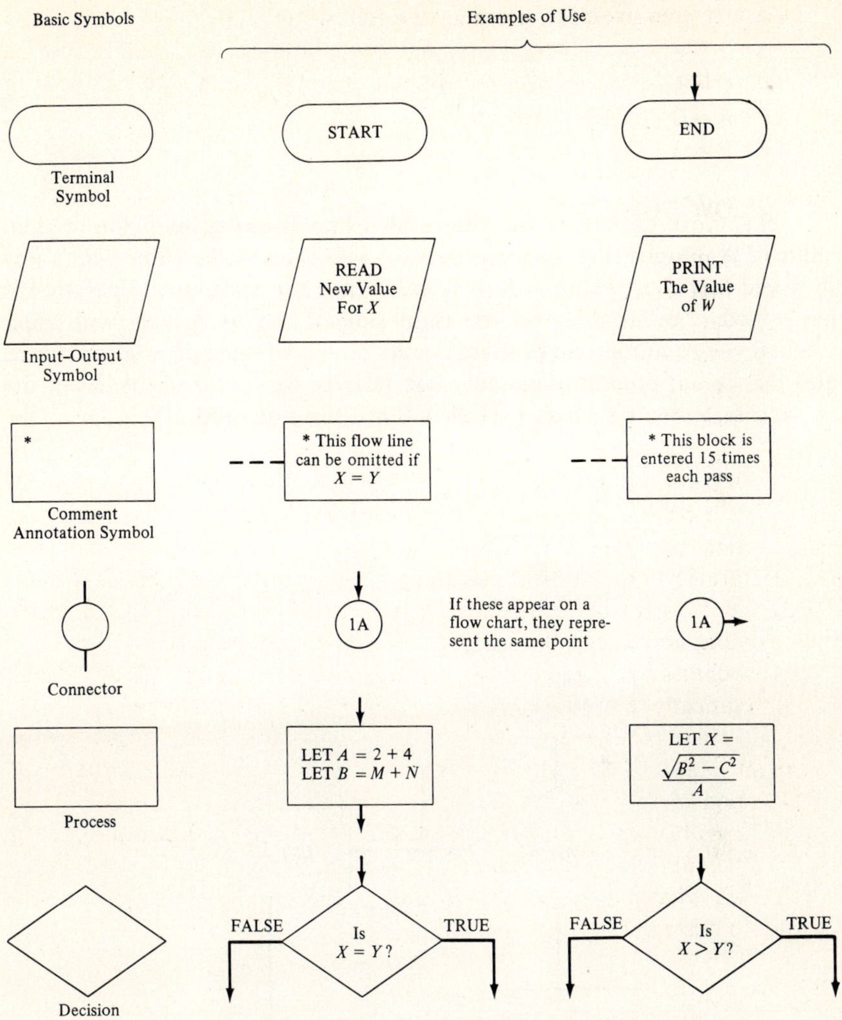

Fig. 5-3 Flow Chart Symbols

Similarly, consider

LET A = 3
LET B = 4
LET C = A∗B
LET A = C + B

The result of the above is that after the assignments have been performed C has value 12, B has value 4, and A has value 16.

As a further example, consider the following:

LET C = A
LET A = B
LET B = C

The above exchanges the values of A and B and gives C the original value of A. Notice that the assignment A = B gives A the value which was in B and leaves the value of B as it was. When the assignment operation is performed, the variables on the right side of the = remain with their original values unless one of them occurs on the left side of = also. Notice also that in our present usage only one variable can occur to the left of the =, and statements such as LET A + B = C are not valid.

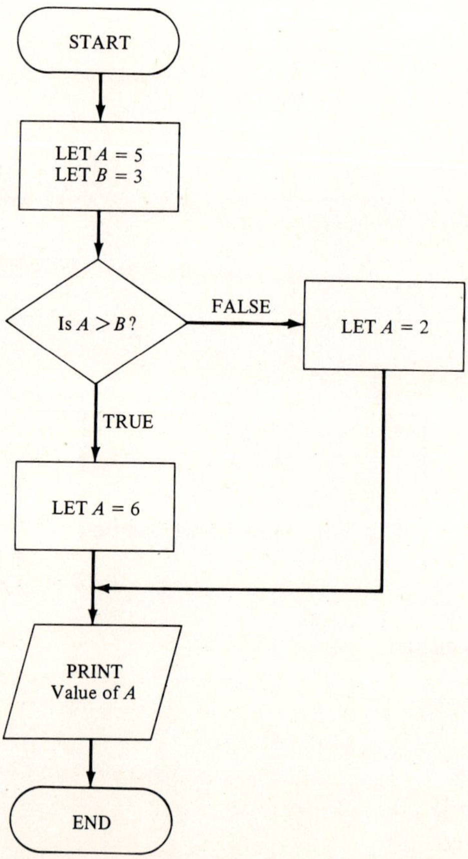

Fig. 5-4 Use of Comparison Operator

As can be seen, the assignment operation corresponds to a BASIC "LET" statement. As a result, this operation can be readily converted into a BASIC statement.

In order to make a decision, a computer often makes comparisons between two values. For instance, an algorithm may have a step where a determination must be made whether the current value of a variable, say A, is greater than the current value of B. The same binary relational symbols $>$, $>=$, $<$, $<=$, $=$ which are used in BASIC will be used to write computer algorithms in flow charts. These symbols are called *relational symbols* or *comparison operators* in computer terminology and are used as follows:

$A < B$	means	A is less than B
$A <= B$	means	A is less than or equal to B
$A > B$	means	A is greater than B
$A >= B$	means	A is greater than or equal to B
$A = B$	means	A is equal to B
$A <>$	means	A is not equal to B

In Figure 5-4 the comparison operator $>$ is used. In the flow chart, first A is given the value 5 and B the value 3. Then the question, "Is A greater than B?" is asked in the decision box. Since A is greater than B, the TRUE flow line is followed, and A is given the value 6, which is printed and the system is stopped.

5-12 SUBALGORITHMS

In Figure 5-5 the decision box plus the assignment statements are used to form a counter which counts the passes through the loop consisting of boxes 3 and 4. First, A is set to 0, F to 1, and N to 5. Then A is set to 1 in box 3 and also the variable F is given the value $F \times A$ which is 1; then the question "IS $A = N$?" is asked. Because A has value 1 and N has value 5, the answer is "No," and so the relation does not hold, and the FALSE exit from the decision box is taken.

This results in box 3 being reentered. A is then incremented from 1 to 2, and F is given the value 2×1 in box 4. Again the question is asked, "IS $A = N$?" by decision box 4. The answer is again "No," and so the FALSE exit is taken, and box 3 is again entered. This is continued for five passes through the loop at which time A will have value 5 and will equal N, so the TRUE exit will be taken this time, the current value of F printed, and the END box entered.

When the final value of F has been calculated, it will be found to be $1 \times 2 \times 3 \times 4 \times 5$ which is defined as the "factorial of 5" and written 5! In

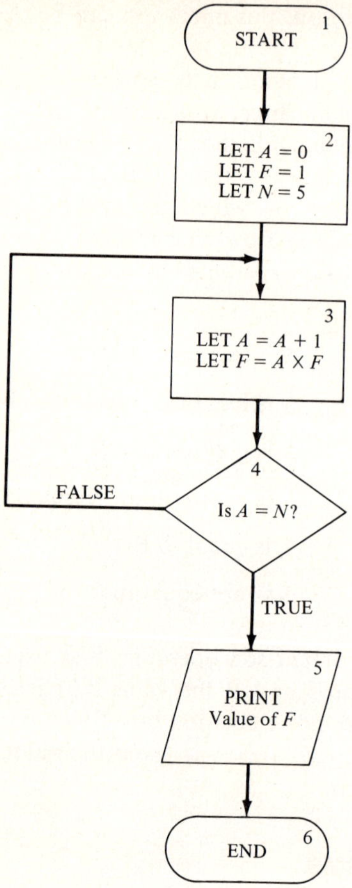

Fig. 5-5 Use of Comparison Operator to Calculate a Factorial

mathematics; it is equal to 120. Compare the flow chart with the factorial program for 7 previously shown in this chapter.

In general, the factorial of the integer N is written N! and is defined as follows:

$$1! = 1$$

$$N! = 1 \times 2 \times 3 \times \cdots \times N$$

This means 1! is 1; $2! = 2$; $3! = 1 \times 2 \times 3 = 6$; $4! = 1 \times 2 \times 3 \times 4 = 24$; $5! = 1 \times 2 \times 3 \times 4 \times 5 = 120$; and so on.

The flow chart in Figure 5-5 will calculate the value of the factorial function for any value of N. Simply place the desired value to the right of the N in box 2 so that N is originally given the value of the integer whose factorial is desired. For instance, to calculate 20! simply write LET N = 20

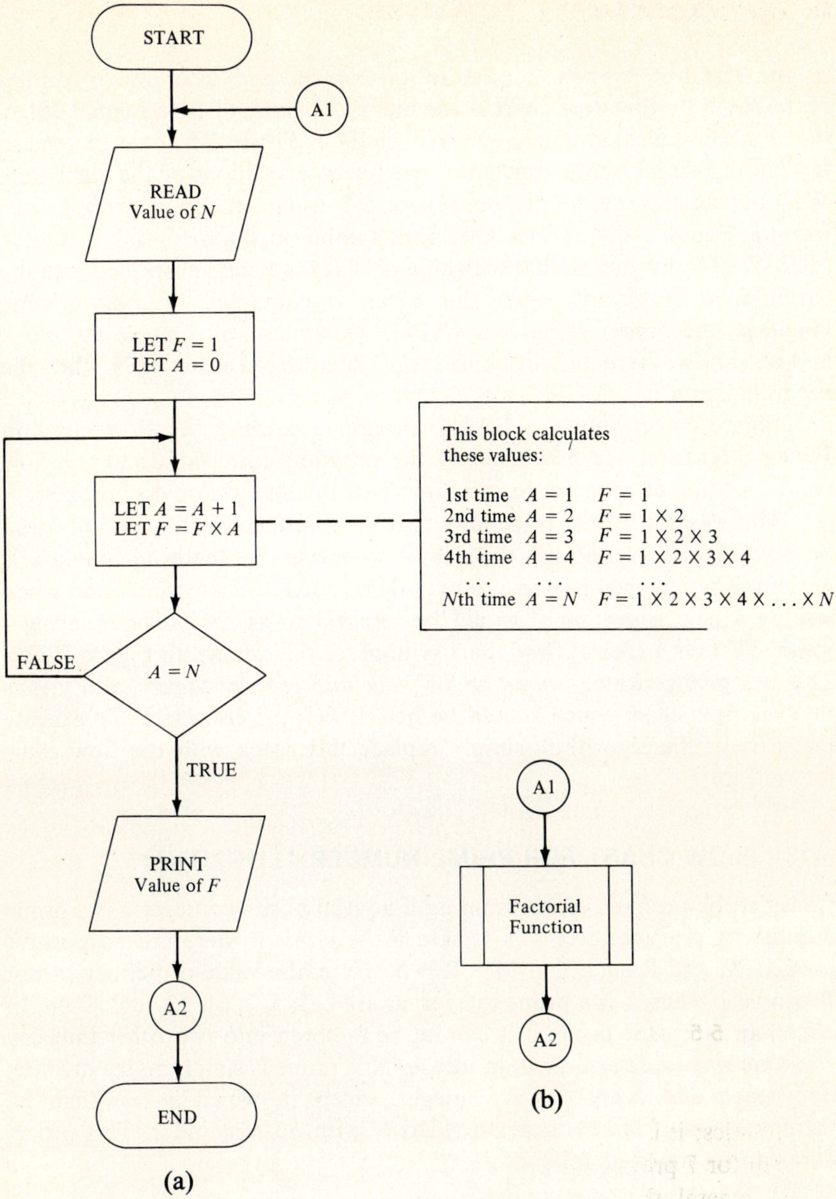


```
10 INPUT N
20 LET F = 1
30 LET A = 0
40 LET A = A + 1
50 LET F = F * A
60 IF A <> N THEN 40
70 PRINT F
80 END
```

(c)

Fig. 5-6 (a) Factorial Function Flow Chart; (b) Predefined Process Symbol; (c) Program for (a)

as the last line in box 2 (instead of N = 5), and after the algorithm represented by this flow chart is executed, the value of F will equal 20!.

Further consideration shows that the N in Figure 5-5 could be read in instead of being given a constant value for all executions of the algorithm. We indicate this by redrawing Figure 5-5 using an input symbol, thus forming Figure 5-6(a). Inside the input symbol in Figure 5-6(a) is written "READ N"; this means that the value of N is read and substituted into the variable N. Naturally, when this block is converted to programming language, the proper READ or INPUT statement will replace the block and all that will remain will be to supply the desired value of N when the program is run.

Figure 5-6(c) shows a BASIC program realizing the flow chart in Figure 5-6(a). Notice how directly the program corresponds to the flow chart.[5] Coding or programming a flow chart is a straightforward process.

This raises a further possibility that the flow chart in Figure 5-6(a) can be used as part of another flow chart whenever the factorial function is desired. The factorial flow diagram is then called a *subalgorithm* and when writing a new algorithm it would be referred to as the *factorial subalgorithm*. There is a special flow chart symbol for this, shown in Figure 5-6(b). This is a *subalgorithm*, *subroutine*, or *predefined process* symbol, and means that the flow chart which should be here is defined elsewhere. To execute this part of the algorithm, simply replace this block with the flow chart referred to.

5-13 FLOW CHART FOR PRIME NUMBER ALGORITHM

Consider the problem of determining if a given positive integer *n* is a prime number. A positive integer N is said to be *prime* if there are no positive integers M and R such that M × R = N. Here, the value of neither M nor R can be 1. Thus, 1 is a prime integer, as are 2, 3, 5, 7, 11, 13, and so on. In effect, an integer is prime if it cannot be factored into two other integers.

One way to determine if an integer N is prime is simply to try dividing it by each and every positive integer, except 1, which is less than N, thereby seeing if some integer divided N with no remainder. This procedure can be stated as follows:

- ***Step 1.*** Read the value of N.

- ***Step 2.*** Is N = 1? If Yes, go to step 7; if No, assign the value 1 to the variable R.

- ***Step 3.*** Add 1 to the current value of R and call this new value R.

[5]A factorial program with input and output statements was also shown in Section 5-5.

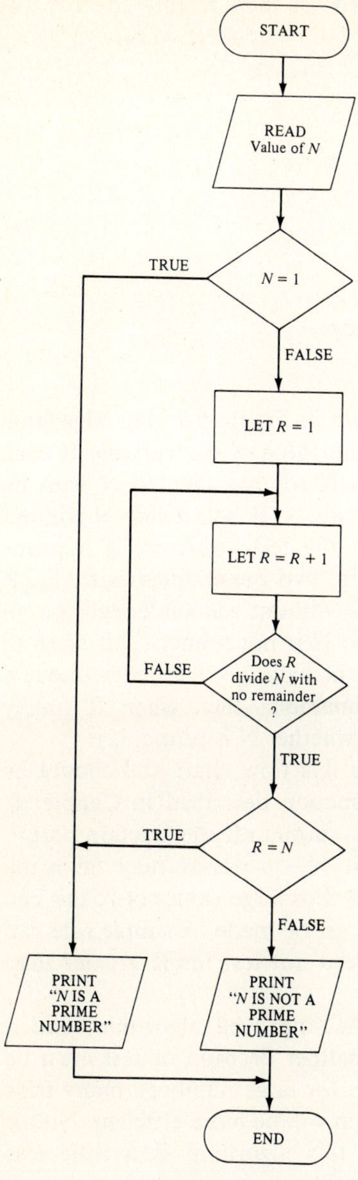

(a)

```
10  INPUT N
20  IF N = 1 THEN 110
30  LET R = 1
40  LET R = R + 1
50  REM THE NEXT STATEMENT TESTS WHETHER R DIVIDES N EXACTLY
60  REM IF IT DOES NOT THE PROGRAM JUMPS TO 40
70  IF N/R <> INT (N/R) THEN 40
80  IF R = N THEN 110
90  PRINT N; "IS NOT A PRIME"
100  GO TO 120
110  PRINT N; "IS A PRIME"
120  END
```

(b)

Fig. 5-7 Prime Number Algorithm Flow Chart

- *Step 4.* Divide N by the current value of R. Is there a remainder? If Yes, go to Step 3.

- *Step 5.* Is $R = N$? If Yes, go to Step 7.

- *Step 6.* Print "N is not a prime number." Stop.

- *Step 7.* Print "N is a prime number." Stop.

A flow chart of this algorithm is shown in Figure 5-7. The algorithm uses the technique of continually raising the value of the variable R each pass through the loop until R is equal to N (or has divided N with no remainder). Notice that when R finally equals N, R will divide N without remainder; this fact is used to terminate the tests when N is a prime integer. When the algorithm reaches Step 5, two possibilities exist: (1) R will be less than N and having divided N without remainder will be an integer less than N which divides N, and so N is not prime; (2) if after all values of R greater than 1 and less than N have been tested without a single division resulting in a nonzero remainder, then when R finally reaches the value of N, we can stop testing whether N is prime; it is.

The program in Figure 5-7(b) realizes this flow chart and should be studied. Statement 70 contains an INT function described in Chapter 8. This simply makes N/R into an integer by cutting off the fraction part.

For a given value of N, notice that $N-1$ passes may be made through the loop consisting of Steps 3 and 4. For large values of N this can mean that many passes through the loop must be made. A simple rule can make this algorithm more efficient: We need not test for R greater than the square root of N.[6]

Figure 5-8 shows a flow chart of the improved algorithm, and a program for this algorithm. In this case, another decision or test must be made each time around the loop, but since, for large numbers, many trips must be made around the loop, the algorithm will be more efficient. Notice for small N (for instance, $N = 2, 3, 4, 5$) this algorithm is a little less efficient, but as N becomes larger, the algorithm improves in comparison with the prior one. Studies of algorithmic efficiency often concentrate on the rate of growth of the number of calculations required by an algorithm as the size of the numbers used increases. In other cases an algorithm is evaluated by seeing if it is efficient for "worse cases."

[6] For if R divides N, then N/R also divides N, and both R and N cannot be larger than $\sqrt{N}$.

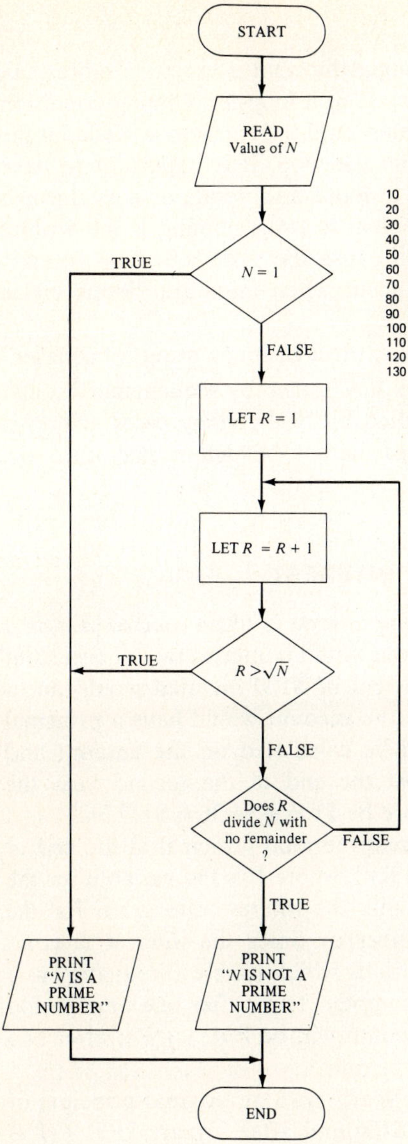

(a)

```
10  INPUT N
20  IF N = 1 THEN 120
30  LET R = 1
40  LET R = R + 1
50  IF R > N ^ (1/2) THEN 120
60  REM THE NEXT STATEMENT TESTS WHETHER R DIVIDES N EXACTLY
70  REM IF IT DOES NOT THE PROGRAM JUMPS TO 40
80  IF N/R <> INT (N/R) THEN 40
90  IF R = N THEN 120
100  PRINT N; "IS NOT A PRIME"
110  GO TO 130
120  PRINT N; "IS A PRIME"
130  END
```

(b)

Fig. 5-8 Improved Prime Number Algorithm

5-14 TERMINATING LOOPS

In general, a sequence of steps in an algorithm that is executed more than once is called a *loop*. Somewhere in any loop a loop-terminating condition must reside, and the loop is then executed until the decision is made by the loop-terminating condition to exit from the loop. It is important to have algorithms that do not get "hung up" in loops and iterate or pass through the loops indefinitely. A common problem in programming is the writing of loops that, with certain inputs, will cause the system to loop forever. This kind of error is more likely to occur when there are "loops inside loops."

So far the flow charts have indexed through loops using a "counter" which went from 1 to N (or from 1 to $\sqrt{N}$), thereby sequencing through the loop some number of times specified by N. In many cases a loop is used for which the number of passes cannot be determined until the problem is run.

5-15 CALCULATING COMPOUND INTEREST

When money is deposited in a bank, the interest is often *compounded on a yearly basis*. This means that, for instance, with an interest rate of 6 percent per year, at the end of 1 year a principal of \$100 invested would accumulate interest of \$6. The second year the account would have a principal of \$106; the 6 percent interest would be calculated on the amount and would then be $0.06 \times \$106 = \$6.36$. At the end of the second year the principal in the account would therefore be $\$106 + \$6.36 = \$112.36$.

If interest is "compounded" N times, the total principal at the end of the Nth compounding will be $P \times (1 + R)^N$, where P is the variable for the original principal deposited, R represents the interest rate given for the basic time period, and N is the number of times the interest is compounded (the number of basic time periods which have expired; the basic time period was a year in the above example). Thus, after one time period N will be 1, and the amount in the account will be $P \times (1 + R)$; after two periods $P \times (1 + R)^2$, and so on.

For a 6 percent rate compounded yearly with an original principal of \$100, after 1 year $\$100 \times (1 + 0.06) = \$106$ and after 2 years $\$100 \times (1 + 0.06)^2 = \$100(1 + 0.12 + 0.0036) = \$112.36$, as was calculated.

We now develop an algorithm which, when presented with an interest rate, will calculate after how many years (for what value of N) the principal in the bank will double. To implement this, we use some fixed initial investment for P; let us use \$1 and then multiply this by $1 + R$ until the value of $(1 + R)(1 + R) \ldots (1 + R)$ exceeds \$2. The flow chart for this is shown in Figure 5-9(a) and the corresponding BASIC program is shown in 5-9(b). The only value which need be read in is R; the flow chart or algorithm then calculates the least N for which $(1 + R)^N \geqslant 2$, and passes

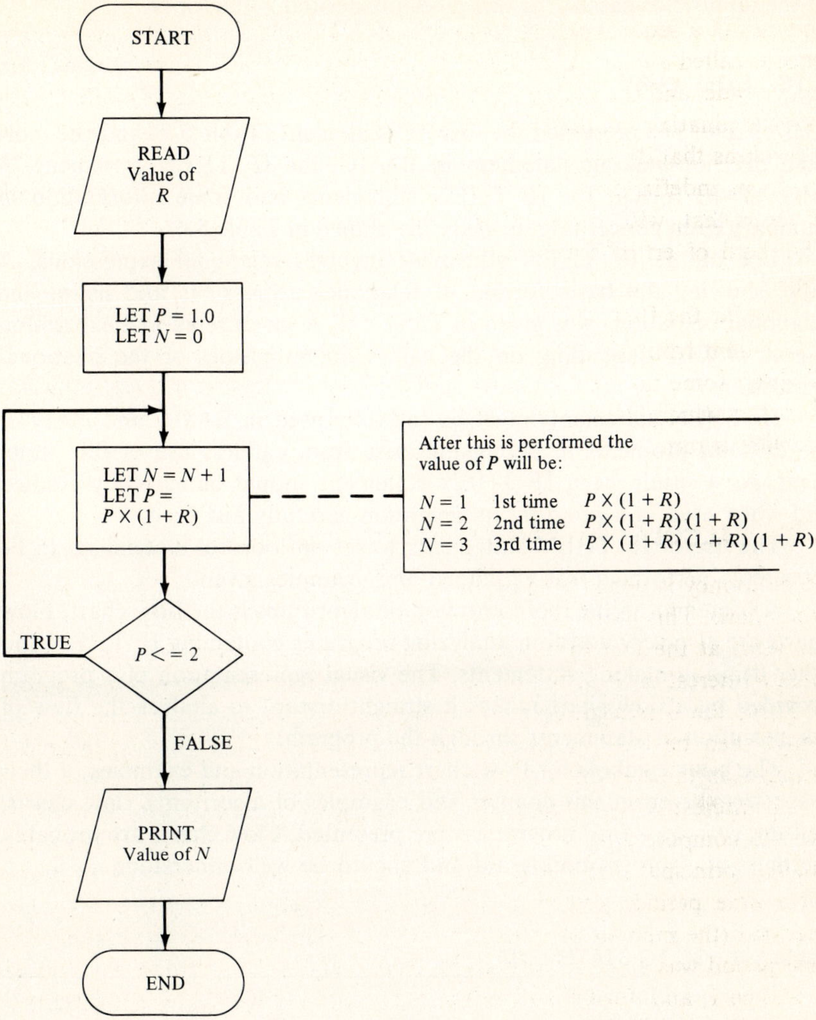

(a)

```
10 INPUT R
20 LET P = 1
30 LET N = 0
40 LET N = N + 1
50 LET P = P * (1 + R)
60 IF P <= 2 THEN 40
70 PRINT "FOR AN INTEREST RATE OF"; R; "MONEY DOUBLES IN"; N; "YEARS"
```

(b)

Fig. 5-9 Compound Interest Program

are made through the loop until this condition is fulfilled. A count is made of the number of passes, for this gives the desired value for N.

5-16 SUMMARY

This chapter has presented the GO TO statement (Table 5-3) and the most used decision-making statement in BASIC, the IF THEN statement. A table of the format for IF THEN statements and some information in summary form concerning its usage are shown in Table 5-4.

Use of the IF THEN statement involves relational expressions. A table showing the basic format of relational expressions and listing the relational operations was given in Table 5-2. A given relational expression is *true* or *false* depending on the values on both sides of the relational expression.

IF THEN statements must be carefully used in BASIC and many of the difficult problems in debugging arise from careless use of this statement. As a result, each IF THEN statement should be carefully studied and when used in a program its operation carefully analyzed.

The use of IF THEN statements to set up loops of statements to be repeatedly performed was explained and examples given.

A basic tool in the representation of algorithms is the flow chart. Flow charts are also very useful in analyzing programs containing IF THEN and other decision-making statements. The visual representation of a program provided by a flow chart makes it straightforward to analyze the flow of the execution of statements through the program.

The basic symbols for flow chart representation and examples of their usage were given in this chapter and examples of algorithms, flow charts, and the corresponding programs were presented. Flow charts are probably the most-used programming aid and should be well understood so that a

Table 5-3 GO TO STATEMENT

The general format is

line number GO TO *line number*

A GO TO statement, when executed, causes the next statement executed to be that at the *line number* following the GO TO.

Examples:

```
30 GO TO 120
50 GO TO 89
```

The first of these statements causes a jump to line number 120 and the second to line number 89.

Table 5-4 IF THEN STATEMENTS

The general form of an IF THEN statement is

line number IF *exp1 rel exp2* THEN *line number*

rel is one of the relational operators >, <, =, >=, <=, <>. exp1 and exp2 are either numeric or string expressions.

Examples:

```
30 IF 3 < 13 THEN 35
40 IF A + 8 < 1.7 * C THEN 50
50 IF "ABLE" = A$ THEN 70
60 IF H$ < = B$ THEN 90
```

If the value of the relational expression consisting of *exp1 rel exp2* is true then the execution of the program continues at the *line number* following the THEN. If the relational expression is false, then the program execution continues in normal sequence with the statement following the IF THEN statement.

The relation of equality holds between two strings if and only if the two strings have the same length and contain identical sequences of characters.

Character ordering in strings is according to the alphanumeric code used in the computer. Normally, however, A precedes B, which precedes C, and so on, up to Z; and 0 precedes 1, which precedes 2, up through 9. Punctuation marks are ordered by the alphanumeric code used in the computer. Also, a "blank" precedes letters, which precede digits, which precede punctuation marks.

---

program can be developed using them and also so the programs of others can be studied using their flow charts.

In some cases, the number of passes through a loop in a program cannot be determined before the program is run. To aid in analysis of a program of this type, flow charts are particularly useful because the visual representation enables one to see how the program makes decisions when run.

Questions

1. What is a relational expression in BASIC?
2. What are the relation operators in BASIC?
3. Modify the program in which someone tries to guess a digit so the guesser gets only two chances.
4. Modify the program which prices masking tape so that Consolidated gives a $12.00 discount on orders.
5. How do you stop a program that is running on your computer?

6. What will be printed if the following program is executed for an input of 5, followed by 20, followed by 40?

```
10 INPUT X
20 IF X < 20 THEN 60
30 IF X = 20 THEN 50
40 PRINT "GOOD"
50 PRINT "BETTER"
60 PRINT "BEST"
70 PRINT
80 END
```

7. Suppose someone pays 1¢ during the first year, 2¢ during the second, 4¢ during the third, and that yearly payments keep doubling. Write a program that will determine the first year for which the payment will be greater than $50,000.00.
8. Write a program to find the sum of all odd integers from 1 to 99.
9. Write a program that reads a value of X with $0 < X < 1$ and then finds an integer I so that $0 < I*X < 50$ and such that I*X is as close to 50 as possible.
10. A company pays an employee $5 per hour if she works 40 hours or less. If she works more than 40 hours, she gets $9.00 per hour for each extra hour. Draw a flow chart and then write a program that will determine an employee's pay.
11. Write a program for which a number is input, and the computer prints back either

    ```
    IT IS TEN
    ```

    or

    ```
    IT IS TWENTY
    ```

    or

    ```
    IT IS NEITHER TEN NOR TWENTY
    ```

    depending on which is the case.
12. Write a program that will determine whether three input numbers could be the sides of a right triangle. Run it for 3, 4, 5, then for 6, 12, 14, then for 5, 12, 13. (A, B, C, can be the lengths of sides of a right triangle provided $C^2 = A^2 + B^2$.)
13. Write a program that converts inches into feet and inches. The printout should read, for an input of 34,

    ```
    34 INCHES EQUALS 2 FEET 10 INCHES
    ```

14. Tennis balls are priced at $2 each if less than ten are purchased, and $1.50 each if at least ten are purchased. Write a program that inputs the number purchased, and printouts the total cost.

15. Draw a flow chart for a program that determines whether a number is between 20 and 30.
16. Footballs are priced at $30 each if less than three are purchased, $18 each if at least three but less than ten are purchased, and $16.00 each if at least ten are purchased. Write a program that will print the cost given the number to be purchased.
17. The fine for speeding is based on how much you exceed the speed limit. Assume the fine is computed as follows:

AMOUNT OVER LIMIT (mi/hr)	FINE
1–10	$10
11–20	$20
21–30	$30
31–40	$40
41 or more	$50

Write a BASIC program to output the following when executed:

```
WHAT WAS SPEED LIMIT?      (to be input)
YOUR SPEED?     (to be input)
THE FINE IS ________ DOLLARS
```

18. Write a BASIC statement that inputs two numbers typed at a terminal into variables X and Y.
19. Write a single BASIC statement that causes a conditional transfer of control to statement 200 if the value of numeric variable A is greater than or equal to 6.
20. What will happen if the following program is executed?

```
10 LET S=2
20 LET X=3
30 LET X=S+X
40 LET X=X+2
50 IF X<50 THEN 20
60 PRINT X
70 END
```

21. What will the printout be?

```
10 LET A=2
20 LET B=5
30 IF A=B THEN 60
40 PRINT "A IS NOT EQUAL TO B"
50 GO TO 70
60 PRINT "A EQUALS B"
70 END
```

21. What will be printed if the following program is executed?

```
10 LET Y = 4
20 LET X = 5*Y
30 PRINT X
40 LET Y = Y + 2
50 PRINT Y
60 IF Y <= 100 THEN 40
70 END
```

22. A parking garage charges a $1.00 minimum fee to park for one hour or less. The garage charges an additional $0.50 per hour for each hour *or part thereof* in excess of one hour. The maximum charge for any given 24-hour period is $10.00. Write a BASIC program that will calculate and print the parking charges for each customer who parks in this garage.
23. Draw a flow chart symbol which indicates that the sum of variables A and B and C is to be assigned to variable P.
24. Draw a single flow chart symbol which indicates that values for variables A, B, and C are to be obtained from a user's terminal.
25. Draw a single flow chart symbol that indicates the end of an algorithm.
26. An instructor decides to award letter grades on an examination as follows:

90–100	A
80–89	B
70–79	C
60–69	D
0–59	F

Write a program to produce the following output when executed:

```
INPUT EXAM GRADE?  (numerical grade is input)
YOUR GRADE IS      (Program types out A, B, C, D, or F)
```

27. Make a flow chart for each of these algorithms:
(a) Input two numbers from a user at a terminal, compute the sum of the numbers, and then print the sum.
(b) Input two numbers from a user at a terminal and print the larger of the two numbers.
28. Examine the operation of the program below by hand for two sets of inputs.

```
10 INPUT A, B, C
20 IF A < B THEN 60
30 IF B >= C THEN 80
40 LET D = A + C
50 GO TO 90
```

```
 60 LET D = A - B
 70 GO TO 90
 80 LET D = A + B - C
 90 PRINT D
100 END
```

29. Suppose Amy Smith deposits \$100 at 7 percent, whereas Joan Johnson deposits \$200 at 2 percent. When will Smith have more money than Johnson?
30. Write a program that inputs a number X with value $0 < X < 1$ and determines how many leading zeros X has. [*Hint*: If X has P leading zeros, then $10^P * X > 1$ but $10^{P-1} * X$ is not greater than 1.]
31. Write a program that will print your name five times.
32. A salesman is paid commission on the following scale:

0–500.00	2 percent
\$500–\$5000	3 percent
over \$5000	5 percent

Prepare a program to input the amount of sales and output of the salesman's commission.

33. The Boston Utility Co. charges for electricity as follows:

KILOWATT-HOURS	COST
0–200	\$10.00
201–1000	\$10.00 + 0.05 for each KWH above 200
1001 and more	\$50.00 + 0.03 for each KWH above 1000

Write a program to input a customer's usage figure for a month from the terminal and then calculate and print the customer's charges for the month.

34. Write a program to input two characters from the keyboard and to then determine the ordering of the characters on your system. For instance, if "A" and "B" are input from the keyboard, the program should print that $A < B$.
35. Using the program developed in the preceding question determine the ordering of the punctuation marks on your keyboard.

Chapter 6
FOR-NEXT and READ-DATA Statements—Correcting Programs

Several statements in BASIC provide a convenience to the programmer and make the language more useful in many classes of problems. One such statement is the FOR statement, which is always used in conjunction with a NEXT statement; it provides for a controlled number of passes through a loop in a BASIC program. Another statement pair is the READ statement, which is always used in conjunction with one or more DATA statements; this statement provides for an easier introduction of values into variables than the repeated use of LET statements.

When control statements are used in programs, and the number of statements in programs increases, the complexity also increases. As programs become more complex, it is inevitable that errors in programs will occur. Therefore, the final sections of this chapter introduce techniques for locating and correcting errors made in preparing a program. Also, the procedures for storing a program in auxiliary, or secondary storage and later recovering it are presented in a final section.

6-1 OBJECTIVES

FOR and NEXT Statements

In many cases a loop consisting of several statements must be repeatedly executed in a program, and the FOR and NEXT statements make it possible for the programmer to easily control the number of passes through this loop. The sections on FOR and NEXT statements provide the programmer with information on this control feature. Study of these statements will add to the programmer's tools for controlling program operation.

READ and DATA Statements

In order to introduce values into variables in a BASIC program, LET statements can be used. However, in order to assign values to a number of variables, a number of LET statements equal to the number of variables must be written. This can be a tedious and error-prone operation. Further, in order to change these values, the LET statements must be rewritten. The READ and DATA statements provide a convenient means for assigning values to variables. Further, by simply retyping the DATA statements, new values for the variables can be conveniently introduced. This subject is treated in detail.

The RESTORE Statement

The RESTORE statement is often used with READ and DATA statements. Its function is to return or restore the order in which values are taken from DATA statements to the first DATA statement in the program. An explanation of the RESTORE statement along with some examples of its usage are given.

Correcting Errors in a Program

The complexity of the BASIC language has now reached the point where complicated and powerful programs can be written. Trouble-shooting new programs (finding and correcting errors in them) then becomes a major task for the programmer. An important point should be made here: *The best way to handle errors is not to let them occur*. After this, the best idea is to have as few errors in the program before running it as is possible. In most cases, this means carefully reading and executing a new program using pencil and paper before placing the program on a computer. It is not a good idea to trouble-shoot a program into existence on the computer.

When errors do occur (that escaped manual checks), it is necessary to have tests to find these errors and then to correct them in a systematic way. This involves having approaches worked out in advance to test a program and locate the errors if the program does not operate properly. This chapter also treats this subject.

Saving a Program in Auxiliary Memory

It is sometimes convenient to store a program in secondary memory where it can be kept from terminal session to terminal session. The procedures for moving a program from work space into secondary memory and for later recalling a stored program are presented and examples given.

6-2 THE FOR AND NEXT STATEMENTS

If computers could only execute program statements once in a fixed statement-by-statement order, their usefulness would be greatly limited. The ability to perform the same string of statements repeatedly greatly enhances the computer's powers. In this section we will examine BASIC's primary statement for repeating a string of statements under program control: the FOR statement. Another statement, the NEXT statement, is always used with a FOR statement.

Here is a short program using a FOR and NEXT statement which will sum five numbers input from a terminal.

```
          10 LET S = 0
          20 FOR I = 1 TO 5
        ⎧ 30 PRINT "INPUT NUMBER"
LOOP    ⎨ 40 INPUT A
        ⎩ 50 LET S = S + A
          60 NEXT I
          70 PRINT "THE SUM OF THE NUMBERS YOU INPUT IS"; S
          80 END
```

The important parts of this program are the FOR and NEXT statements. The FOR I = 1 TO 5 says "repeat the statements up to (and including) the NEXT statement with values of I from 1 to 5." The NEXT statement marks the end of the loop in the program to be repeated. Figure 6-1 shows this program in flow chart form.

When the program is executed, S is first set to 0, then the FOR statement gives I its starting value, which is 1, and establishes a test or limit value for I, which is 5. The statements up to the NEXT are then executed. When the NEXT statement is reached, I is incremented by 1, giving I a new value of 2, and the computer goes back to the statement after the FOR statement, statement 30. Another value is then input into A and when the NEXT statement is reached, I is incremented to 3 and statement 30 again executed.

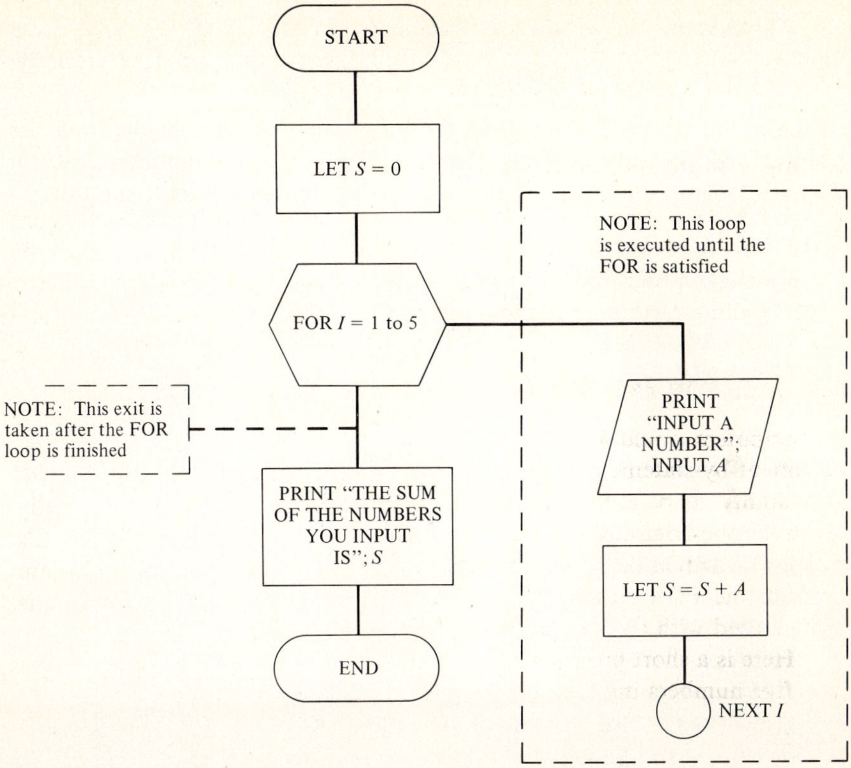

Fig. 6-1 Adding Several Numbers Using a Programmed Loop

The result is that statements 30 through 60 are repeated 5 times and I is given the values 1, 2, 3, 4, and 5 in succession. Each time an input value is read from the terminal and added to the current sum.

When the NEXT statement is reached after the fifth pass through the *loop* consisting of statements 30 through 60, I has value 5 and the limit for I, which was 5, has been reached. As a result, the statement after the NEXT statement (that is, statement 70) is executed. This results in the sum being printed along with an appropriate statement.

It is important to note that there actually is a variable I stored in computer memory and that this variable takes the values 1 through 5 while the loop is executing.[1] The values of this variable may be used or printed during execution of the loop.

[1]The value of I will be 5 *during* the final pass and will be 6 *after* the final pass through the loop, that is, when statement 70 is executed. This will be dealt with later.

For example, if we add the statement

```
25 PRINT "I NOW EQUALS"; I
```

to the above program, each time the program runs through the loop the terminal will print the current value of I. If we input the numbers 2, 9, 15, 24, and 23 from the terminal, the terminal's printout will look like this:

```
I NOW EQUALS 1
INPUT NUMBER
 ?2
I NOW EQUALS 2
INPUT NUMBER
 ?9
I NOW EQUALS 3
INPUT NUMBER
 ?15
I NOW EQUALS 4
INPUT NUMBER
 ?24
I NOW EQUALS 5
INPUT NUMBER
 ?23
THE SUM OF THE NUMBERS YOU INPUT IS 73
```

The numbers 2, 9, 15, 24, and 23 were input from the terminal, and the sum was printed by the computer.

Here is a program that sums the integers from 1 to 20:

```
10 LET S = 0
20 FOR I = 1 TO 20
30 LET S = S + I
40 NEXT I
50 PRINT "THE SUM OF ALL INTEGERS FROM 1 TO 20 IS"; S
60 END
```

When this program is run, I takes the values $1, 2, 3, \ldots, 20$ and each time I is added to S when statement 30 is performed. When statement 40 is reached the twentieth time through the loop, I has value 20 and the computer sees that this is the test or limit value and so executes the statement following the NEXT instead of going back to the statement after the FOR. This results in execution of the PRINT statement.

Consider this FOR statement:

```
10 FOR K = 2 TO 6
```

in this statement, 2 is called the *initial value* and 6 is called the *limit*.

To be more precise, the format of the above FOR statement is as follows:

line number FOR V = *initial value* TO *limit*

The V here can be any numeric variable (A, B, I, Al, and so on). The "initial value" is the starting value for V (the numeric variable) and this value is incremented until it reaches (or exceeds) the limit. The initial value and limit can be numeric expressions (which include both numbers and numeric variables). For example, all of these are acceptable:

```
FOR I = 1 TO N
FOR A = M TO N + 2
FOR S = K TO A1*2
```

The expression

```
FOR S = K TO A1*2
```

will cause S to first have the value of K when the FOR is first executed and to then be incremented by 1 until it reaches the value of Al*2. For example, if K = 5 and Al = 6 when the FOR is reached, then S will have values 5, 6, 7, . . . , 12.

We now examine a program where the limit is input from the terminal. Since the factorial function has been introduced in Chapter 5 we we will again use this as an example. The program that follows can then be compared with previous programs. The point here is that the FOR-NEXT statements do not add to the capabilities of BASIC if we have IF THEN's but the FOR simplifies writing many programs.

Suppose we wish to know the value of the product of all positive integers up to and including any given integer N. (This is called the factorial of N and is generally written N!.) For instance, the product of all positive integers less than or equal to 3 is $1 \times 2 \times 3 = 6$. The product of all positive integers less than or equal to 5 is $1 \times 2 \times 3 \times 4 \times 5 = 120$.

Here is a program to input a value N and find its factorial:

```
10 LET P = 1
20 INPUT N
30 FOR M = 1 TO N
40 LET P = P*M
50 NEXT M
60 PRINT "THE PRODUCT OF ALL INTEGERS FROM 1 TO"; N; "IS"; P
70 END
```

Here are two typical printouts:

```
?4
THE PRODUCT OF ALL INTEGERS FROM 1 TO 4 IS 24

?8
THE PRODUCT OF ALL INTEGERS FROM 1 TO 8 IS 40320
```

The control variable in a FOR statement can be incremented by values other than 1. This is done by adding another section to the FOR statement with the word STEP followed by the increment desired. As an example:

```
FOR I = 1 TO 7 STEP 2
```

will cause the control variable I to take the values 1, 3, 5, and 7. As another example:

```
10 LET S = 0
20 FOR K = 2 TO 11 STEP 3
30 LET S = S + K
40 NEXT K
50 PRINT S
60 END
```

This will cause K to have values 2, 5, 8, and 11; the value printed will be 26.

6-3 RULES CONCERNING FOR AND NEXT STATEMENTS

Considerable flexibility is given in the rules for usage of the FOR and NEXT statements in BASIC. Care must be taken when other than the conventional forms of the FOR statements are used, however. The complete format of a FOR statement is

FOR V = *initial value* TO *limit* STEP *increment*

Numeric variable (called "control variable") — Numeric expressions

The STEP *increment* section of this statement is optional as has been noted. The *increment* value is a 1 when the STEP *increment* section is omitted.

Most of the freedom in the usage of FOR statements comes because the initial values, limit, and increment can all be numeric expressions. As a result, they cannot only be integers as we have used so far, but also numeric variables, expressions such as A + 0.5*B, negative values such as

−2.5, −21.7, and so on. Thus, a FOR statement can look like this:

```
FOR A = B TO C1*0.5 STEP P1/2.6
```

The statements from the FOR statement up to and including the NEXT statement are called a "FOR block." Let us call the initial value I and the STEP increment value S. Then the block is to be repeated with the control variable having value I, I + S, I + 2S, I + 3S, ... until I + MS equals the limit value or I + (M + 1) × S exceeds the limit value.

Thus we can have

```
FOR I = 0 TO 1 STEP 0.1
```

This will result in execution of the FOR block with I having values 0, 0.1, 0.2, ..., 0.9, 1.0.

Great care must be taken when such constructions are used, however. Integers, both positive and negative, can be exactly represented in most machines. Decimal fractions may not be directly represented, however. As a result, the 0.1 above may not be directly representable (it would appear as 0.099999, for example), although the above will probably work as expected.

A FOR statement such as

```
FOR I = 1 TO 0 STEP −0.1
```

may not work as expected, however, and should be tested before use.

FOR blocks can be *nested* (this means one FOR block can be written inside another FOR block), as shown in this example:

```
10 LET S = 0
20 FOR I = 1 TO 4
30 FOR K = 1 TO 3
40 LET M = I + K
50 NEXT K
60 NEXT I
70 PRINT S
80 END
```

The first time the LET statement is executed, I and K each have value 1. The second time I will have value 1 and K value 2, the fourth time I will have value 2 and K value 1, and the final time I will have value 4 and K will have value 3.

An example of a program that uses the full FOR statement follows. We wish to generate a table of Fahrenheit and the corresponding Centigrade temperatures for some temperature interval to be input from the terminal and with some number of regularly spaced temperatures also input from the terminal.

First we input the lowest and highest temperatures (in Fahrenheit) to be listed. Then we input the number of temperatures to be listed.

```
 10 PRINT "INPUT LOWEST TEMPERATURE FOR TABLE"
 20 INPUT L
 30 PRINT "INPUT HIGHEST TEMPERATURE FOR TABLE"
 40 INPUT H
 50 PRINT "INPUT NUMBER OF ENTRIES FOR TABLE"
 60 INPUT N
 70 PRINT "        TEMPERATURES"
 80 PRINT "FAHRENHEIT", "CENTIGRADE"
 90 LET D = (H - L)/(N - 1)
100 FOR F = L TO H STEP D
110 LET C = (F - 32)*(5/9)
120 PRINT F, C
130 NEXT F
140 END
```

Statements 10 through 60 input a lowest and highest temperature and the number of entries for the table. Statement 90 calculates the number of degrees between temperatures in the table entries (the N − 1 is because both highest and lowest temperatures will be used). Thus this increment, or interval, is used to step the FOR statement. The temperature F, in degrees Fahrenheit, then is stepped by the FOR statement in increments of D from H to L degrees. For each F the corresponding Centigrade temperature C is calculated and both are printed.

A typical run of this program looks like this:

```
INPUT LOWEST TEMPERATURE FOR TABLE
 ?10
INPUT HIGHEST TEMPERATURE FOR TABLE
 ?90
INPUT NUMBER OF ENTRIES FOR TABLE
 ?9
        TEMPERATURES
FAHRENHEIT      CENTIGRADE
10              -12.2222
20              -6.66667
30              -1.11111
40               4.44444
50               10
60               15.5556
70               21.1111
80               26.6667
90               32.2222
```

FOR *V* = *Initial value* TO *limit* STEP *increment*
Statements in FOR block
NEXT *V*

(a)

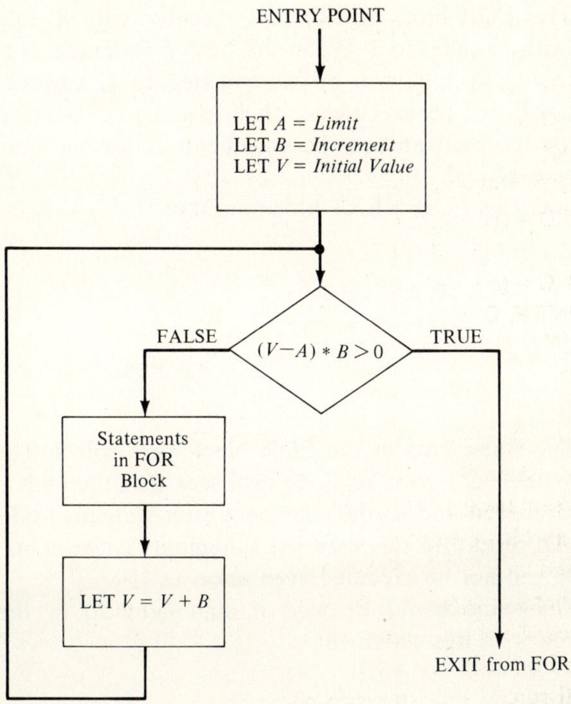

(b)

Fig. 6-2 For-Next Statement Flow Diagram Using IF and Assignment Operations. (a) FOR-NEXT Statement Format; (b) Flow Diagram of FOR-NEXT Statements Operation

Being able to set the increment as well as the starting and final values for the step variable in a FOR statement can be used to advantage in programs of this type, as can been seen.

A good way to examine the operation of FOR-NEXT statements is using a flow chart as shown in Figure 6-2. Examination of the flow chart will often aid in resolving problems with negative numbers as limits or increments. A program detailing FOR-NEXT operation is also given in the summary and this can be useful in difficult constructions.

On the following page are some further comments concerning FOR-NEXT usage.

1. Consider a FOR-NEXT block in this form:

```
10 FOR K = 1 TO 4 STEP 2
   - - - - - - - - - - - -
50 NEXT K
   - - - - - - - - - - - -
```

This FOR block will first be executed with K equal to 1 and then with K equal to 3. When the NEXT statement is reached and K is equal to 3, K will be incremented to 5, however, the FOR block will not be executed with K equal to 5 because this value exceeds the limit and so the statements following line number 50 will be executed.

2. Consider this FOR-NEXT block outline:

```
10 LET A = 5
20 FOR K = A TO 4 STEP 2
   - - - - - - - - - - - -
60 NEXT K
   - - - - - - - - - - - -
```

The statements in the FOR block here will not be executed. When statement 20 is read, control sees that the limit has already been exceeded and so the statement after statement 60 is executed next. To repeat, in this case the statements between statements 20 and 60 will not be executed even once.

The same could be said if statement 20 in the above is replaced with this statement

```
20 FOR K = 2 TO -3 STEP 2
```

Again the limit has been exceeded before the FOR block is executed. (Incrementing the control variable by 2 will never cause it to reach −3 so the limit is considered to be exceeded; examine the flow chart in Figure 6-2.)

3. Here are three more statements for which the statements in the FOR block will be passed over and not executed:

```
20 FOR K = 1 TO 3 STEP -2
20 FOR K = 2 TO 0
20 FOR K = 6 TO 3 STEP 2
```

Before the FOR block is executed each time computer control examines the limit, current value of the control variable and increment and only executes the statements in the FOR block when it is possible to equal or exceed the limit by adding more increments to the current value of the control variable.

6-4 THE READ AND DATA STATEMENTS

Numbers have been introduced into program operation using either LET statements or INPUT statements in the programs so far. Another way to enter data is through READ and DATA statements. Briefly, a READ statement makes an assignment of values to one or more variables and DATA statement(s) list the data to be used in these variables.

As an example, consider

```
10 DATA 10, 25, 35
20 READ A, B, C
30 LET D = A + B + C
40 PRINT "IF A, B, C = "; A; ","; B; ", AND"; C; "THEN A + B + C = "; D
50 END
```

When this program is translated, the DATA statement will be read but not executed. When the READ statement is executed, the computer will look for the first DATA statement in the program (the one with the smallest line number). It will then assign the values in that statement to the variables in the READ statement in order of occurrence. For the above example, the value 10 will be assigned to A, 25 to B, and 35 to C. The computer will then perform the calculation for D and finally print

```
IF A, B, C = 10, 25, AND 35 THEN A + B + C = 70
```

Here are some rules concerning READ and DATA statements.

RULE 1

The DATA statements can occur anywhere in the program before the END.

The statements

```
10 DATA 10, 20, 15
20 READ A, B, C
30 LET D = A + B + C
```

assign the same value to A, B, and C as

```
10 READ A, B, C
20 DATA 10, 20, 15
30 LET D = A + B + C
```

and the following gives the same result:

```
10 READ A, B, C
20 LET D = A + B + C
30 DATA 10, 20, 15
```

RULE 2

When several DATA statements are in a program, data are taken from them in order with the first (lowest line number) statement used first, the second (second lowest line number) statement used second, and so on.

Consider, for instance,

```
10 READ A, B, C
20 DATA 10
30 DATA 20
40 DATA 30
50 LET D = A + B + C
```

This puts 10 into A, 20 into B, and 30 into C. So does

```
10 READ A, B, C
20 DATA 10
30 DATA 20, 30
40 LET D = A + B + C
```

and so does

```
10 DATA 10, 20
20 READ A, B, C
30 DATA 30
40 LET D = A + B + C
```

and so does

```
10 DATA 10
20 READ A, B, C
30 LET D = A + B + C
40 DATA 20, 30
```

RULE 3

Multiple READ statements read in order from multiple DATA statements. Consider the statements

```
10 READ A, B
20 READ C, D
30 DATA 10, 20
40 DATA 30, 40
50 LET X1 = A + B + C + D
```

The above gives values 10 to A, 20 to B, 30 to C, and 40 to D. So does

```
10 DATA 10
20 READ A
30 DATA 20, 30, 40
40 READ B, C
50 READ D
60 LET X1 = A + B + C + D
```

and so does

```
10 DATA 10, 20
20 READ A, B, C
30 READ D
40 LET X1 = A + B + C + D
50 DATA 30, 40
```

The READ and DATA statements simplify the job of assigning values to variables in programs. Several LET statements can replace READ and DATA combinations, but if a number of variables must be assigned values, the READ and DATA statements will be found to be more convenient. More importantly, by simply changing the values in the DATA statements, a program can be rerun with new values for the variables.

RULE 4
READ statements may contain character string variables as well as numeric variables and DATA statements may contain character string constants as well as numeric constants. In most systems, character string constants in DATA statements must be enclosed in quotation marks. Therefore, programs such as the following are legal:

```
10 READ A, B$, C, D$
20 DATA 3, "TIMES", 4, "EQUALS"
30 LET E = A*C
40 PRINT A; B$; C; D$; E
50 END
```

If this program is run, the computer will print

```
3 TIMES 4 EQUALS 12
```

The type of datum in a list of data elements must correspond to the type of variable to which it is assigned. For example, the word "TIMES" cannot be assigned to the variable C. Statements such as the following would therefore not be legal:

```
10 READ A$, B
20 DATA 5, "EQUALS"
```

6-5 TEACHING PROGRAMS

Computers are now used as part of educational programs in both schools and industry. Often, the computer is used to print a question and then check the answer, thus printing a statement telling if the answer is right or wrong and perhaps correcting the user in some way.

To illustrate the fundamental ideas let us develop a program using DATA and READ and also a FOR-NEXT loop. The program is to ask the terminal user to guess the name of the capital of a state, to then check the response, and give the correct answer if necessary.

The following is a typical interchange between computer and terminal user when this program is used:

WHAT IS THE CAPITAL OF MASSACHUSETTS	Computer asks question
?BOSTON	Answer is input by user
RIGHT	Computer says "RIGHT"
WHAT IS THE CAPITAL OF MISSOURI	Another question from computer
?DALLAS	Answer
NO IT'S JEFFERSON CITY	Answer is wrong so computer
WHAT IS THE CAPITAL OF TEXAS	gives right answer
?AUSTIN	
RIGHT	
WHAT IS THE CAPITAL OF CALIFORNIA	
?LOS ANGELES	
NO IT'S SACRAMENTO	

The program to generate this exchange follows:

```
10 REM CAPITALS PROGRAM
20 REM A. J. KEEN, 8/9/81
30 REM S$ IS THE STATES VARIABLE, C$ IS THE CAPITALS, AND,
40 REM G$ IS THE GUESS
50 FOR K = 1 TO 4
60 READ S$, C$
70 PRINT "WHAT IS THE CAPITAL OF ";S$
80 INPUT G$
90 IF C$ = G$ THEN 120
```

```
100 PRINT "NO IT'S "C$
110 GO TO 130
120 PRINT "RIGHT"
130 NEXT K
140 DATA "MASSACHUSETTS", "BOSTON"
150 DATA "MISSOURI", "JEFFERSON CITY"
160 DATA "TEXAS", "AUSTIN", "CALIFORNIA", "SACRAMENTO"
170 END
```

Here are some important points concerning the program.

1. The DATA statements contain state and capital values in pairs. The READ statement reads a state into S$ and then a capital into C$. This is repeated each pass through the loop consisting of the FOR and NEXT statement.
2. The FOR and NEXT statements are set up to sequence four times through the loop. Each pass through the loop reads a pair capital and state values into C$ and S$; there are four such pairs in the DATA statements.
3. To change the states and capitals only the DATA statements need to be changed. To increase the number of states and capitals only the final value in the FOR statement needs to be changed.
4. Quotation marks should be used around character strings in DATA statements, although some systems will tolerate their absence.

To further show the flexibility of this overall scheme for a program, the above program has been converted to one which tests for a knowledge of chemistry by asking for the abbreviations for various chemical names.

Each pass through the program the name of the chemical is printed and the terminal user (student) is asked to give the corresponding chemical abbreviation. If the answer is correct, RIGHT is printed; if the answer is wrong, a NO and the correct answer is printed. Because the construction of this program is so similar to that of the preceding guessing program a detailed description of its operation will not be given. By adding alternate questions based on whether a given answer was right or wrong, a program that coaches the student and also progresses at the student's learning rate can be developed.

The following program is typical of a program used in many training programs in industry where employees are taught and sometimes graded using a computer. (The computer can be programmed to count the number of answers right and wrong and prints this later. The questions at the end of the chapter develop this idea.)

```
10 REM CHEMISTRY PROGRAM
20 REM A. J. KEEN, 8/9/81
30 REM C$ IS THE CHEMICAL ELEMENTS NAME
```

```
 40 REM A$ IS THE ABBREVIATION AND G$ IS THE GUESS
 50 FOR K = 1 TO 4
 60 READ C$, A$
 70 PRINT "WHAT IS THE ABBREVIATION FOR ";C$
 80 INPUT G$
 90 IF G$ = A$ THEN 120
100 PRINT "NO. IT'S ";A$
110 GO TO 130
120 PRINT "RIGHT"
130 NEXT K
140 DATA "ALUMINUM", "AL", "BORON", "B"
150 DATA "GADOLINIUM", "GD", "NEPTUNIUM", "NP"
160 END
```

Here is a typical run from this program:

```
WHAT IS THE ABBREVIATION FOR ALUMINUM
 ?AL
RIGHT
WHAT IS THE ABBREVIATION FOR BORON
 ?BO
NO. IT'S B
WHAT IS THE ABBREVIATION FOR GADOLINIUM
 ?GD
RIGHT
WHAT IS THE ABBREVIATION FOR NEPTUNIUM
 ?NE
NO. IT'S NP
```

6-6 PROCESSING DATA ORGANIZED IN RECORDS

When large amounts of data are to be processed by a computer, the organization of the data is an important factor. The most straightforward way to organize data, and one which often makes good sense, is to simply establish what is called a *record* format and then list the records to be processed one right after the other. This organization is called a *flat file* in business data processing.

For example, suppose we have a sales force consisting of several sales personnel and the number of salespeople can vary from time to time. Each salesperson has a name and a base rate for hours worked. The salespeople are paid at their base rate for each hour worked up to 40 hours and are paid time-and-a-half for each hour over 40. In addition, the salespeople are paid a percentage on what they sell and this percentage also varies from salesperson to salesperson. For each salesperson there are five factors to be considered in calculating the weekly pay check. These are:

1. Salesperson's name
2. Base pay rate
3. Number of hours worked
4. Amount sold
5. Percentage to be paid on total sales (commissions)

To organize these data into a record we simply list the values in order. In data processing, each set of five values would be called a *record*. Here is a typical record.

John A. Reston, 9.50, 45, 2500.00, 0.02

First let us draw a flow diagram showing how to calculate a payroll. This is shown in Figure 6-3(a). The next step is to refine this description of the program to be developed. This consists of:

1. Assigning variables to the inputs and outputs.
2. Writing the READ statement to read the data for each salesperson.
3. Calculating hourly pay for each salesperson.
4. Adding hourly pay to commission and printing the total pay for each salesperson.

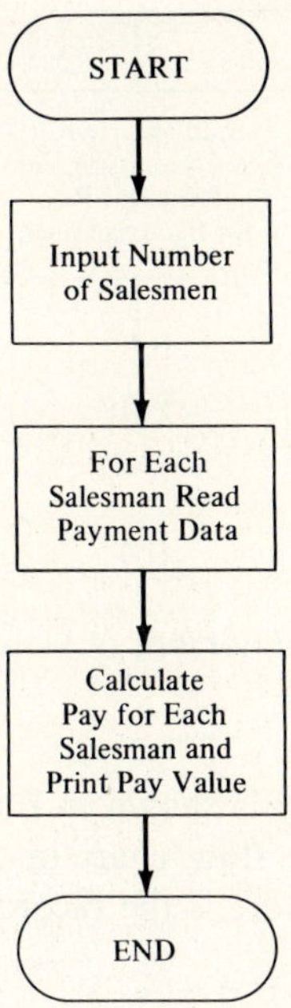

(a)

Fig. 6-3 (a) Calculating Pay for Sales Force—An Overview

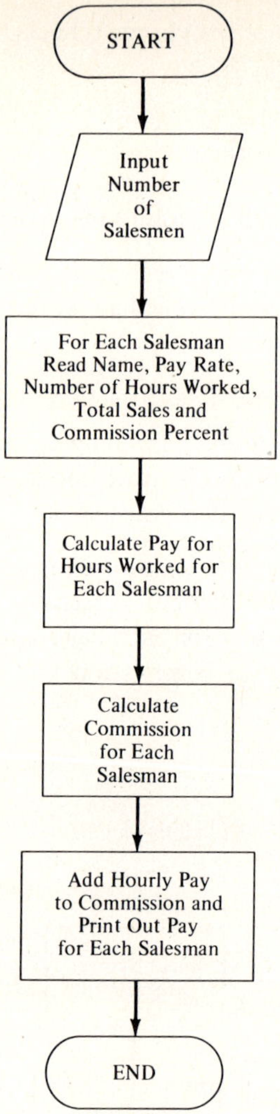

(b)

Fig. 6-3 (b) Refinement of Flow Chart of pair (a)

A flow chart for this step is shown in Figure 6-3(b). At the next level of program development the flow chart in Figure 6-3(b) is broken into final details [Figure 6.3(c)]. Here is the record format again.

John Keyes,	*5.50,*	*46,*	*2245.00,*	*0.02*
Salesperson's name	Base pay rate	No. of hours worked	Total sales	Commission on sales (2 percent)

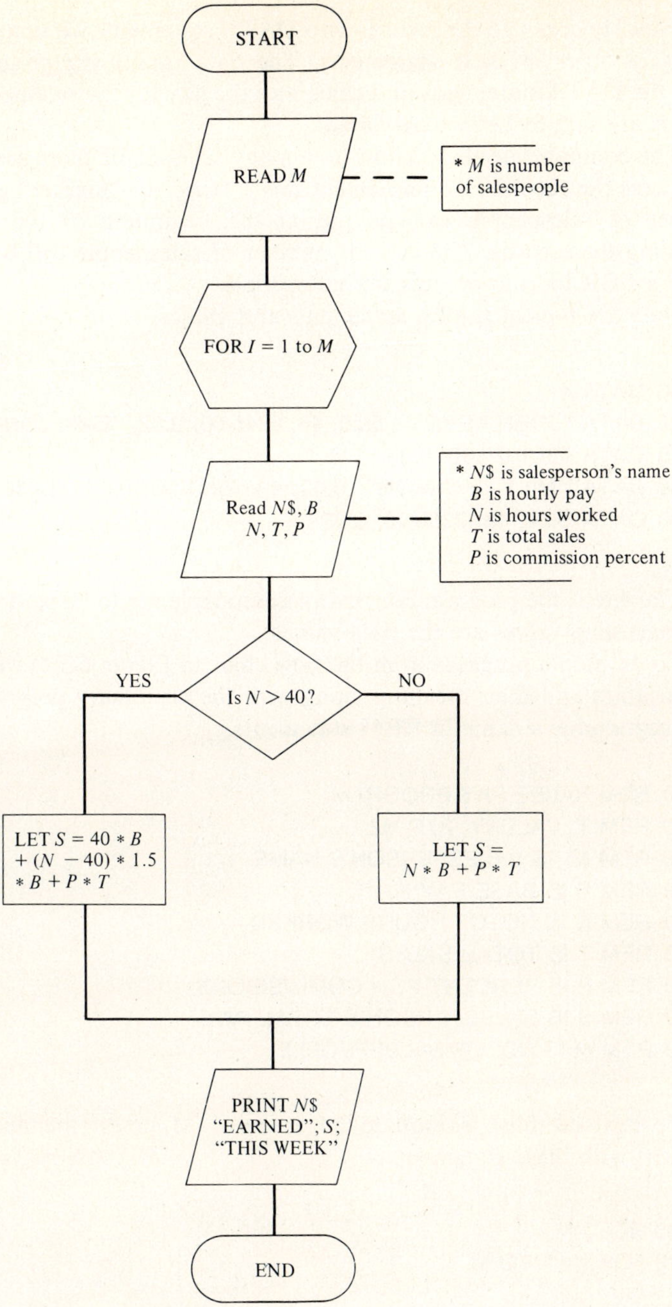

(c)

Fig. 6-3 (c) Final Flow Chart for Program to Calculate Pay for Sales Force

Now, to organize the records into DATA statements we simply list the values in order in these statements. The data processing program then reads the DATA statements and calculates the pay for the salespeople. The records are said to be in *fixed format*.

The computer needs to know how many salespeople there are in order to process the records. To implement this a "flag" or "marker" giving the number of salespeople can be put at the beginning of the data list preceding the records. The current number of salespeople will be used to set up a FOR loop to process the salespeople.

Here are typical DATA statements and values.

```
50 DATA 4
60 DATA "JOHN KEYES", 5.50, 46, 2245.00, 0.02, "EMIL JONES", 4.50
70 DATA 42, 1025.00, 0.03
80 DATA "MILT JACKSON", 6.00, 44, 2251.00, 0.02, "DON SMITH",
90 DATA 5.50, 43, 2200.00, 0.03
```

The 4 tells the program how many salespeople are to be paid this time. The remaining values are the data values.

To develop a program from the flow chart in Figure 6.3(c) we first list the variables and their meaning along with the customary program name and programmer's name in REM statements.

```
10 REM SALES PAY PROGRAM
20 REM T. VALERY, 2/5/82
30 REM N$ IS SALESPERSON'S NAME
40 REM B IS BASE PAY RATE
50 REM N IS NO. OF HOURS WORKED
60 REM T IS TOTAL SALES
70 REM P IS PERCENT FOR COMMISSIONS
80 REM S IS SALESPERSON'S TOTAL PAY
90 REM M IS NO. OF SALESPEOPLE
```

We next establish a loop to be executed M times (the number of salesmen) with these statements:

```
100 READ M
110 FOR I = 1 TO M
```

The program segment to calculate pay begins by reading values from the DATA statements for N$, B, N, T, and P.

```
120 READ N$, B, N, T, P
```

```
 10 REM SALES PAY PROGRAM
 20 REM T. VALERY, 2/5/82
 30 REM N$ IS SALESPERSON'S NAME
 40 REM B IS BASE PAY RATE
 50 REM N IS NO. OF HOURS WORKED
 60 REM T IS TOTAL SALES
 70 REM P IS PERCENT FOR COMMISSIONS
 80 REM S IS SALESPERSON'S TOTAL PAY
 90 REM M IS NO. OF SALESPEOPLE
100 READ M
110 FOR I = 1 TO M
120 READ N$, B, N, T, P
130 IF N > 40 THEN 160
140 LET S = N*B + P*T
150 GO TO 170
160 LET S = 40*B + (N - 40)*1.5*B + P*T
170 PRINT N$;" EARNED $"; S; "THIS WEEK"
180 NEXT I
190 DATA 4
200 DATA "JOHN KEYES", 5.50, 46, 2245.00, 0.02
210 DATA "EMIL JONES", 4.50, 42, 1025.00, 0.03
220 DATA "MILT JACKSON", 6.00, 44, 2251.00, 0.02
230 DATA "DON SMITH", 5.50, 43, 2200.00, 0.03
240 END
```

(a)

```
READY
RUN

SALES.P

JOHN KEYES EARNED $314.4 THIS WEEK
EMIL JONES EARNED $224.25 THIS WEEK
MILT JACKSON EARNED $321.02 THIS WEEK
DON SMITH EARNED $310.75 THIS WEEK
```

(b)

Fig. 6-4 Salary Calculations Based on Sales. (a) Program to Calculate Salaries; (b) Run from Program (a)

Now we write a segment to calculate the pay for each salesperson and then increment I by 1.

```
130 IF N > 40 THEN 160
140 S = N*B + P*T
150 GO TO 170
160 LET S = 40*B + (N - 40)*1.5*B + P*T
170 PRINT N$; "EARNED $"; S; "THIS WEEK"
180 NEXT I
```

The above loop will be executed as many times as there are salespeople, printing an appropriately labeled statement for each pay value calculated. (In actual practice, this might be on checks.)

Adding the desired DATA statements and an END statement will complete this program. A complete program and a run is shown in Figure 6-4.

The above shows development of a program to process data listed in DATA statements in a fixed format. The use of a number in a DATA statement to set up a FOR-NEXT loop to process the data (records) the required number of times was also illustrated. The above program illustrates several common programming practices in processing data. Notice that to process the pay records each period only new DATA statements with the required data need be entered.

6-7 THE RESTORE STATEMENT

Another BASIC statement used with DATA and READ statements is the RESTORE statement. When a RESTORE statement is executed by the BASIC systems translator, it restores or returns the order in which values are taken from DATA statements to the first value in the first DATA statement.

Consider this program:

```
10 DATA 5, 10, 15
20 DATA 20, 30, 40
30 READ A, B, C
40 RESTORE
50 READ E, F, G
60 PRINT A, B, C, E, F, G
70 END
```

This program will read 5 into A, 10 into B, and 20 into C. Then the RESTORE statement will cause the selection of data values to be restored to the first value in the first statement so that E will be given value 5, F will be given value 10, and G will be given value 15.

Here is another example.

```
 10 DATA 5, 10
 20 DATA 20, 30
 30 DATA 40, 50
 40 READ A, B, C
 50 RESTORE
 60 READ E, F
 70 RESTORE
 80 READ G
 90 PRINT A, B, C, E, F, G
100 END
```

The values assigned will be as follows: A = 5, B = 10, C = 20, E = 5, F = 10, and G = 5.

The values in the DATA statements are kept in a list and the BASIC translator maintains a pointer which points to the data value to be used each time a READ statement calls for a value. When a RESTORE statement is executed the pointer is reset to the beginning of the list of values in the DATA statements.

The location of the DATA statements in the program does not matter with regard to the RESTORE statement. This following program assigns 10 to A, 20 to B, 10 to C, and 20 to D.

```
10 READ A, B
20 RESTORE
30 READ C, D
40 PRINT A, B, C, D
50 DATA 10, 20, 30
60 DATA 40, 50
70 END
```

The RESTORE statement is primarily useful in conjunction with control statements such as the FOR-NEXT statement combination; examples will be given in the following chapter.

6-8 ERRORS IN BASIC PROGRAMS

There are several different types of errors that can occur in BASIC programs and different types of errors are generally found at certain points in program development.

One often encountered type of error is found by the translator program when the new program is entered. You may have already encountered such errors and quite often they are simply typing errors. For example, if you enter the statement

```
20 LCT X = 20
```

when you mean

```
20 LET X = 20
```

the translator will detect this error and print a comment such as

```
INVALID STATEMENT IN LINE 20
```

This comment from the computer can come at one of two times. In most systems the translator would write the error message when the system command RUN is given, and instead of running the program would print this *error comment* along with any others it found. In a few systems, lines are scanned by the translator as they are entered and the comment would be typed just after you hit the ⟨CR⟩ (or return) key signaling a statement was to be entered in the work space.

The above type of error is called a *syntax* error in computer circles. The word *syntax* refers to all the rules of the language including spelling rules, rules for line numbers, rules for number formation, and so on. For instance, suppose we attempt to enter this statement

```
30 LET X = 9,998
```

A *syntax* error has been committed, for BASIC does not allow commas in numbers. The translator will respond with a comment such as

```
LINE 30 CONTAINS AN INVALID NUMBER AFTER THE EQUALS SIGN
```

Syntax errors are generally easy to fix if the rules of BASIC are well understood. Sometimes illegal variables are used (such as AB); often quotation marks are missing such as in

```
40 PRINT "ENTER X
```

In each case, the translator will find the error and comment on it. Occasionally, however, the translator's comments may be hard to interpret. There is no general rule for dealing with this because there are so many kinds of errors that can be made.

If you cannot find the error referred to, it is a good idea to:

1. List the program.
2. Check the typing carefully. Sometimes O's and 0's or I's and 1's are confused in statements.
3. Go back and check the rules for statement usage and format.

Syntax errors also include errors such as writing a GO TO statement which calls for a jump to a line number that does not exist in the program. Another error is not including an END statement. The computer is an inflexible machine and requires great care and careful organization on the part of the programmer.

The more difficult errors to locate are generally not syntax errors but errors in program construction. The BASIC translator cannot determine what you want done. For example, if you want to sum the even numbers from 2 to 10 and write

```
10 LET S = 0
20 LET N = 1
30 LET S = S + N
40 LET N = N + 2
50 IF N < = 10 THEN 30
60 PRINT S
70 END
```

the computer cannot determine that you have written a program which sums the odd numbers from 1 to 9. It cannot even determine if your program is complete nonsense. For example, if you write

```
10 LET X = 20
20 GO TO 50
30 LET X = 30
40 IF X < Y THEN 30
50 PRINT "THIS IS NONSENSE"
60 END
```

This program is nonsense but the syntax is perfect. Each statement follows the BASIC rules and the program can be run with no trouble.

The hard part of programming is therefore preparing a program that does what you want it to do. Programmers are on their own here, and programming aids such as flow charts and the error checking technique to follow are all intended to assist in the sometimes difficult practice of programming.

6-9 MANUAL CHECKING OF A BASIC PROGRAM

An important step in the development of a program is that of checking a written draft of the program. If the program is short or has a simple construction with few control statements, it may be possible to simply check the program by reading it carefully and asking yourself what happens when each statement is executed. For more complicated programs this will not be adequate, however, and a more rigorous check of a program using a technique similar to that which will be described is necessary.

The careful reading and checking of programs by the programmer (or another programmer) is very important in the development of large systems or programs. In a famous program development project at IBM in which structured programming (to be discussed later) was used and in which the "chief programmer" techniques were originated,[2] each program was read and checked by the program's author and at least one other programmer before it could be operated on the machine. The idea behind this is that programs must be carefully checked before they are operated, or else, in the process of correcting errors, more errors may be introduced. If programs are carefully planned and then carefully checked using paper and pencil before operation on the computer, they will be relatively error free and testing and finding errors on the computer will be straightforward and not likely to introduce more errors.

It is sometimes difficult to get beginners to check their programs away from the terminal, but anyone who has spent hours trying to find an elusive error at a terminal (and introduced other errors in the process) can appreciate the value of paper and pencil checking. Similarly, if you have an error you cannot locate, it is often wise to leave the terminal and check the program carefully using pencil and paper.

A good technique for program checking will now be presented. To develop it we will use the following program:

```
 10 LET S = 0
 20 LET N = 1
 30 PRINT "INPUT GRADE"
 40 INPUT G
 50 IF G = 999 THEN 90
 60 LET S = S + G
 70 LET N = N + 1
 80 GO TO 30
 90 LET A = S/N
100 PRINT "THE AVERAGE GRADE IS"; A
110 END
```

This program inputs a set of grades from the terminal. To signal the computer that the last grade has been entered the terminal operator enters 999. When the 999 is read, the computer is to print the average of all the grades which were entered along with the statement "THE AVERAGE GRADE IS".

Terminating the inputting of data using a number (999 in this case) that would not occur in data (grades will be from 0 to 100) is a widely used

[2]See Harlan Mills' papers in the references.

programming technique and we will encounter versions of this technique in several programs.

The programmer uses a variable N to count the number of grades entered and a variable S to sum the grades as they are entered. After all grades have been entered, S is divided by N and this gives the average grade. We should note that this program contains no remarks in order to simplify the following description. (It should be improved by adding comments in several places.)

To test this program using pencil and paper, we first set up a simple problem to which we have the answer. Let us use grades of 70, 80, and 90 for which the average will be 80.

Now, our procedure is to operate the program a statement at a time and see if it works as desired. First, we examine the statement

```
10 LET S = 0
```

On our paper we now write

S
0

Now we examine the next statement:

```
20 LET N = 1
```

Operating this statement in our mind, thereby simulating the computer's operation, we add to our record the variable N and its starting value:

S	N
0	1

Statement 30 causes the line INPUT GRADE to be printed on the terminal. We mentally input a 70 at line 40 and this is read into the variable G and we write (again simulating the computer's action)

S	N	G
0	1	70

We now mentally test G in the statement

```
50 IF G = 999 THEN 70
```

Since G does not equal 999 we proceed to statement 60 and find a new S, calculated by

```
60 LET S = S + G
```

Since S is 0 and G is 70, we have a new S and must mark out the old S and enter the new value, 70, as follows:

S	N	G
~~0~~	1	70
70		

At line 70 we have

```
70 LET N = N + 1
```

Since N is 1 on our paper, a new N is calculated with value 2 and we write as follows:

S	N	G
~~0~~	~~1~~	70
70	2	

The statement

```
80 GO TO 30
```

causes a transfer of control back to statement 30.

The above process now continues for the inputting of the values 80 and 90. At this point, we have

S	N	G
~~0~~	~~1~~	~~70~~
~~70~~	~~2~~	~~80~~
~~150~~	~~3~~	90
240	4	

We are now at location 30. Then INPUT GRADE is typed by line 30 and G is input as 999 giving

S	N	G
~~0~~	~~1~~	~~70~~
~~70~~	~~2~~	~~80~~
~~150~~	~~3~~	~~90~~
240	4	999

Now, when line 50 is executed we have G equal to 999 and so a jump to 90 is taken and we next operate

```
90 LET A = S/N
```

Since S is 240 and N is 4, this gives A = 60. We dutifully write

S	N	G	A
~~0~~	~~1~~	~~70~~	60
~~70~~	~~2~~	~~80~~	
~~150~~	~~3~~	~~90~~	
240	4	999	

Statement 90 caused this (erroneous) value of 60 for the average to be printed. Clearly something is wrong. To find it we note that S should be 70 + 80 + 90 which is 240, as it should be. N, however, should be 3 and it is 4. An examination of the program shows the error; statement 20 should be modified to read

```
20 LET N = 0
```

We substitute this in the program and try the checking procedure again. This time we have

S	N	G	A
~~0~~	~~0~~	~~70~~	80
~~70~~	~~1~~	~~80~~	
~~150~~	~~2~~	~~90~~	
240	3	999	

The average now has the correct value and we are ready to keyboard the program.

If the above checking procedure seems tedious (you may have figured out the error in advance of the check), be assured that for more complicated programs it is worth the effort. You might also remember that many highly skilled programmers are using this (or a similar technique) at their job each day.

6-10 TESTING PROGRAMS

An important step in program preparation is that of testing a given program. The preceding section described a technique for checking a program using pencil and paper. When a program is finally in the computer, however, it should be carefully operated to locate any possible errors. Sometimes errors are hard to find and require much testing.

It is a good idea to try negative numbers and 0 in programs if they are possible inputs. Sometimes loops respond in unforeseen ways to negative numbers and thus they should be checked.

It is sometimes a good idea to add print statements in the program to print values as the program is operated. For example, in the program to average grades as in the preceding section the following PRINT statement might be added:

```
75 PRINT G, S, N
```

As grades are entered using the original (erroneous) program we will get a printout which lists the values of G, S, and N as program operation progresses. A careful examination of the values will uncover the error in the original LET statement for N.

If many variables are used, it is a good idea to label the variables. In this case we might have

```
75 PRINT "G = "; G, "S = "; S, "N = "; N
```

This technique sometimes uncovers errors in control statements when we find a print where variable values are listed in unexpected places during a run.

Testing a program requires good judgment on the part of the programmer. Imagining errors that might occur and developing tests to seek out these errors is also a good procedure to follow.

6-11 SAVING PROGRAMS IN SECONDARY (AUXILIARY) MEMORY

As the written programs become longer and more complex it becomes more and more desirable to save them in the computer's secondary or backup memory and not have to re-enter them each time they are needed. Also, being able to save a program in the computer from terminal session to terminal session permits modification, correction, and improvement of a program over a long time period. Saving programs in memory also enables the collecting of a "library" of programs for computer use.

Because each computer user is assigned a work space by BASIC and because this space is generally limited in size, program storage for any substantial time period will generally be on some secondary (auxiliary) memory device such as disks or tape (see Chapter 1).

Fortunately, BASIC systems often provide an easy-to-use feature which makes saving a program straightforward. Unfortunately, the procedure varies slightly from system to system. However, the procedure is similar for most systems.

The key point in all systems is that each saved program must be named. The reason for this is that it is this name that is used when the program is retrieved. For example, suppose on Wednesday we save a program called JOB and later sign off. On Friday, we write and save a program called NOTICE. Then, on the next Monday we sign on again. Now in order to retrieve JOB and run it we must call it by name because we have also saved another program. The programs could be numbered, of course, but most users prefer names to numbers because they are easier to remember and can even roughly indicate the program's function. This becomes increasingly important as the number of programs saved become larger.

The naming of the program is therefore an important step in saving it and we now examine the three most used procedures for naming.

1. In some systems a program *must* be named before it is written. In these systems the computer will generally type NEW or OLD before a program can be entered into work space. The user then types NEW if writing a NEW program and OLD if calling for a program previously stored (this will be discussed). When NEW is typed, after the ⟨CR⟩ is depressed the computer will ask for the name of the new program, the user will type it, followed by a ⟨CR⟩, and the program can then be entered.[3]
2. In some systems the program is named after it has been entered. In these systems the user types NAME, followed by the chosen program name, and a ⟨CR⟩. For example, to name a program TRIG we would type

   ```
   NAME TRIG ⟨CR⟩
   ```

   In other systems the systems command word to give a program a name is RENAME. To use this and name the same program we would type

   ```
   RENAME TRIG ⟨CR⟩
   ```

   The reason for the use of RENAME instead of NAME is that a program called JOB may have been stored in secondary memory. We then call for the program by the name JOB, get it in our work space, and modify it. During this time period the BASIC system

[3]Different systems have different rules for naming programs. If you start your name with an alphabetic character and use no more than five alphanumeric characters in the name it will probably be acceptable.

still keeps the name JOB associated with the unaltered program. Now we wish to store our new modified program but still wish to continue storing the old JOB program. To do this we "rename" the modified program MOD, for example, and then store it. Later, we can call for either MOD or JOB. (Using RENAME to name a new program simply assigns a name to the program.)[4]

3. In some systems, the program is named in the same system command which stores it in memory (this will be discussed).

Now having dealt with the naming of programs, the saving of programs is easy. In almost all BASIC systems, if the program in work space has already been named, to save it is secondary memory we simply type the system command

```
SAVE
```

This will cause the program to be stored in memory.

In some systems the naming of a program and the saving of the program are combined. In these systems the same systems command is used. For example, in one system to save a program named JOB we type

```
SAVE JOB
```

This causes the program in work space to be saved in secondary memory and given the name JOB.

In another BASIC system the systems command would be

```
SAVE "JOB"
```

In this system the program name must be enclosed in quotation marks, otherwise it has the same name as before.

Having saved a program in memory, how do we call it? The procedures in different BASIC systems are remarkably similar. Here is an example where the systems command word is GET and the program to be moved from secondary storage into the work space is JOB, which has previously been stored.

```
GET JOB
```

This causes a copy of the program JOB to be moved from secondary storage into work space. If we now type LIST, the program JOB will be

[4]There is probably no reason to prefer RENAME to NAME. In either case we are simply "naming" the program. In systems that use NAME and not RENAME you can still call a program from memory and give a new name using the NAME command.

listed. If we type RUN, the program JOB will be run. It would be nice if all systems used GET (or some other word) as the systems command word to retrieve a program from secondary storage into work space, but they do not. The following are commands to load a program JOB from secondary memory into work space for three different systems:

```
GET JOB
LOAD JOB
OLD JOB
```

The GET has been discussed; the words OLD and LOAD perform the same function in different BASIC systems.

If we already have a program in our work space and get a program from memory, in most systems the program in memory will be added to the program already in work space. Suppose we have in our work space

```
10 PRINT "NOW"
20 END
```

If we call for the program named MIX in memory and MIX is as follows:

```
15 PRINT "MIX"
20 END
```

the result in work space will be

```
10 PRINT "NOW"
15 PRINT "MIX"
20 END
```

Notice the END statement occurs only once. If the two END statements had been numbered differently, both would be in the program in work space. To prevent this addition of programs, you must remember to delete what is in the program work space[5] before calling a program in memory unless you really want to add them together. If you just signed on (logged in), this will be no problem because work space is clear. Also, remember that if you call a program and two statements have the same line number, the BASIC system will delete the statement from the program originally in memory.

Another systems command now needs to be discussed. How do we delete programs that have been saved in memory? Sometimes we have a new, improved program and no longer need the old one. In some cases we

[5]To delete a program in work space you simply type SCR, SCRATCH, CLEAR, or NEW, depending on your system. See Chapter 2.

may be near exceeding our storage allocation and must clean up a little. Here is the systems command that causes a saved program named JOB to be destroyed in one system.

```
KILL JOB
```

This dramatic systems command causes the destruction of JOB in secondary memory. It does not affect the program currently residing in the user's work space.

The following are systems commands that do the same thing in three other systems.

```
DELETE JOB
UNSAVE JOB
PURGE JOB
```

You must find the one that will work on your system.

If you save many programs, you may sometimes wish a list of all these programs you currently can call from secondary storage. A list of the programs in your secondary storage can generally be obtained by typing one of the following:

```
CAT
CATALOG
FILES
```

You should find what works in your system if you intend to store many programs.

One final point should be made. When a program is moved from secondary memory into the user's work space, the name of the program moves with it. If the program is then modified, an attempt to replace the (changed) program in secondary memory using the same name may fail and cause the computer system to complain about two programs with the same name by giving the user a message. You can avoid this problem by (1) destroying (KILLing, DELETEing, and so on) the program in secondary memory and then (2) moving the program in work space into secondary memory. An alternate solution is to rename the program in work space, store it, and then destroy the original of the program that is still in secondary memory.

6-12 SUMMARY

The first sections of this chapter introduced the FOR and NEXT statements which can be used to control the execution of a block of statements in a BASIC program. Table 6-1 shows the format for the FOR and NEXT

Table 6-1 FOR AND NEXT STATEMENTS

The general formats are

line number FOR *v* = *initial value* TO *limit* STEP *increment*

line number NEXT *v*

v is a simple *numeric variable*

Initial value, *limit*, and *increment* are *numeric expressions*.

The clause "STEP increment" is optional. If it is omitted, the *increment* is assumed to be 1.

Examples:

```
30 FOR X = 1 TO 15
60 ...
70 NEXT X

20 FOR I = A TO B STEP C
   ...
80 NEXT I

50 FOR M = A + 5.2 TO C - 15 STEP 3*D
   ...
60 NEXT M
```

The FOR and NEXT statement are defined in conjunction with each other. The sequence of statements beginning with a FOR statement and continuing up to and including the first NEXT statement with the same control variable is called a "FOR block." FOR blocks can be nested (that is, one can contain another), but they cannot be interleaved, that is, a FOR block or FOR and NEXT statement must contain the entire FOR block begun or ended by that statement. Also, nested FOR blocks cannot use the same control variable.

In the absence of a STEP clause in a FOR statement the increment is assumed to be +1.

A statement must not jump into the middle of a FOR block (except for a RETURN statement).

If a statement such as this is reached

```
30 FOR I = 6 TO 5 STEP 2
```

The FOR block will not be executed and control will pass directly to the statement after the NEXT. Also, if a statement such as

```
40 FOR N = 1 TO 4 STEP 2
```

is reached, N will first take value 1 and then value 3. When the NEXT statement is reached, N will be incremented to 5, but because 5 is greater than the limit 4, control will pass to the statement following the NEXT statement and the loop will not be executed with N equal to 5.

The action of the FOR and NEXT statements can be defined in terms of LET, IF THEN, and GO TO statements. This can be shown by defining a FOR and NEXT statement in its most general form and then show a program containing FOR, IF THEN, and GO TO statements which does the same thing.

Here is the FOR-NEXT block.

FOR *v* = *initial value* TO *limit* STEP *increment*

NEXT *v*

Here is the equivalent code:

```
        LET A = limit
        LET B = increment
        LET V = initial value
line 1  IF (V − A)*B > 0 THEN line 2
          --------
          --------
        LET V = V + B
        GO TO line 1
line 2  REM
```

Here *v* is any simple "numeric" variable, A and B are variables that cannot be used elsewhere in the program, and *line 1* and *line 2* are line numbers associated with the FOR block.

---

statements, also pointing out some of the important features of usage in these particular statements. Although the FOR and NEXT statements could be replaced using IF THEN statements, the FOR and NEXT statements provide a powerful tool to the programmer for controlling operations.

The READ and DATA statements are also very useful in programming because they enable the programmer to organize his or her introduction of values into variables. Also, by retyping the DATA statements on the terminal, new values for variables can be conveniently introduced into a program. The READ and DATA statements present convenient methods for the assignment to variables as well as a method whereby later versions of programs can be conveniently generated. Table 6-2 gives information on the READ and DATA statement.

The sections on locating and correcting errors in programs first presented some details on the location of syntactic errors in a program along with the kind of errors that can be located by the compiler or translator for BASIC. A programming technique wherein a program was operated by a programmer using pencil and paper to determine how the

Table 6-2 THE DATA, READ, AND RESTORE STATEMENTS

General forms:

line number DATA *datum, . . . , datum*

line number READ *variable, . . . , variable*

line number RESTORE

Datum is a numeric constant, a string constant, or an unquoted string (if allowed). *Variable* is a numeric or string variable.

Examples:

```
30 DATA 15, "SAM", 20
40 READ A, B$, C

20 DATA 20, 30, "ABLE"
30 READ A, B, C$
40 RESTORE
50 READ M1, D$, M2
```

The data from all DATA statements in the program are collected into a list (sequence) of data elements in the order in which they occur in the DATA statements. There is a single list, not separate lists of strings and numbers. When the execution of a program encounters a DATA statement, the program proceeds with no effect.

Each READ statement causes variables in the variable list to be assigned values, in order, from the list of data elements gathered from the DATA statements. Conceptually, a pointer is set to point to the first data element when the program operation is begun, and as each variable in the variable list for a READ statement is encountered it is assigned the data element being pointed to and the pointer is moved to the next data element in the list of data elements.

A RESTORE statement resets the pointer to the beginning of the list when executed. This causes the next READ statement executed to read from the beginning DATA statement.

The type of a datum in the list of data elements must agree with the type of the variable to which it is assigned. For example, the word "ABLE" cannot be assigned to a variable X but can be assigned to X$.

---

program functions when it is operated on the computer was then explained. By carefully simulating the program operation using paper and pencil a programmer can often locate errors that could not be found through a less-organized examination of the program's operation.

The techniques for testing and locating errors in programs are important tools that the programmer must learn.

As the complexity of programs increases it becomes desirable to store programs in secondary memory for extended periods of time. Procedures for accomplishing this and for retrieving the stored programs have been

Table 6-3 SYSTEMS COMMANDS TO CLEAR THE PROGRAM IN WORK SPACE

TYPICAL COMMANDS
SCRATCH
SCR
NEW
ELIMINATE
CLEAR
Your System ____________

Table 6-4 SYSTEMS COMMAND TO MOVE A PROGRAM FROM SECONDARY MEMORY TO WORK SPACE

TYPICAL COMMANDS
GET *program name*
OLD *program name*
LOAD *program name*
OLD: *program name*
Your System ____________

Table 6-5 SYSTEMS COMMAND TO MOVE A PROGRAM FROM WORK SPACE TO SECONDARY MEMORY

TYPICAL COMMANDS
SAVE
SAVE *program name*
Your System ____________

Table 6-6 SYSTEMS COMMAND TO NAME THE PROGRAM IN WORK SPACE

TYPICAL COMMANDS
NAME *program name*
RENAME *program name*
RENAME: *program name*
Your System ____________

presented along with some details on naming the programs. Tables 6-3 through 6-6 present systems commands for several systems for these functions.

QUESTIONS

1. What will be printed by this program?

```
10 FOR A = 1 TO 5
20 PRINT A*2;
30 NEXT A
40 END
```

2. What will be printed by these programs?

(a)
```
10 FOR I = 1 TO 6
20 PRINT I*3
30 NEXT I
40 END
```

(b)
```
10 FOR I = 1 TO 6 STEP 0.5
20 PRINT I*2
30 NEXT I
40 END
```

3. What will be printed by these programs?

(a)
```
10 FOR I = 5 TO 0 STEP -0.3
20 PRINT I
30 NEXT I
40 END
```

(b)
```
10 FOR I = 10 TO 2 STEP 0.4
20 PRINT I
30 NEXT I
40 END
```

(c)
```
10 DATA 5, 10, 15, 20
20 READ A, B, C
30 PRINT A, B, C
40 END
```

4. What will be printed by this program?

```
10 FOR I = 10 TO 5 STEP -0.5
20 PRINT I;
30 NEXT I
40 END
```

5. What will be printed by these programs?

(a)
```
10 DATA 5, 2.3
20 DATA 6, 2.7
30 READ A, B, C
40 READ D
50 PRINT A, B, C, D
60 END
```

(b)
```
10 DATA 6
20 DATA 7
30 READ A, B, C
40 READ D
50 PRINT A, B, C, D
60 DATA 4, 5.5, 7
70 END
```

6. Operate this program on your terminal.

```
10 REM INTEREST ON A 5% LOAN
20 REM JACK JONES 2/16/81
30 REM P IS PRINCIPAL, D IS ORIGINAL
40 REM DEPOSIT AND N IS NO OF YEARS
50 READ D
60 PRINT "DEPOSIT"; "PRINCIPAL",
70 FOR N = 1 TO 10
80 LET P = D*1.05^N
```

```
 90 PRINT D, P, N
100 NEXT N
110 DATA 100
120 END
```

7. Trace the operation of the above program as if you were debugging it.
8. This program does the same calculations as that in Question 6 but allows for an input of the principal, balance, number of years, and interest rate in a DATA statement. Insert the necessary DATA statement and operate this program on your terminal.

```
 10 REM INTEREST ON A LOAN
 20 REM JACK JONES 2/20/81
 30 REM P IS PRINCIPAL, D IS ORIGINAL DEPOSIT,
 40 REM Y IS MAX NO. OF YEARS AND I IS INTEREST RATE
 50 READ D, Y, I
 60 PRINT "DEPOSIT", "PRINCIPAL", "INTEREST RATE", "YEARS"
 70 FOR N = 1 TO Y
 80 LET P - D*(I + 1)↑N      or      (I + 1)^N
 90 PRINT D, P, I, N
100 NEXT N
110 END
```

9. Draw a flow chart of the program in Question 8 and then trouble-shoot this program using the technique in this chapter by testing it both by hand and then by computer for test values you select.
10. Prepare a program to print the following table:

0	5	10	15	20
25	30	35	40	45
180	185	190	195	200

11. Write a program to print the following table:

NUMBER	SQUARE	CUBE
1	1	1
2	4	8
3	9	27
⋮	⋮	⋮
10	100	1000

12. Write a program to produce the following table:

CELSIUS	FAHRENHEIT
0	32
10	50
20	68
⋮	⋮
100	

13. Write a program so that, for DATA 3, 5; the printout is

```
3 OUT OF 5 EQUALS 60 PERCENT
```

Change the DATA statement and test for 6 out of 20.

14. Assume a DATA statement (or several DATA statements) that contains a list of positive numbers of unknown length. The end of the list is marked with the number −999. Write a BASIC program to print out the sum of the numbers in the list.

15. The Fibonacci number sequence begins with 1, 1; then each succeeding number in the sequence is the sum of the two previous ones. The Fibonacci sequence for seven numbers is

1, 1, 2, 3, 5, 8, 13

Write a BASIC program that will print the first 20 numbers in the Fibonacci sequence.

16. Write a program that takes a data list of first and last names like DATA "TOM", "JONES", "JIM", "PLUNKETT", and so on, and has a printout of the form

```
LAST NAME    FIRST NAME

JONES        TOM
PLUNKETT     JIM
```

17. Prepare a program to read the following DATA statements and then to list the people who received a B both semesters. Try it on another data list. END marks the end of the list.

```
DATA "JONES", "A", "B", "SMITH", "A", "B", "KENT", "C", "A"
DATA "FOREST", "A", "B", "MANTI", "D", "B", "MOORE", "B", "B"
DATA "END", "A", "B"
```

18. Each set of three data numbers gives the year, the first-half sales, and the second-half sales. DATA 1978, 30, 27, 1979, 20, 14, 1980, 30, 25, 1981, 40, 30. Using a FOR-NEXT loop (FOR K = 1 TO 4), write a program that will compute the total sales for each year, and format the printout as follows:

YEAR	FIRST-HALF SALES	SECOND-HALF SALES	TOTAL SALES
1978	30	27	57
1979	20	14	34
1980	30	25	55
1981	40	30	70

19. In this DATA statement, the data gives the sales for the 12 months of the year. DATA 30, 50, 14, 10, 9, 19, 18, 14, 35, 31, 21, 15. Write a program that will print out this table.

MONTH	MONTH'S SALES	TOTAL TO DATE
JAN	30	30
FEB	50	80

20. The data statements below contain information on college students. The numbers are in pairs; the first number tells if the student is male or female (1 for male and 2 for female) and the second number gives age. Write a program to find the average age for males and the average age for females. The number −99 is used to indicate the end of the data.

```
10 DATA 1, 17, 1, 19, 2, 18, 2, 17, 1, 19, 1, 17
20 DATA 1, 17, 2, 18, 2, 17, 2, 18, -99
```

21. Trace this program as if you were debugging it.

```
 10 LET X = 0
 20 LET V = 0
 30 FOR I = 2 TO 7 STEP 2
 40 FOR J = 10 TO 0 STEP -5
 50 LET Y = Y + J
 60 PRINT X, Y
 70 NEXT J
 80 LET X = X + 2
 90 NEXT I
100 END
```

22. Trace this program as if you were debugging it.

```
10 READ A, B, C, X, Y
20 DATA 5, 6, 4, 2, 3
30 LET Z + A↑X + B*C↑4
40 FOR P = 1 TO 4
50 LET Q = A/B/C
60 LET R = P + Q
70 NEXT I
80 PRINT Z, P, Q, R,
90 END
```

23. Write a program that will print your name nine times.
24. What will be printed if this is run?

```
15 FOR Y = 10 TO 1 STEP -2
20 PRINT Y,
30 NEXT Y
40 END
```

25. What will be printed if this is run?

```
10 FOR A = 1 TO 3
20 FOR B = 1 TO 4
30 PRINT A + B
40 NEXT B
50 NEXT A
60 END
```

26. Write a program that converts two data numbers representing yards and feet, respectively, into inches. For example, for DATA 2, 3 the printout should be:

```
2 YARDS AND 3 FEET EQUALS 108 INCHES
```

27. Write a program to find the largest number in any list of numbers in a DATA statement with a "flag" consisting of −99 to indicate the end of the numbers.
28. Write a program that will find the average of three data numbers listed in a DATA statement.
29. The following DATA statement gives information on three salespeople.

```
10 DATA 0713, 52, 0719, 86, 0744, 61
```

The first pair of data numbers gives the salesperson's identification and how many sales he had in a given week. Write a program that will print out

```
SALESPERSON #        HAD THE MOST SALES
```

30. Write a program that examines a DATA statement which gives the number of pins a bowler knocked down with each ball he threw during a game of bowling and then calculate the final score.
31. A DATA statement contains a list of positive numbers with the last number a flag −99. Write a program to determine if the numbers are in ascending order.
32. A DATA statement contains a list of positive and negative numbers from −100 to +100. A flag of −999 indicates the end of the list. Write a program to determine how many positive, negative, and zero numbers are in the list.
33. On Mars a 100-lb person (on earth) would weigh 38 lb. On Jupiter a 100-lb person (on earth) would weigh 264 lb. Write a program that inputs your weight on earth, asks if you are on Jupiter or Mars, and then outputs your weight on that planet.
34. The formula to calculate the monthly payment M on a loan of P dollars at a yearly interest rate of I for Y years is

$$M = \frac{I*P/12}{1 - (I/12 + 1)^{-12 \times Y}}$$

Develop a program to input P, I, and Y and output M.
35. Write a program to print a table of monthly payments versus interest rates for a \$10,000.00 loan for 20 years at rates of from 9 to 12 percent in increments of 0.05 percent.

36. Grades for the students in a class are listed in a DATA statement. A flag of −999 indicates the end of the list. Write a program to find the highest and lowest two grades in the class.
37. At John's restaurant, the cash register enters into a DATA statement the price of each meal and type of meal as each meal is paid for. The transactions are in pairs with the type of meal first: 1 for breakfast, 2 for lunch, 3 for dinner and the cost second. For example, DATA 1, 2.30, 3, 5.40, −99 means a breakfast at 2.30 and a dinner at $5.40. The −99 marks the end of the transactions. Develop a program to read the DATA statement and calculate the gross sales and the sales in each meal category.

Chapter 7
Developing Programs—Functions

BASIC has a special facility in the translator to supply the user with several sections of program that have already been written and stored in the memory. These program modules are "called" using function notation; the BASIC feature is known as *implementation supplied functions*. Use of BASIC's function notation makes it possible for the programmer to use sections of programs that have been written by expert programmers to perform often needed functions.

This chapter introduces implementation supplied functions and then develops a program using a top-down procedure which utilizes several of these functions.

The subjects of top-down program development, error-free programming, structured programming, and making programs readable are then introduced. These techniques are part of the current trend toward making program development more systematic and improving programming techniques.

7-1 OBJECTIVES

Implementation Supplied Functions

Often used functions, such as square root, absolute value, log, sine, and tangent are provided by the BASIC system through the use of function notation in programs. This subject is introduced and examples of usage are given.

Top-Down Program Development

There are several general strategies for program development, but many large computer programming organizations are now using and recommending a strategy called "top-down program development." An example program is first developed using the top-down procedure and then this general subject is discussed.

Good Programming Practice

There is an area of study which deals with how programs should be developed and written and what practices make for good programs. This area includes structured programming, making programs readable, and several other general topics. Some of the leading ideas in this area are introduced in the final sections of this chapter.

7-2 FUNCTIONS—SQR

The BASIC system provides a set of previously programmed functions that simplify writing many kinds of programs. These functions range from rounding, taking a square root, and finding the absolute value, to trigonometric functions. The "square root" function provides a good example. Finding the square root of a number (the square root of X is a nonnegative number A such that $A \times A = X$) requires a section of program. To simplify writing programs where a square root is needed, a feature is included in BASIC so that simply writing SQR(X) will return the square root of X. Consider, for example,

```
10 LET X = 36
20 LET Y = SQR(X)
30 PRINT X; Y
40 END
```

When this program is run it will print

```
36  6
```

Here Y was given the value of SQR(X) when X equals 36.

The X in SQR(X) is called the *argument* of the function and the value in parentheses must be 0 or a positive number. When the BASIC translator reads the SQR it knows the square root of the value in parentheses must be found; therefore it runs a section of program that has already been written and stored to find this value. The use of the function notation SQR( ) tells the translator what is to be done.

Another program similar to the above follows:

```
10 FOR X = 1 TO 20 STEP 2
20 LET Y = SQR(X)
30 PRINT "FOR X = "; X; "SQR(X) = "; Y
40 NEXT X
50 END
```

Here is the printout from this program.

```
FOR X = 1 SQR(X) = 1
FOR X = 3 SQR(X) = 1.73205
FOR X = 5 SQR(X) = 2.23607
FOR X = 7 SQR(X) = 2.64575
FOR X = 9 SQR(X) = 3
FOR X = 11 SQR(X) = 3.31662
FOR X = 13 SQR(X) = 3.60555
FOR X = 15 SQR(X) = 3.87298
FOR X = 17 SQR(X) = 4.12311
FOR X = 19 SQR(X) = 4.3589
```

The general form for the square root function is SQR(*expression*). The expression in parentheses can be any numeric expression, so this includes SQR(100) which will have value 10; SQR(10 + 80 + (2*5)) which will also have value 10; also, SQR(2*X) which will have value 6 if X has value 18; and so on.

If X has a negative value in SQR(X), then your BASIC system will probably print some sort of error message. You might try a case and see what happens (or ask) so you will understand if this condition arises.

7-3 FUNCTIONS—INT

Another function supplied by BASIC is the INT function.[1] The BASIC expression INT(X) returns the greatest integer which is less than or equal

[1]INT is a contraction of INTEGER.

to X. Thus INT(3) has value 3, INT(3.5) has value 3, INT(−4.16) has value −5, INT(102.9) has value 102, and so on. Here is a short program.

```
10 DATA 1.2, -1.2, 40.9
20 FOR K = 1 TO 3
30 READ X
40 LET A = INT(X)
50 PRINT "IF X = "; X; "THEN INT(X) = "; A
60 NEXT K
70 END
```

This will cause the printing of

```
IF X = 1.2 THEN INT(X) = 1
IF X = -1.2 THEN INT(X) = -2
IF X = 40.9 THEN INT(X) = 40
```

Notice that the INT function does not "round" a number, which means making the number into the nearest integer. For example, if we round 39.9, the value is 40 because 40 is the closest integer to 39.9. (The INT function *chops* or *truncates* a number in computer programming jargon.)

You can round a number to the nearest integer, however, using INT, by simply adding 0.5 to the number. Thus, to round 39.9, we form INT(39.9 + 0.5); to round 18.2, we form INT(18.2 + 0.5); and, in general, to round X we write INT(X + 0.5).

As an example of the use of INT, we consider a problem in biology. A researcher has 100 fruit flies and lets them breed for 5 years. The researcher then counts them and finds 789 flies. What is the yearly rate at which the fruit flies have multiplied? Knowing this, the biologist can, for instance, predict how many fruit flies will exist in 10, 15, or any other year in the future.

The formula for making this calculation is as follows: Let G be the growth rate as a decimal fraction, B the beginning number, F the final number, and Y the number of years. Then

$$G = (F/B)^{1/Y} - 1$$

An important point should now be made. The formula given returns a decimal fraction (for example, 0.07934). Suppose what is wanted is a percentage correct to two places. Simply multiplying by 100 will convert to percentage form (0.07934 is 7.934 percent); however, we also desire to round the number to the nearest percent. Here is a statement to take a number G and convert it to a percentage Q rounded to the nearest percent.

```
10 LET P = INT(G*100 + 0.5)
```

A program using the above formula for the biology problem follows:

```
 10 REM BIOLOGY PROGRAM
 20 REM I. G. FLUX, 5/6/81
 30 REM G IS GROWTH RATE, B BEGINNING NUMBER, F FINAL
 40 REM NUMBER
 50 REM Y IS NUMBER OF YEARS, P IS G CONVERTED TO PERCENT
 60 REM FORM
 70 DATA 100, 789, 5
 80 READ B, F, Y
 90 LET G = (F/B)^(1/Y) - 1
100 LET P = INT(G*100 + 0.5)
110 PRINT "IF"; B; "FLIES BECAME"; F; "FLIES IN"; Y;
120 PRINT "YEARS THE GROWTH RATE";
130 PRINT "WAS"; P; "PERCENT"
140 END
```

Here is a printout from a run of this program:

```
IF 100 FLIES BECAME 789 FLIES IN 5 YEARS THE GROWTH RATE
WAS 51 PERCENT
```

The way statement 100 works is: G is given the value 0.511525 when 90 is executed; this is multiplied by 100, giving 51.1525, which is now in percentage form but not rounded. Adding 0.5 gives 51.6 and taking the INT function gives the final value 51 which is G converted and rounded to the nearest percent.

In performing business calculations, quite often percentages or decimal fractions are used, and the results of calculations should be in dollars and cents, but the actual numbers arrived at have too many digits. This requires rounding and the INT function can be used for this.

For example, suppose a department store has a sale. On some items the store gives 25 percent off and on others 1/3 off. Suppose a customer buys item A at 25 percent off and item B at 1/3 off; what should be charged?

Suppose we write

```
10 LET P1 = A*0.75
20 LET P2 = B*(2/3)
```

This gives us the conversion for 25 percent off and 1/3 off.

Now, if A costs \$2.35, then 2.35×0.75 is 1.7575. We cannot charge this, however; what is needed is to round 1.7575 to 1.76 and to charge \$1.76. Similarly, if B costs \$2.00, then $2.00 \times (2/3)$ is 1.33333 and here we wish to charge \$1.33.

The solution to this problem is to first convert the price from dollars and cents to cents by multiplying by 100 and then to round by adding 0.5 and then taking the INT function. Dividing by 100 will then convert back to dollars and cents. Here is how the variable P1 can be rounded using this technique.

```
LET P1 = INT(100*P1 + 0.5)/100
```

We can round P2 similarly:

```
LET P2 = INT(100*P2 + 0.5)/100
```

A more complicated single statement can be used to reduce the price by 25 percent and then to round as follows:

```
LET P1 = INT(100*(A*0.75) + 0.5)/100
```

To reduce the price by 1/3 we write

```
LET P2 = INT(100*(B*2/3) + 0.5)/100
```

What should be noted here is the use of INT to round a number in decimal form to the nearest integer.

7-4 FUNCTIONS—ABS

The ABS function returns the absolute value of an argument. Therefore ABS(X) returns the magnitude of X (the "positive or absolute value of X"). If X equals −9, then ABS(X) equals 9; if X equals 12, then ABS(X) equals 12; if X equals −39.6, then ABS(X) equals 39.6.

Any numeric expression can be in the parentheses for the ABS function. As examples: ABS(−2 + 1) has value +1; ABS(−3 − 4) has value +7; ABS(X + 2) has value +1 if X has value −3; ABS(3 + 0.2 − 4) has value 0.8.

The ABS function is very useful in finding out if a value in the computer is "near" some number. For example, suppose we have performed several calculations and wish to test variable X for value 0. Unless the calculations have all been with integers, X may have some very small value near 0 but not exactly equal to 0. For example, if X has the value 0.00001 and we write

```
IF X = 0 THEN 80
```

then a jump to 80 will not be made. However, we may consider 0.00001 "close enough" so that the jump should be made.

This point should be carefully considered. Even simple calculations can lead to small errors in number representation, just as is the case for hand calculators.

Consider, for example, the following:

```
10 LET X = 1
20 LET Y = 3
30 LET A = 3
40 LET B = 2
50 LET C = (X/Y) + (B/A - 1)
60 IF C = 0 THEN 100
```

There is a good chance C will not equal 0 and the jump to 100 will not be taken because 1/3 and 2/3 cannot be represented exactly in a digital computer, although they can be represented to as many digits as desired.[2]

To get around this problem, we can test to see if C has value 0 as follows:

```
60 LET C = ABS(C)
70 IF C < 0.0001 THEN 100
```

The reason for the use of the ABS function is as follows: Suppose C has value −13; this is not very close to 0 but if we test using IF C < 0.0001, then C will pass the test but is too large to be near enough 0 for our purposes. If we form ABS(C), however, then the result will be positive, regardless of C's original sign, and the IF test can be used satisfactorily.

This test procedure can be used to find if B equals C, also. The statements are as follows:

```
60 LET D = ABS(B - C)
70 IF D < 0.0001 THEN 100
```

The above should be carefully checked to make sure the point is understood. Calculations with integers are exact in BASIC but calculations with decimal fractions can lead to small errors.

Functions can be composed in BASIC. The expression LET Y = SQR(ABS(X)) will first find the absolute value of X, which will always be nonnegative, and will then find the square root of that value.

[2]The value of 1/3 is 0.3333... in digital form but the number of 3s can only be finite because the computer is finite (BASIC tends to use five or six 3s).

Consider this program.

```
10 LET A = -50.41
20 LET B = INT(SQR(ABS(A)))
30 PRINT "THE ROUNDED DOWN, SQUARE ROOT OF THE";
40 PRINT "ABSOLUTE VALUE OF"; A; "IS"; B
50 END
```

This will print the value of INT(SQR(ABS(−50.41))), which is 7.

7-5 MECHANIZING BUSINESS PROCEDURES

There is a continuing effort to organize and make more methodical the practices engaged in by businesses. In large and small business organizations managers continually are on the lookout for procedures that can be followed to better organize or make more efficient an organization's operation.

Business procedures are everywhere. For example, using a credit card causes a salesperson in a business accepting that credit card to follow some procedure that has been worked out for checking and validating your card, billing you, and so on.

Many of the procedures used in business can be completely defined (computer scientists would call them algorithms). As a result, they can often be mechanized in one manner or another and in many cases can even be computerized.

An example of a commonly encountered operation is making change. For example, if the operator of a cash register knows the total for some purchase and is given some money, then change must generally be returned, and this change often involves several bills and coins of differing types.

Change making can be made a completely mechanical operation and we will now examine how. (Several automatic cash registers are available which implement the calculations to be shown.) We will develop the program using what is called a *top-down* procedure. First, the overall outline of the procedure will be developed, then this will be refined into more explicit steps and a flow chart prepared. Finally, the program will be written.

This follows accepted practice. First a problem is "roughed out" or described at a system or general level. Then more and more details are added until all the exact details of the procedure have been arrived at.

To begin, we assume a customer has made a purchase and so we have a sale price for an item. Also, the customer has offered some money to pay for the item. This could be a single bill or coin or it could be several bills and coins. In any case, the change will be the difference between the price and the amount offered. The correct number of bills and coins to make change must then be calculated, so that the change value is equal to the difference between the sale price and the amount given by the customer.

For example, suppose the item purchased is a clock and the price is \$11.53. The customer offers a ten dollar bill and a five dollar bill. This makes \$15.00 and the difference to be returned to the customer would be \$15.00 − 11.53 = \$3.47. To "make change" we would then give the customer three one dollar bills, a quarter, two dimes, and two pennies.

An overview of this procedure shows two parts can be separated out.

1. The sales price and amount offered by the customer are entered and the difference or change value calculated.
2. The different coins and bills needed to make correct change are determined and printed.

We now have a first procedure which is very general and requires considerable refinement or breaking down into explicit steps. Figure 7-1 shows a flow chart for this procedure.

Our next steps are to refine and make more detailed each of the two steps above. We first approach step 1, the inputting of sales price and amount offered by the customer. First, the price of the item should be tested to see if it is zero or negative. If this is the case we choose to print "THERE IS SOME MISTAKE" and ask for another input.

Now, is the amount offered greater than or equal to the sales price? This should be tested and if the difference is negative, the offer is too small and the statement "YOU NEED MORE" will be printed. Then the customer must enter a new number for his offer.

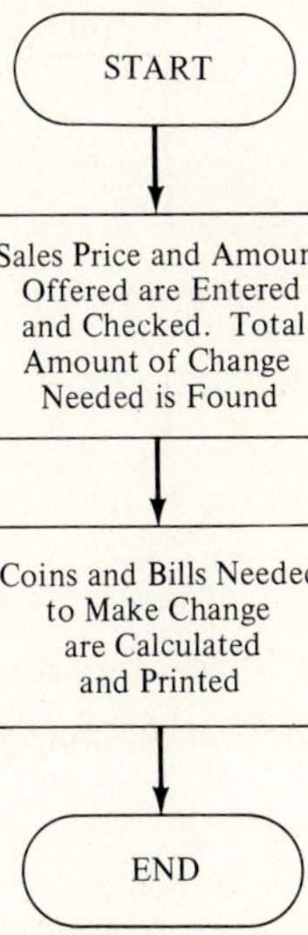

Fig. 7-1 General Steps for Change-Making

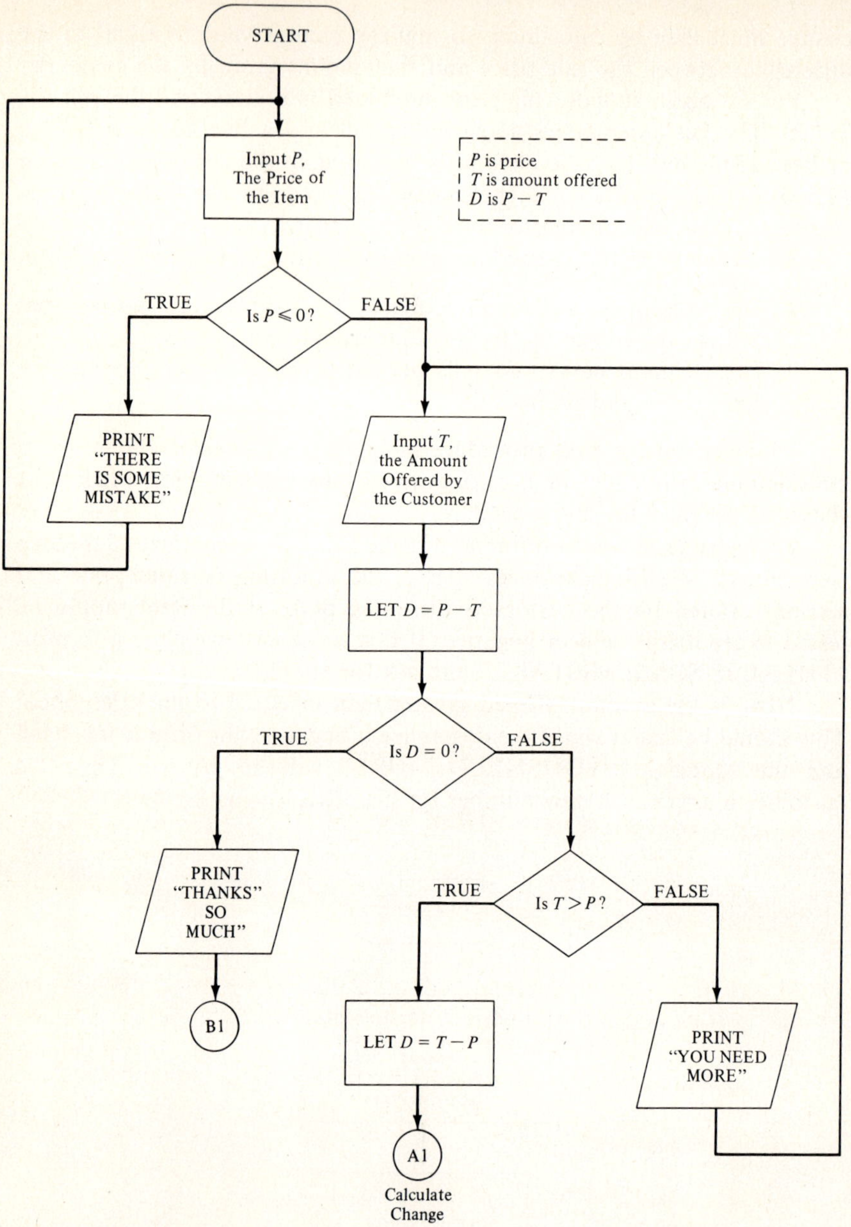

Fig. 7-2 Input Section of Change-Making Program

This completes the outline of the steps to be taken for the input section of the program. We now know that an acceptable sales price and offer from the customer have been made. Before drawing our flow chart we assign variable names as follows:

> P is the price of the item being sold.
> T is the amount offered by the customer.
> D is the difference between P and T (that is, $P - T$).

A flow chart can now be drawn for this part of the overall procedure (algorithm). This is shown in Figure 7-2.

The calculation of the bills and coins to be given to the customer requires more thought. First, we limit the bills available to ten, five, and one dollar bills and coins to quarters, dimes, nickels, and pennies.

Now, how do we calculate change? If we must make change for $3.00 in ones, we know that three ones will do. If we must make change for $4.05, we know that four ones and one nickel will do. A little examination shows that we mentally start checking with the largest bill at our disposal, in this case a ten dollar bill, and see if we can use one or more of these. If we can, we subtract the total tens given from the total change value to be made up and do the same thing for fives, then for ones, quarters, dimes, nickels, and finally pennies.

To make this more precise, let us again use D as the variable for the difference or change to be made. To see if we can use one or more tens in our change, we divide 10 into D and see how many times it "goes." If the answer is 0, that is, if $D < 10$, we use no tens and move on to fives. To make this more precise, we form $D/10$ and then round down. In BASIC this translates into the statement

```
LET M = INT(D/10)
```

If M is 0, then no tens can be used; however, if M is greater than 0 (it will be an integer, remember), this will be the number of tens to be used.

Now, if M = INT(D/10) is a nonzero integer, we will give the customer M tens and then subtract M times 10 from D, calling the new difference D, also. The same basic steps will then be performed for five dollar bills.[3] The upper left corner of Figure 7-3 shows this part of the procedure for ten dollar bills.

The procedure is basically the same for five dollar bills, except that M = INT(D/5) is found instead of M = INT(D/10). Also, note the D used here is the remainder after the tens used have been subtracted from the original D.

[3] This corresponds to our normal way of making change. If we make change for 7.25, we see that one five can be used. We then subtract 5.00 from 7.25 giving 2.25 and "make change" for 2.25 but using one dollar bills as the largest to be used.

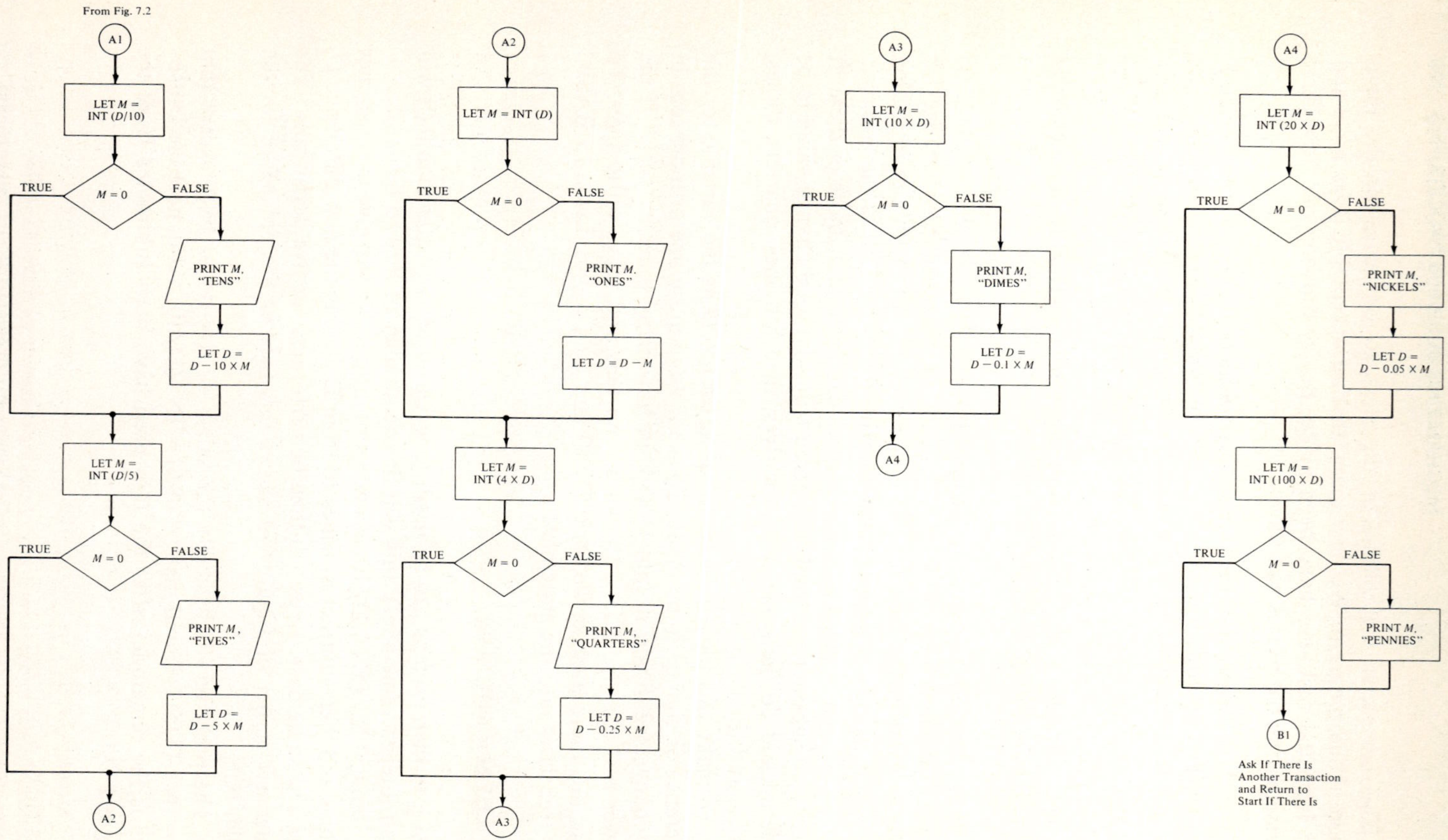

Fig. 7-3 Making Change

We can now draw the flow charts for calculating the number of fives, ones, quarters, dimes, nickels, and pennies. This is shown in Figure 7-3 and the complete BASIC program is shown in Figure 7-4.

Here are some notes on the final program.

1. When T, the amount offered, is subtracted from the sales price P and the difference P − T is tested for 0 to see if no change is required, the value of P and T can be decimal fractions. There may be a small offset after we subtract because the numbers may not be exactly represented; thus we proceed as follows:

   ```
   300 LET D = ABS(P − T)
   310 IF D < 0.001 THEN 930
   ```

   The above two statements form P − T; convert this to a positive number if it is negative and then see if the result is less than 0.001. If this is the case, we consider it to be effectively zero and simply print "THANKS SO MUCH" because no change is needed.
2. The statement

   ```
   430 LET D = D + 0.001
   ```

   adds a small increment to D to make sure that statements such as

   ```
   470 LET M = INT(D/10)
   ```

   do not result in a lower integer than desired. This is insurance against an inexact computer representation of some number. An alternate solution to this problem would be not to add the 0.001 but to make statement 470 like this:

   ```
   470 LET M = INT(D/10 + 0.001)
   ```

   The same would be done to statements 540, 610, 680, 750, 820, and 890.
3. The user of the program is asked at the end of the program whether another transaction is desired. This consists of statements 970, 980, and 990. If the user wants to stop, statement 1000 prints a THANK YOU and the program ends.

An important point has now been reached in program preparation. This change-making program is complex enough to warrant use of some of the programming techniques to make programs "readable" and to aid in their analysis.

```
100 REM CHANGE MAKING
110 REM P. L. MATTHEWS, 3/5/79
120 REM
130 REM THIS PROGRAM INPUTS A SALES PRICE, P,
140 REM AND AN AMOUNT OFFERED, T. THE PROGRAM
150 REM THEN CALCULATES THE CHANGE TO BE RETURNED.
160 REM
170 PRINT "PLEASE ENTER THE PRICE OF THE ITEM"
180 INPUT P
190 REM
200 REM SEE IF P IS NOT 0 OR NEGATIVE
210 REM
220 IF P > 0 THEN 250
230 PRINT "THERE IS SOME MISTAKE"
240 GO TO 170
250 PRINT "HOW MUCH ARE YOU GIVING US?"
260 INPUT T
270 REM
280 REM CHECK FOR EXACT PAYMENT OFFER THEN FOR ENOUGH
290 REM
300 LET D = ABS(P - T)
310 IF D < 0.001 THEN 930
320   IF T > P THEN 380
330     REM
340     REM PAYMENT OFFER IS NOT ENOUGH
350     REM
360     PRINT "YOU NEED MORE"
370     GO TO 250
380   PRINT
390   PRINT
400   PRINT
410   PRINT "THAT'S TOO MUCH, HERE'S YOUR CHANGE"
420   PRINT "======================"
430   LET D = D + 0.001
440   REM
450   REM CALCULATE NUMBER OF TENS NEEDED
460   REM
470   LET M = INT(D/10)
480   IF M = 0 THEN 540
490     PRINT M; "TENS"
500     LET D = D - 10*M
510     REM
520     REM CALCULATE NUMBER OF FIVES NEEDED
530     REM
540   LET M = INT(D/5)
```

Fig. 7-4 Change-Making Program. (a) Program

```
550   IF M = 0 THEN 610
560      PRINT M; "FIVES"
570      LET D = D - 5*M
580      REM
590      REM CALCULATE NUMBER OF ONES NEEDED
600      REM
610   LET M = INT(D)
620   IF M = 0 THEN 680
630      PRINT M; "ONES"
640      LET D = D - M
650      REM
660      REM CALCULATE NUMBER OF QUARTERS NEEDED
670      REM
680   LET M = INT(4*D)
690   IF M = 0 THEN 750
700      PRINT M; "QUARTERS"
710      LET D = D - 0.25*M
720      REM
730      REM CALCULATE NUMBER OF DIMES NEEDED
740      REM
750   LET M = INT(10*D)
760   IF M = 0 THEN 820
770      PRINT M; "DIMES"
780      LET D = D - 0.1*M
790      REM
800      REM CALCULATE NUMBER OF NICKELS NEEDED
810      REM
820   LET M = INT(20*D)
830   IF M = 0 THEN 890
840      PRINT M; "NICKELS"
850      LET D = D - 0.05*M
860      REM
870      REM CALCULATE NUMBER OF PENNIES NEEDED
880      REM
890   LET M = INT(100*D)
900   IF M = 0 THEN 930
910      PRINT M; "PENNIES"
920      GO TO 940
930 PRINT "THANKS SO MUCH"
940 PRINT
950 PRINT
960 PRINT
970 PRINT "DO YOU WANT TO BUY MORE? TYPE YES OR NO."
980 INPUT Z$
990 IF Z$ = "YES" THEN 170
1000 PRINT "THANK YOU FOR YOUR PURCHASE. BYE."
1010 END
```

Fig. 7-4(a) (*Continued*)

```
PLEASE ENTER THE PRICE OF THE ITEM
 ?1.00
HOW MUCH ARE YOU GIVING US?
 ?27.43

THAT'S TOO MUCH, HERE'S YOUR CHANGE
====================================
 2 TENS
 1 FIVES
 1 ONES
 1 QUARTERS
 1 DIMES
 1 NICKELS
 3 PENNIES

DO YOU WANT TO BUY MORE? TYPE YES OR NO.
 ?YES
PLEASE ENTER THE PRICE OF THE ITEM
 ?5.22
HOW MUCH ARE YOU GIVING US?
 ?33.99

THAT'S TOO MUCH, HERE'S YOUR CHANGE
====================================
 2 TENS
 1 FIVES
 3 ONES
 3 QUARTERS
 2 PENNIES

DO YOU WANT TO BUY MORE? TYPE YES OR NO.
 ?NO
THANK YOU FOR YOUR PURCHASE. BYE.
```

Fig. 7-4 (*Continued*) (b) Program run

The primary rules used in Figure 7-4 will be used in the remaining programs in this book. These are:

1. The name of the program, programmer, and date are placed in REM statements at the beginning of the program.
2. A description of the program's function and the major variables used are included in a heading using REM statements.
3. The statements following IF statements are indented two spaces up to the point where the THEN may transfer control (unless an IF

can transfer control to a lower THEN statement number, in which case no indentation is used).

4. The statements in a FOR loop up to the NEXT are indented by four spaces.
5. REM statements are used to clarify program operation. Vertical spacing around REM statements (through the use of REM statements followed by all spaces) is used to set them off. Notice that a REM followed by spaces is skipped over by the translator just like other REM statements.

The intent of the above is to make programs readable and understandable. More discussion of this follows later in the chapter.

It is possible to shorten the program in Figure 7-4. Notice that in Figure 7-3 a block of statements with the same shape is repeated and in Figure 7-4 a block of similar statements is repeated for tens, fives, ones, quarters, dimes, nickels, and pennies. The values in the LET statements and print statements change each time, however. This offers the possibility of making the seven similar blocks in Figures 7-3 and 7-4 into a single block and repeating it seven times using a FOR-NEXT loop. The values in the LET and PRINT statements can be changed using DATA statements. To set this up we form the following FOR loop:

```
490 FOR I = 1 TO N
500         READ A$, C
510         LET M = INT(D/C)
520         IF M = 0 THEN 550
530             PRINT M; A$
540             LET D = D - C*M
550 NEXT I
```

The N in the FOR statement is given the value 7 by a READ statement

```
480 READ N
```

and a DATA statement

```
650 DATA 7
```

The values read into A$ and C are pairs of values "TENS", 10; "FIVES", 5; and so on, from DATA statements. A complete program using this loop is shown in Figure 7-5. This program should be carefully examined to see how the use of the FOR loop and DATA statements makes it possible to shorten and structure the program in Figure 7-4.

```
100 REM CHANGE MAKING, VERSION 2
110 REM P. L. MATTHEWS, 3/5/79
120 REM
130 REM THIS PROGRAM INPUTS A SALES PRICE, P,
140 REM AND AN AMOUNT OFFERED, T. THE PROGRAM
150 REM THEN CALCULATES THE CHANGE TO BE RETURNED.
160 REM
170 PRINT "PLEASE ENTER THE PRICE OF THE ITEM"
180 INPUT P
190 REM
200 REM SEE IF P IS NOT 0 OR NEGATIVE
210 REM
220 IF P > 0 THEN 250
230   PRINT "THERE IS SOME MISTAKE"
240   GO TO 170
250 PRINT "HOW MUCH ARE YOU GIVING US?"
260 INPUT T
270 REM
280 REM CHECK FOR EXACT PAYMENT OFFER
290 REM
300 LET D = ABS(P - T)
310 IF D < 0.001 THEN 570
320   IF T > P THEN 380
330     REM
340     REM PAYMENT OFFER IS NOT ENOUGH
350     REM
360     PRINT "YOU NEED MORE"
370     GO TO 250
380   PRINT
390   PRINT
400   PRINT
410   PRINT "THAT'S TOO MUCH, HERE'S YOUR CHANGE"
420   PRINT "======================"
430   LET D = D + 0.001
440   RESTORE
450   REM
460   REM THIS LOOP CALCULATES THE CHANGE FOR D
470   REM
480   READ N
490   FOR I = 1 TO N
500   READ A$, C
510   LET M = INT(D/C)
```

Fig. 7-5 Improved Change-Making Program

```
520          IF M = 0 THEN 550
530             PRINT M; A$
540             LET D = D - C*M
550       NEXT I
560       GO TO 580
570 PRINT "THANKS SO MUCH"
580 PRINT
590 PRINT
600 PRINT
610 PRINT "DO YOU WANT TO BUY MORE? TYPE YES OR NO."
620 INPUT Z$
630 IF Z$ = "YES" THEN 170
640 PRINT "THANK YOU FOR YOUR PURCHASE. BYE."
650 DATA 7
660 DATA "TENS", 10, "FIVES", 5, "ONES", 1
670 DATA "QUARTERS", 0.25, "DIMES", 0.10
680 DATA "NICKELS", 0.05, "PENNIES", 0.01
690 END
```

Fig. 7-5 (*Continued*)

7-6 PROGRAM DEVELOPMENT

The following are four important aspects of the development of a program: (1) documentation; (2) making the program readable and understandable; (3) having a systematic program development procedure; and (4) using control structures such that the program is logically structured.

The first of these considerations is documentation. Documentation generally includes (1) the flow charts[4] that are used to visually illustrate the structure of the program and operations performed by the program; (2) any written materials that accompany the program (such as a description of the program's operation, function, and any special characteristics); and (3) the remarks within the program itself that make it possible to understand the various sections of the program.

The techniques for making the program readable are many. A program should be written in a manner that does not include the use of tricks or "cute" obscure statements. Also, the program should not be overly complicated so that another programmer can later readily understand the program. There are many other aspects of this subject, however, and these

[4]Some program developers prefer other techniques for describing programs in the early stages. These include "pidgen English" and several other "English-like" languages. We emphasize flow charts because they are widely used and will be encountered by all programmers.

include making the program readable by indenting control structures, spacing between mathematical symbols and relation symbols, and naming variables so they convey their function. These techniques will be discussed in a later section.

Development of a program generally proceeds in several stages. It is a good idea to clearly plan what the stages of development will be. Studies of possible programming developments have concentrated on two overall approaches that have particular names: *top-down programming* and *bottom-up programming*. (However, several other approaches can be used.) At present, the most widely studied and publicized technique is the top-down programming development procedure and this will be described.

A great deal has been written about a subject called *structured programming* in the past few years. Several large programs within both government and industrial application areas using structured programming were very successful. Subsequent comparisons of similar programs which did not use structured programming techniques, to the structured programs showed the structured programs to have several advantages. Two advantages are lower programming costs and fewer errors. Additionally, structured programs are thought to be *maintainable* in the sense that updating these programs or making changes is more straightforward than in programs which contain control structures of other types. This will be discussed in the final sections of this chapter.

7-7 DOCUMENTATION

We have already placed emphasis on some fundamental practices in documenting a program. First, the author of the program, date of the program, and as descriptive a title of the program as possible should always accompany a program. Remember, it is not only other programmers who will be interested in a program, it is also the original author who, after not seeing a program for some time, may find it difficult to identify and understand. Further, if the same program exists in several versions, these versions should be documented so that the latest and most correct program is readily identifiable.

Flow charts are, of course, a basic form of documentation and many industrial and government concerns require flow charts with each program they purchase.

Other important considerations in documenting a program concern whether or not a description of the program's operation should be included as part of the program (using REMARK statements) or whether a separate written description of the program should be made. Again, most contracts for program development require a complete description of the program's operation, including a list of all inputs and outputs and any conditions of operation.

Another important documentation practice concerns listing, in REMARK statements, all variables to be used in a program at the beginning of the program. When possible, variable names should be assigned so that the purpose of the variable in a program is easily remembered. For example, profit can be named P, interest can be I, loss can be L, and so on. This is useful both in developing a program and in tracing its operation at a later date. Remember that all of these practices aid in debugging programs, which is very important in program development.

Documentation should be a part of the regular programming practice. A program should be documented as it is developed and not at the end in a desperation effort. The documentation should be planned in the initial stages of program development and programs should be developed in parallel with the documentation.

7-8 MAKING PROGRAMS READABLE

Making programs easy to read can be approached in several ways. An important consideration in making a program easy to read is the alleviation of any tricks or hard to understand practices in developing the program. A program should be written in as straightforward and understandable way as is possible. This is not only of great value to others who may wish to understand the programs operation, but it also is important in debugging a program when a small glitch has developed. (An unforeseen twist in an ingenious scheme may cause a program to fail under certain conditions.)

In BASIC, the translator pays no attention to spacing in statements. The following statement can be written in these ways and will run the same.

```
20 GO TO 60
20 GOTO 60
20    GO   TO   60
```

The first example seems the best, although the GO TO is often written in a single word GOTO.

Arithmetic expressions can often use spacing to convey meaning because the translator program ignores spaces (you cannot space numbers of course, 64.5 should not be written 64. 5).

It is a good idea to use spaces around +'s and −'s and to group more closely operations to be performed first. Here are some examples.

GOOD	BAD
A + B*C	A + B * C
(A − X)/Y	(A − X) / Y
A + B^2	A + B ^ 2

```
100 REM                         BUBBLE SORT
110 REM                         F. K. WILLIAMS, 4/18/81
120 REM
130 REM * THIS PROGRAM SORTS A LIST OF NUMBERS IN A *
140 REM * DATA STATEMENT INTO ASCENDING ORDER USING THE *
150 REM * BUBBLE SORT TECHNIQUE *
160 REM
170 DIM L(50)
180 READ N
190 REM          ** READ IN LIST **
200 REM
210 FOR I = 1 TO N
220     READ L(I)
230 NEXT I
240 REM
250                 GOSUB 350
260 REM
270 PRINT "THE SORTED LIST IS"
280 FOR I = 1 TO N
290     PRINT L(I); ",";
300 NEXT I
310 STOP
320 REM
330 REM          ** SORT CODE FOLLOWS **
340 REM
350     LET M = N - 1
360     LET X$ = "YES"
370     FOR I = 1 TO N
380     IF X$ = "NO" THEN 520
390         FOR J = 1 TO M
400         LET X$ = "NO"
410             IF L(J) < = L(J + 1) THEN 490
420 REM
430 REM          ** SWAP VALUES **
440 REM
450                 LET Q = L(J)
460                 LET L(J) = L(J + 1)
470                 LET L(J + 1) = Q
480                 LET X$ = "YES"
490         NEXT J
500         LET M = M - 1
510     NEXT I
520     RETURN
530 DATA 6, 9, 5, 4, 10, 12, 9
540 END
```

Fig. 7-6 Bubble Sort Using a Programming Style to Emphasize REMs

Each of the above pairs of numeric expressions will be executed identically by BASIC but the leftmost expressions are much easier to read and better express the intent of the programmer.

Using parentheses is also a good idea and often eliminates errors in programming. If we want to add A to B and then divide the sum by C, a mistake can be generated by writing

```
A + B/C
```

Writing (A + B)/C will eliminate this error and make the expression clear.

Often, in order to make programs more readable and to convey better the logical structure of the program, control structures are indented. In BASIC the two primary control structures are the IF THEN statement and the FOR-NEXT statement. By indenting FOR loops and jump blocks for IF THEN's in programs by successive amounts, a feeling for the operation of the program can be given.

The rules for indentation and spacing in programs have been given in the preceding section. Other systems are in existence for indenting and spacing but the rules explained before are widely accepted and used. As an example of a program that uses "stars" (asterisks) and other spacing to set off REM statements examine Figure 7-6. This shows the same program as in Figure 10-4 but using a different programming style.

The purpose of the indentation of FOR loops and statements following IF THEN's is to display the control structure of the program more clearly. Even if at this point the functioning of the program in Figure 7-6 (or 10-4) cannot be understood, the FOR-NEXT and IF THEN control statements operation can be figured out by examining the program because of the indentation.

7-9 TOP-DOWN PROGRAMMING

The subject of top-down programming is a very popular one and entire books and many papers have been written on this subject. The basic idea behind top-down programming is as follows: The problem (or task) is stated first in general terms. Then the problem is broken into successively smaller pieces (steps to be taken) until the level of detail is such that all parts of the program can be written.

Quite often the top-down approach proceeds in levels. Figure 7-7 shows two levels in program development. First, the overall task (or problem) is stated in general terms. This is shown in Figure 7-7(a), a payroll processing program. Then the statement of the task is broken down into finer steps. In this case, at the next level we have a division of the employees into salaried and hourly pay categories as shown in Figure 7-7(b). The next or third level could then be flow charts of the procedure to calculate hourly and salaried pay and to record sick leave, vacation

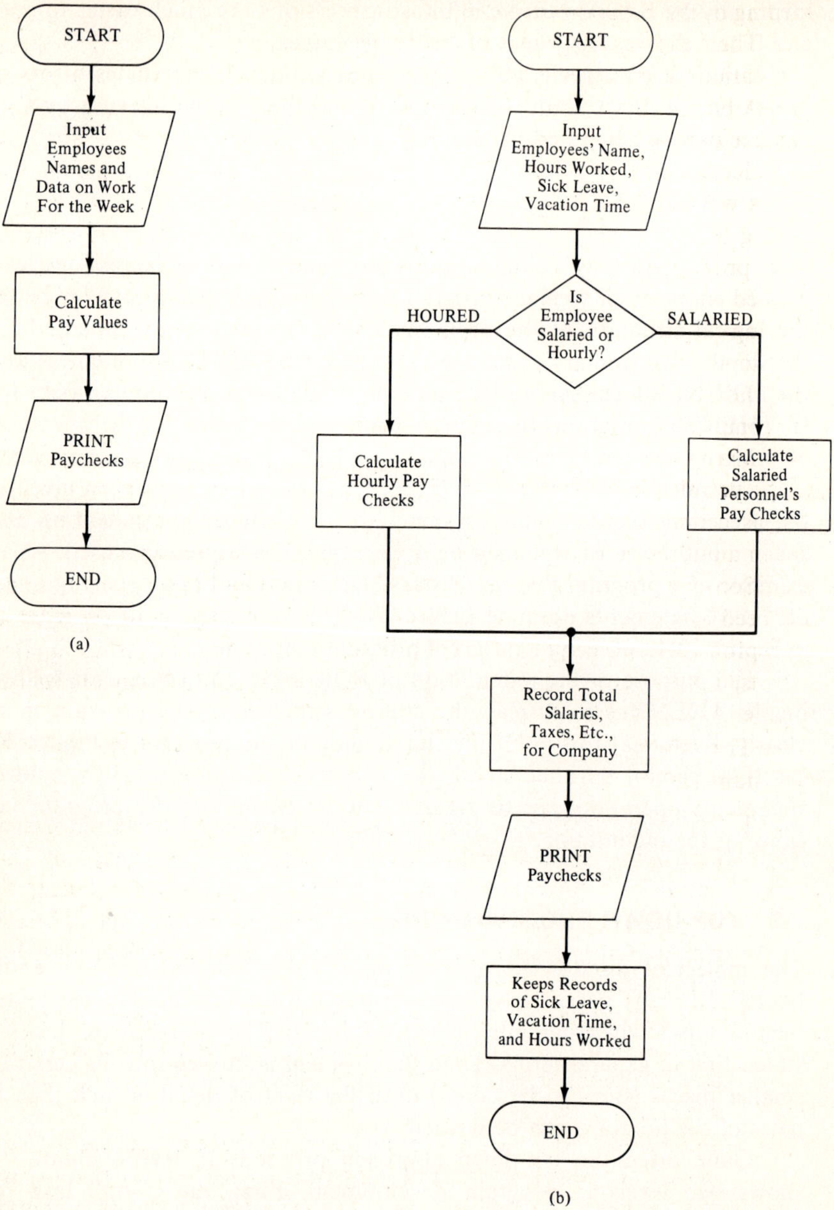

Fig. 7-7 First Two Levels in Program Development. (a) Level 1; (b) Level 2

time, and hours worked. Finally, the fourth level would be the actual writing of the program in BASIC.

The other approach, bottom-up programming, starts by developing the various subprograms or sections of program to perform parts of the job. A bottom-up procedure programmer or programming team might first write a section of program to print the checks for example, then a section to calculate hourly pay, then a section to input employees' names and hours worked. The programmer (or programmers) would then start combining the pieces of program by writing the necessary linking statements. The programmer (or programmers) would think of more things that needed doing as the project developed and would add and coordinate the piecing together of the program as additional parts of programs were developed. The documentation might proceed along with the programming but the final documents stating overall program organization would only be completed near the end of the project.

Most large programs were developed in a bottom-up manner in the early years of computer program development. Programmers wrote programs for the parts of the problem or task that they could immediately begin and worked out other parts as the programming progressed.

Some of the details concerning how a top-down programmer should proceed are still being studied. Many of the arguments concern whether the problem (task) should be described in the early stages using flow charts, English language statements, or some English-like high-level language. All of these approaches have different advocates.

The following ideas are in just about every approach to top-down programming:

1. The task (problem) is approached from the "top" in that the overall program is first described using either English language or flow chart form. Successive levels of design consist of refining the original sections. At each level of development the task is broken into modules or pieces and each module is then broken into finer detail in the next level.
2. The early stages of development are documented using flow charts or English language statements and only during the final stages are actual programs in BASIC, FORTRAN, COBOL, and so on, written.
3. Details are postponed and only broad generalities are worked with in early stages of program development. When top-down programming is used, the problem must be well understood and all details worked out early on. This is an excellent feature of this approach and we use it in this book. The change-making program is an example. First, the general idea was presented; then a rough but complete overall procedure was developed. A flow chart followed this, giving details of the computational stages and control structure of the problem. Finally, a BASIC program was written.

4. The program is developed using modules or blocks where each module contains only a reasonable number of statements. Some program developments limit modules to one page of statements, some to less than 50 statements, and so on. The individual modules are tested as they are developed. In BASIC the primary mechanism for modularization is the use of subroutines to be defined in Chapter 9.

Clearly specifying the inputs and outputs and all variables to be used as early as possible is another feature of top-down programming.

Large programs require several steps or levels using the top-down procedure. For smaller programs, when it is possible for a person to visualize easily the entire program, the top-down ideas which are most advantageous consist of (1) clearly understanding the problem before coding begins; (2) laying out details of the program in English or a flow chart early on; (3) carefully specifying inputs and outputs before coding begins; and (4) testing pieces of the program when possible before assembling these pieces into the entire program.

Both top-down and bottom-up programming emphasize the development of modules or sections of code independently of other sections. The idea is to break the problem into clearly defined pieces and to develop these pieces in as independent a manner as possible. More on this will be found in the following section on structured programming and the chapter on subroutines.

7-10 STRUCTURED PROGRAMMING

The history of structured programming goes back to some work in the mid-1960s by E. W. Dijkstra in the Netherlands. It was Dijkstra's position that GO TO statements, if used excessively, were a sign of bad programming practice.[5]

Dijkstra persisted in his position and began developing alternate control structures along with ways to prove that programs written with these structures were correct. He also advocated top-down design, and structured programming is almost always used in conjunction with top-down design.

Other programmers began studying Dijkstra's work and developing new control structures. Proving programs correct and other related aspects of "GO-TO-less" programming became topics for research in both educational and commercial organizations.

[5]Two early and well-known papers on this subject are: Dijkstra, E. W., "Programming Considered as a Human Activity," *Proc. of IFIP Congress 65*, Spartan Books, Washington, D.C., 1965. Dijkstra, E.W., "GO-TO Statement Considered Harmful," Letters to the Editor, *Communications of the ACM*, March 1968. There are a number of more recent papers and books in the references.

A major step forward was taken when Harlan Mills, of IBM, ran two large programming projects using ideas of his own, his fellow workers, and Dijkstra.[6] The second of these projects, an information retrieval project for the *New York Times* newspaper, was widely acclaimed and gave considerable support to the ideas that were becoming known as *structured programming*.

Since the early work, structured programming has become fashionable in programming circles and its many advocates are now having a considerable impact on several aspects of program preparation and also new programming language development.

It must be said that many programmers oppose the ideas of structured programming and at this time most programmers probably use only selected techniques from the structured programming box of programming tools. Also, the structured programming advocates do not completely agree on all aspects of the subject.

The ideas behind structured programming is to increase programmer output primarily by enforcing certain rules on the programmer which are intended to reduce the errors made in preparing programs, thereby reducing the check out and debugging time required. Structured programming is also intended to make programs clearer and more readable.

The essence of structured programming concerns the development of programs using modules that have only one entry and one exit point. Figure 7-8(a) shows the basic layout for a structured program in its early block diagram stages. The program modules are executed one after the other until the end is reached. Inside a module there may be decision elements, loops, and/or control structures.

Figure 7-8(b) shows a nonstructured program at the same stage of development. Notice that modules can have several inputs and outputs and there are jumps back and forth between modules. Figure 7-8(c) shows a "bottom-up" layout where operation of the modules is sequenced by the main program. In this layout the modules can be interconnected in any order and jumps can be made back and forth between "main programs" and "lower level" modules.

The control structures in structured programming are quite similar to the IF THEN and FOR-NEXT structures in BASIC and these are acceptable to structured programming advocates if used properly. However, to force the writing of programs in a structured form several other control structures are advocated by structured program developers and these can be found in "structured BASIC" systems (they are sometimes called "extended" BASIC systems).

[6]Mills, H. "Top-Down Programming in Large Systems," from *Debugging in Techniques in Large Systems*, Prentice-Hall, Englewood Cliffs, N.J., 1971. See also Linger, R. C., Mills, H. D., and Witt, B. I., *Structured Programming, Theory and Practice*. Addison-Wesley, Reading, Mass., 1979.

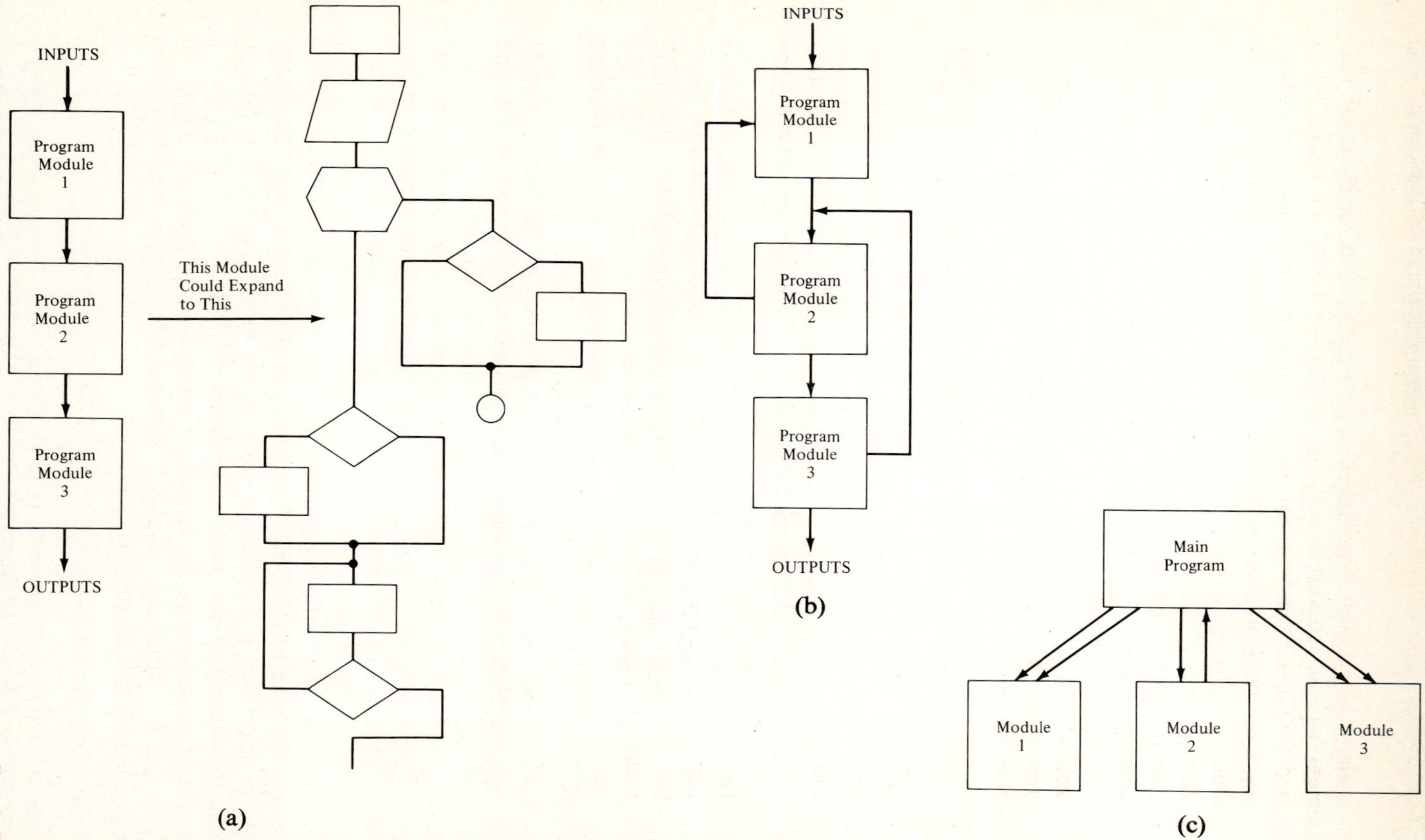

Fig. 7-8 Program Layouts for Several Styles. (a) Structured Programming Layout; (b) Nonstructured Program Layout; (c) Bottom-Up Program Layout

It should now be pointed out that it can be proved that the GO TO statement can be eliminated if the control structures in either ANSI standard BASIC or the structured systems are used. Sometimes, however, the program arrangement seems a little strained and this leads to much use of "almost" structured programming (few GO TO's in a program). The best known proof of the fact that GO TO's are not necessary is that of Bohm and Jacopini[7] who showed any program that can be written with any control statements (including GO TO's) can be written using only the IF THEN ELSE and DO WHILE statements (structures) which will now be introduced.

Here is an example of a typical structured programming with the IF THEN ELSE statement in a program.

```
100 IF X > 0 THEN 110 ELSE 130
110 LET A = B + C
120 LET D = A*2
130 -----
```

This is from a system called "BASIC-Plus" and is called a "single alternative decision structure." Notice that both places where jumps can be made are called out and that in either case the program section is straight line in that it does not jump backward or around another section of code.

Here is a similar structure for a system called "DARTMOUTH BASIC:"

```
100 IF X > 0
110 THEN
120      LET A = B + C
130      LET D = A*2
140 IF END
```

We have indented a section of program to illustrate how the above works. If X > 0 when the section of program is reached, then A is made equal to B + C and D is made equal to A times 2. If X is less than or equal to 0, the IF END is immediately jumped to and statements 120 and 130 are eliminated. Notice with this construction you cannot "jump around" in the program but must proceed directly through the statements. Figure 7-9(a) shows this structure in flow chart form.

[7]Bohn, C. and Jacopini, G., "Flow Diagrams, Turing Machines and Languages with Only Two Formation Rules," *Communications of the ACM*, Vol. 9, No. 4, May 1966.

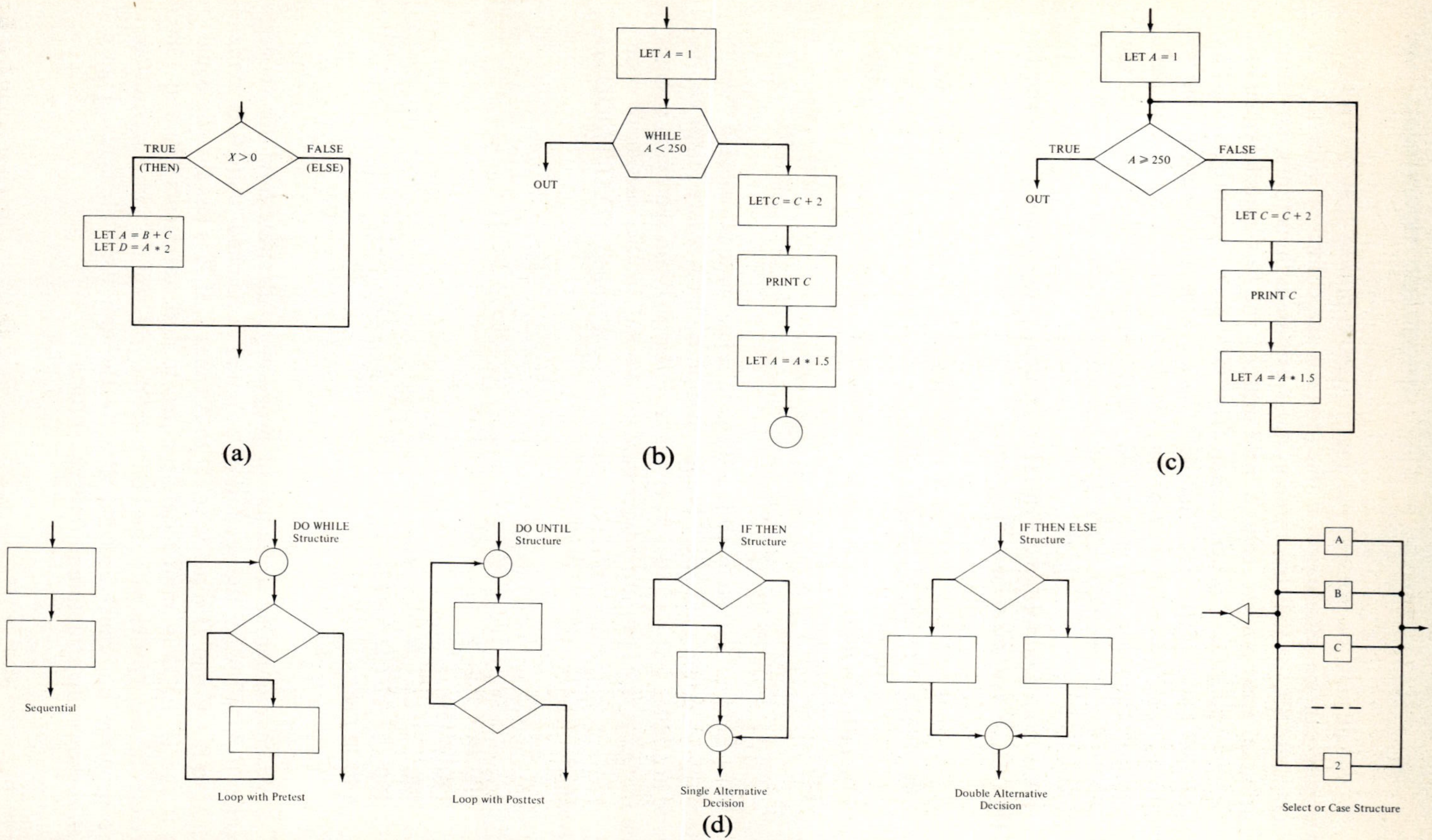

Fig. 7-9 Control Structures. (a) Control Structure for IF THEN ELSE Statement; (b) Flow Chart for WHILE Structure; (c) Equivalent ANSI Code for WHILE Structure; (d) Basic Control Structures in Structured Programming

For completeness here is our ANSI BASIC doing the same thing:

```
100 IF X > 0 THEN 120
110 GO TO 150
120 REM THEN
130       LET A = B + C
140       LET D = A*2
150 REM IF END
```

There is a "structured" control structure similar to the FOR-NEXT control structure in ANSI BASIC. The control structure is called a WHILE loop in BASIC Plus.

```
100 LET A = 1
110 WHILE A < 250
120       LET C = C + 2
130       PRINT C
140       LET A = A*1.5
150 NEXT
```

Here is the same WHILE loop in DARTMOUTH BASIC:

```
100 LET A = 1
110 DO WHILE A < 250
120       LET C = C + 2
130       PRINT C
140       LET A = A*1.5
150 LOOP
```

Notice that there is a single entry point and a single exit point from each section of program. In each case the loop up to the LOOP or NEXT statement[8] is performed until A equals or exceeds 250.

The same structure can be programmed in our ANSI BASIC.

```
100 LET A = 1
110 REM DO WHILE A < 250
120 IF A > = 250 THEN 170
130       LET C = C + 2
140       PRINT C
150       LET A = A*1.5
160       GO TO 120
170 REM END OF LOOP
```

[8] These are the *loop-terminating* statements.

Notice this contains a GO TO (in essence the WHILE statements also contain a GO TO in their structure) and that an IF THEN is used to test in the same manner as the WHILE does. (In order to simulate some of the structured program statements in ANSI BASIC the GO TO is useful.) Figures 7-9(b) and (c) show the above structures.

The general forms of the structures now in use in structured programming are shown in Figure 7-9(d). Notice the single entry and exit point for each. The case or select structure selects a single block from several blocks and is included in some of the newer systems. The structures in Figure 7-9(d) should be carefully studied because use of these structures in preparing programs will generally improve the overall quality of a program.

There is a considerable body of written material on structured programming and this section is of necessity only introductory. Control structures are still under study and in development and no systems can now be said to be the last word. The intention here is to present some of the fundamental ideas. The references list several books and papers expanding on this subject.

More about modules and modular programs can be found in the chapter on BASIC subroutines and the GOSUB statement.

7-11 SUMMARY

This chapter introduced a BASIC system feature called "implementation supplied functions" which facilitates the writing of many programs. This BASIC system facility enables a programmer to use sections of program previously written by expert programmers and maintained by the BASIC system in computer memory. These sections of program are called from memory by the BASIC programmer using the same function notation used in mathematics. A description of the INT, SQR, and ABS functions was given in this chapter along with examples of their usage. Other functions will be introduced in following chapters.

Some general information on automating business procedures was presented followed by a specific example, that of making change. In this example, a program was developed which calculates the change for a specific transaction.

The important subject of program development was then discussed. Some procedures and a general methodology now exist which facilitate the preparation of correct programs. Several subjects in this general area were discussed, including documentation, making programs readable, top-down programming, and structured programming.

In each of these subjects there is ongoing research and discussion, but a knowledge of existing techniques is important in large program preparation.

Examples of control structures for structured programs were presented along with structured program statements from several new systems. Structured programs can be written in ANSI BASIC or in any of the standard systems; the new systems simply facilitate (or even necessitate) the writing of structured programs.

The techniques for program development described in this chapter will be used in following chapters.

Questions

1. Give the value of A after the following statements are executed.

   (a) 10 A = SQR(49)
   (b) 10 A = SQR(64)
   (c) 10 B = 39
   20 A = SQR(B + 42)

2. Give the value of A after the following statements are executed.

   (a) 10 A = INT(6.4)
   (b) 10 A = INT(− 6.4)
   (c) 10 A = INT(SQR(65))
   (d) 10 A = SQR(INT(64.8))

3. Write a BASIC statement that will round a value stored in the variable X to the nearest integer and place that value in the variable B.
4. Write a BASIC statement that will round a value stored in the variable C to the nearest tenth (one digit to the right of the decimal point) and will store this value in the variable A.
5. Modify the Biology program which calculates growth percentage so the printout is rounded to one fraction digit.
6. Write a BASIC statement to reduce a price P by 35 percent and then to round the result to dollars and cents.
7. Write a BASIC statement to reduce a price P by 43 percent and then to round the result to dollars and cents (two decimal digits).
8. In BASIC, a commonly used test to see if a number A is an integer is the following:

   ```
   20 IF A = INT(A) THEN 60
   ```

   If A is the same as INT(A), then A is an integer and the transfer to statement 60 will be taken; if A is not an integer, the next statement in sequence will be executed.

   The above test can fail to operate properly if calculations are performed on the numbers before the test is made. For example, the fourth root of 81 is 3; that is, $3^4 = 81$. We might expect, then, that these statements would cause a jump to location 70:

   ```
   20 LET A = (81)^(1/4)
   30 IF A = INT(A) THEN 70
   ```

   In actual practice, after testing several BASIC systems, the jump was never taken because instead of 3, some number close to 3, such as 2.99998 was always given to (81)^(1/4). To get around this problem, the following test to see if A is "close enough" to integer value is more reliable.

```
20 IF ABS(A − (INT(A + 0.002)) < 0.005 THEN 70
```

The value of A is incremented by 0.002 in case the value of A is slightly less than an integer (2.99998, for example, in which case INT would round it down to 2). Use this statement on the value A = (81)^(1/4) on your computer and also the preceding one and see which one works.

9. Jim's age minus one is the square of an integer and next year it will be the cube of an integer. Find Jim's age (which is less than 100) using a BASIC program. (You may need the information in Question 8.)
10. After finding the age in Question 9, write a program to find when the age will be the cube of an integer.
11. Modify the program in Figure 7-4 so that it will make change in the English system (using Pounds, and so on).
12. Modify the program in Figure 7-5 so that it makes changes in the English system (using Pounds, and so on).
13. The cash register is out of nickels. Modify the program in Figure 7-5 so it will still make change.
14. The cash register is out of quarters. Modify the program in Figure 7-5 so it will still make change.
15. Modify the program in Figure 7-5 so that it does not test for a negative or zero value when an amount is offered, but simply sees if the amount is sufficient to cover the sales price, printing some appropriate statement if the amount offered is enough.
16. What are your preferred techniques for making a program readable? List at least three things you think should always be done.
17. Compare top-down and bottom-up programming, listing advantages and disadvantages.
18. The overall (first) flow chart for small problems when top-down programming is used is often quite simple but for large problems it can be fairly complicated. Discuss this aspect of top-down programming.
19. Draw a flow chart of a nonstructured program.
20. What is the chief characteristic of the control structures in structured programming?
21. Show why the WHILE statement more or less forces the programmer to write a structured program.
22. Show how to make an IF THEN statement so it functions like a GO TO statement.
23. A well-known method for figuring depreciation is to subtract a fixed percentage of the original value of the item each year (a \$100 item depreciated at 10 percent would be valued at \$90 at the end of the first year, \$80 at the end of the second, and so on). A second method for depreciation is to subtract a fixed percentage of the *present* value each year (a \$100 item depreciated at 10 percent would be valued at \$90 at the end of the first year, $\$90 - (0.1 \times 90) = \$81$, at the end of the second year, and so on). Write a program to accept as input the original value, the depreciation rate, and number of years N which will

produce a table showing the depreciated value for the first, second, third, ... *N*th year using both depreciation methods.

24. A common multiple of three numbers A, B, and C is an integer exactly divisible by all of them. The *least common multiple* (LCM) is the smallest such multiple. For example, the LCM of 2, 3, and 6 is 6. Write a BASIC program to find the LCM of three numbers input from the terminal.
25. Three integers A, B, C are called a *pythagorean triple* if

    $$A^2 + B^2 = C^2$$

    Write a BASIC program to compute all pythagorean triples with A and B less than 25.
26. Write a BASIC program to find all sets of three integers, X, Y, and Z that give the same result when multiplied or added. That is,

    $$X * Y * Z = X + Y + Z$$

    Let X, Y, and Z be less than 25.
27. Find all squares less than 50 that can be written as the difference of two squares. For example,

    $$3^2 = 5^2 - 4^2$$

28. Write a program to find four different integers A, B, C, and D for which

    $$A^B \times C^D = ABCD$$

    Let A, B, C, and D be less than 50.
29. Write a program to find four different integers A, B, C, and D less than 50 that satisfy $A^3 + B^3 + C^3 = D^3$.
30. Every integer can be expressed as a product of its prime factors in only one way. For example,

    $$7 = 7 \times 1$$
    $$14 = 7 \times 2 \times 1$$
    $$30 = 3 \times 2 \times 5 \times 1$$
    $$36 = 3 \times 3 \times 3 \times 2 \times 2 \times 1$$

    Write a BASIC program that will find the prime factors of any given integer input from a terminal.
31. All prime numbers except 2 are odd, so any two consecutive primes greater than 3 must have a distance that is equal to or greater than 2. Pairs of primes that differ by 2 are called *twin primes*. For example, the following number pairs are twin primes:

    3, 5   5, 7   11, 13   17, 19

    Write a BASIC program to find all twin primes less than 250.
32. A *Mersenne prime number* M_p is a prime with a value

    $$M_p = 2^p - 1$$

    where p is another prime. The first three Mersenne primes are

    $$M_2 = 2^2 - 1 = 3$$
    $$M_3 = 2^3 - 1 = 7$$
    $$M_5 = 2^5 - 1 = 31$$

    Find the first ten Mersenne primes.

33. An integer is *perfect* if it is the sum of its prime factors; for example,

$$6 = 1 + 2 + 3$$
$$28 = 1 + 2 + 4 + 7 + 14$$

Write a program that determines whether or not an integer input from a terminal is perfect.

34. A ball is dropped from a height of 10 feet. It bounces to one-half the distance from which it was dropped on each bounce. What is the total distance the ball travels before it stops? (Assume that the ball has stopped bouncing when it hits the ground for the fifteenth time.)
35. Write a program to read in a list of integers and to determine which, if any, are prime numbers.
36. Write a program to read an integer and print the number of 1s, 2s, 3s, . . . , 9s in the integer. *Hint*: To extract the rightmost digit from a number n, try

```
LET D = N - INT(N/10)*10
```

37. Write a program to sum the digits in a number and print it. For example, the sum of the digits in 347 is 14.
38. Assume a customer in a bank makes an initial deposit (which is read in from an input statement) and then deposits \$100.00 each month into his account. If the interest is compounded monthly, write a program to calculate the amount in the account after 10 years.
39. A linear equation in one unknown has the form $AX + B = 0$. Here X is the unknown and A and B are constants. For example, if $A = 5$ and $B = 10$, then the linear equation is $5X + 10 = 0$ and a value of X which satisfies this equation is -2. Write a program to input values of A and B and to then find a value of X to satisfy the equation. (In some cases, any X satisfies the equation and in some cases no X can satisfy the equation. Test for this.)
40. An equation of the form $AX^2 + BX + C = 0$ is called a *quadratic equation*. X is the unknown and a value of X which makes the equation true is called a *root* of the equation. Write a program to input values of A, B, and C and then to find and print values of X (roots) to satisfy the equation. Limit your roots to real values (no complex numbers) and test for cases where no roots exist.
41. Write a program to input the lengths of three sides of a triangle into a program and then find the area of the triangle. The area is given by

$$A = \sqrt{S(S-X)(S-Y)(S-Z)}$$

where $S = \dfrac{X+Y+Z}{2}$. Print the area and lengths of the sides.

Chapter 8 Simulation and Graphics—More Functions

Computers are often used to simulate[1] complicated situations in business, economics, and science. For example, large computer simulators consisting of long programs are used to simulate the economy and provide the government with information to predict economic conditions. Other programs simulate airframes under stress, buildings in earthquakes, population decline in an epidemic, and so on. The BASIC RND function plays an important role in most BASIC simulation programs, and is introduced here. The RND function is also often used in computer games, several of which are explained and their programs shown.

In many cases it is useful to display results using a graph instead of simply listing numbers or generating a table. Some principles in graphics programs and a graphics program that plots the graph of a function within given limits is presented in this chapter along with the operating details.

[1]To *simulate* a system is to represent that system using a model. The model is then used to gain information about the system being simulated. Computer simulations use a model of the system being simulated consisting of a program.

8-1 OBJECTIVES

The RND Function

The RND function is used to generate random numbers in BASIC programs. Using RND properly requires a knowledge of how RND works and several programming techniques that are introduced here. After studying this chapter, programs to generate and use random sequences of numbers in some prescribed interval can be written.

Making Decisions Using Random Numbers

Techniques for choosing between alternatives using random numbers are described and illustrated with examples.

The DEF Statement and Number Rounding

In BASIC, it is possible for a programmer to define useful functions through the use of the DEF (for DEFINE) statement. This can shorten and simplify many programs. The function and usage of the DEF statement is discussed. Then a technique for rounding numbers through the use of the DEF statement is given.

The TAB Function

BASIC provides a TAB function in PRINT statements to position characters on a page. This function can be used to format any printout and is particularly useful in graphics programs.

Graphics Programs

A simple graphics program to print values of a function in graphical form is shown and explained. A more useful program is then introduced that will print values of a function in intervals set up by the programmer.

8-2 THE RND FUNCTION

An interesting and useful feature in BASIC is the RND (for RANDOM) function. The RND function generates a sequence of random numbers. These numbers can be used in many ways, ranging from simulations in the social sciences, biology, physics, and so on, to the game playing programs that are now so popular. In business, random numbers can be used to simulate business situations and help in decision making.

The use of computers in simulation is, in fact, an important factor in computer usage. In many situations the possibilities are so complex in structure they cannot be completely analyzed. (Consider a model of the nation's economy, for example.) What can often be done, however, is to assign probabilities to things that may happen and to then program the entire system's interactions using random number-generating facilities to determine which paths are taken (which decisions are made) through the program. By then running the program many times and examining the outputs, analyses of what the system might do can be developed. Some of these concepts will be clearer after more discussion of the RND function.

The RND function, unfortunately, varies somewhat in its usage from BASIC system to BASIC system. Fortunately, the variations are small and generally easy to manage. The ANSI standard and most computers simply use RND to give this function. Other systems (HP, for example) use RND(0). You must find exactly how this function is written in your system, but it is likely that RND or RND(0) will work.

If we write

```
10 LET X = RND
```

or in some systems

```
10 LET X = RND(0)
```

when statement 10 is executed, the variable X will be given a value that is a random number. When the translator reads the RND it generates a number that is greater than or equal to 0 and less than 1. The assignment operator equals then places the value in X.

Here is a short program to print five random numbers:

ANSI Standard		Other Systems
	10 FOR I = 1 TO 5 20 LET A = RND 30 PRINT A, 40 NEXT I 50 END	10 FOR I = 1 TO 5 20 LET A = RND(0) 30 PRINT A, 40 NEXT I 50 END

This program prints five numbers in order on a line and each of these numbers will be fractions from 0 to (but not including) 1. That is, the RND random number generated each time is a number greater than or equal to 0 and less than 1. A typical printout for the above program might be

```
0.254976    0.114659    0.874301    0.493056    0.764211
```

The program operates as follows: The FOR loop causes the LET statement to be executed five times. Each time the RND function generates a number from 0 to 1 and this value is stored in the variable A. The PRINT statement then prints this value.

In each BASIC system the RND function generates random numbers using one of a number of techniques which have been developed by mathematicians. You can think of the RND function as follows, however. (We assume a BASIC system having six digit numbers.) Suppose we write each possible decimal fraction with 6 digits, including all 0's, on a separate slip of paper. We will then have 10^6 pieces of paper, each with a different fraction written on it. We throw these slips of paper in a bowl and mix them up. Then each time the RND is reached we choose one, use its value for RND, and then return it to the bowl and mix the slips again.

The above program can be more simply written as follows. The LET was only used to show how values can be introduced into variables from the RND.[2]

```
10 FOR I = 1 TO 5
20      PRINT RND,
30 NEXT I
40 END
```

In most systems, if you run the above program twice (or more) you will get the same sequence of numbers.[3] This is to enable testing programs. To make the RND give a different sequence each time, a RANDOMIZE statement must be used and placed before the RND. (If several RND's are used, a single RANDOMIZE statement will work for all the RND's in a program.) Our program then becomes

```
10 RANDOMIZE
20 FOR I = 1 TO 5
30      LET A = RND
40      PRINT A,
50 NEXT I
60 END
```

You should try the above program on your terminal at the first opportunity to see the results and get some feeling for the RND function.

Two other points need to be made here.

1. If your system uses the form RND(0), the 0 is a "dummy" value and you could use RND(1), RND(15), or whatever you choose; there will be no difference in the output values generated. Use of RND(0) each time is suggested, however.

[2] Only RND will be used in the following examples. If your system uses RND(0), simply use this form instead.

[3] In HP systems the sequence will vary each time.

2. To generate random sequences that are the same each time a program is run on Hewlett Packard (HP) Computer BASIC, you should use a RND(−1) on the first occurrence of the RND and a RND(0) thereafter. No RANDOMIZE statement is required in HP BASIC, unless a RND(−1) is encountered the sequence will vary each time.

8-3 USING THE RND IN TESTS AND GAMES

Many programs designed to test knowledge and many learning programs use the RND to generate different sequences of tests. Game programs also make wide use of the RND function.

First, an important programming technique in using the RND function needs to be understood. If it is necessary to generate random integers from 0 to 10 instead of a fraction from 0 to 1, this can be done by a LET statement as follows:

```
10 LET A = INT(11*RND)
```

or

```
10 LET A = INT(11*RND(0))
```

depending on your system. Multiplying the RND value, which is from 0 to 1, by 11 gives a value from 0 to (up to but not including) 11; then taking the integer value with the INT statement cuts off the fraction part, giving an integer from 0 to 10 (including 10).

The following[4] gives integers from 0 to 15:

```
10 LET A = INT(RND*16)      10 LET A = INT(RND(0)*16)
```

These statements give a random integer from 5 to 10:

```
10 LET A = INT(RND*6) + 5      10 LET A = INT(RND(0)*6) + 5
```

The following gives a random number, including fractions, from 0 to 10 (not including 10):

```
10 LET A = RND*10      10 LET A = RND(0)*10
```

[4]The general rule is as follows:

INT(RND*R) + S

R: Number of different integers wanted

S: Starting value

The following statements give a random number including fractions from 5 to 10 (but not including the number 10).

```
10 LET A = RND*5 + 5        10 LET A = RND(0)*5 + 5
```

It is now possible to show an application of the RND function in game programs. The first game requires a player to guess a number (an integer from 1 to 5) that has been generated by a RND statement.

```
 10 REM GUESS PROGRAM
 20 REM P.ABLE, 8/7/81
 30 REM
 40 REM G IS THE PLAYERS GUESS, A IS THE RANDOM NUMBER
 50 REM
 60 PRINT "TYPE AN INTEGER FROM 1 TO 5, TO QUIT TYPE -1"
 70 LET A = INT(RND*5) + 1
 80 INPUT G
 90 IF G = -1 THEN 150
100   IF G = A THEN 130
110         PRINT "WRONG, TRY AGAIN"
120         GO TO 80
130   PRINT "RIGHT"
140   GO TO 60
150 END
```

The player is asked to type an integer from 1 to 5. He can quit playing by typing −1. The Computer generates a random integer from 1 to 5, sees if the integer is equal to the input G in statement 80; if it is, prints RIGHT; if not, prints WRONG, TRY AGAIN, then asks for another number. Understanding this program will help in much that follows and you should operate the program, if possible, before proceeding.

8-4 A PROGRAM TO ILLUSTRATE DECISION PROCESSES

A more interesting guessing program that uses the ABS and RND functions along with several IF statements, including one which examines a character string and makes a decision based on its value, will now be developed.

The program generates a random integer between 1 and 10. A player is then asked to guess this number and to continue guessing until the number is correct. When the player guesses the number the computer is to print RIGHT; if the number input is incorrect, the player is to be "coached" by a statement saying the guess is too high or too low, or, if the guess is very close, a statement saying the guess is close. This will help shorten the game and a skillful player can learn to get the answer very quickly.

The variables used will be the guess value G, the random number R, and the difference between the guess and the random number; that is, D = ABS(G – R). Here are the possibilities, and what should be printed for each.

1. If D is 0 the player has won and we print RIGHT.
2. If D is 1 the player is very close and we print

   VERY CLOSE, TRY AGAIN

3. If D is 2 the player is nearly right and we print

   CLOSE, TRY AGAIN

4. If D is greater than 2 we tell the player if he is high or low so he can improve his guess.

In this same program, after each game the player will be asked if he or she wishes to continue playing or quit. The player is to type P to continue playing and Q to quit.

A flow chart of a program to realize all of these possibilities is shown in Figure 8-1. The program can now be written, including the decision processes.

Here are some REM statements to summarize the program and identify the variables.

```
10 REM GUESS AND BE COACHED PROGRAM
20 REM A.B. PRESS, 2/4/81
30 REM THE PROGRAM ASKS A PLAYER TO GUESS A NUMBER
40 REM FROM 1 TO 10. IT THEN COACHES THE PLAYER
50 REM UNTIL THE NUMBER IS GUESSED
60 REM G IS THE PLAYERS GUESS, R THE RANDOM NUMBER,
70 REM D IS THE DIFFERENCE IN G AND R,
80 REM AND V$ IS INPUT TO PLAY AGAIN OR QUIT
```

Now, referring to the flow diagram, statements are written to (1) generate a random number from 1 to 10; (2) input the number; and (3) ask the player to input a number from 1 to 10. These statements are:

```
 90 LET R = INT(10*RND) + 1
100 PRINT "TRY AND GUESS A NUMBER. IT IS BETWEEN 1 AND 10"
110 INPUT G
```

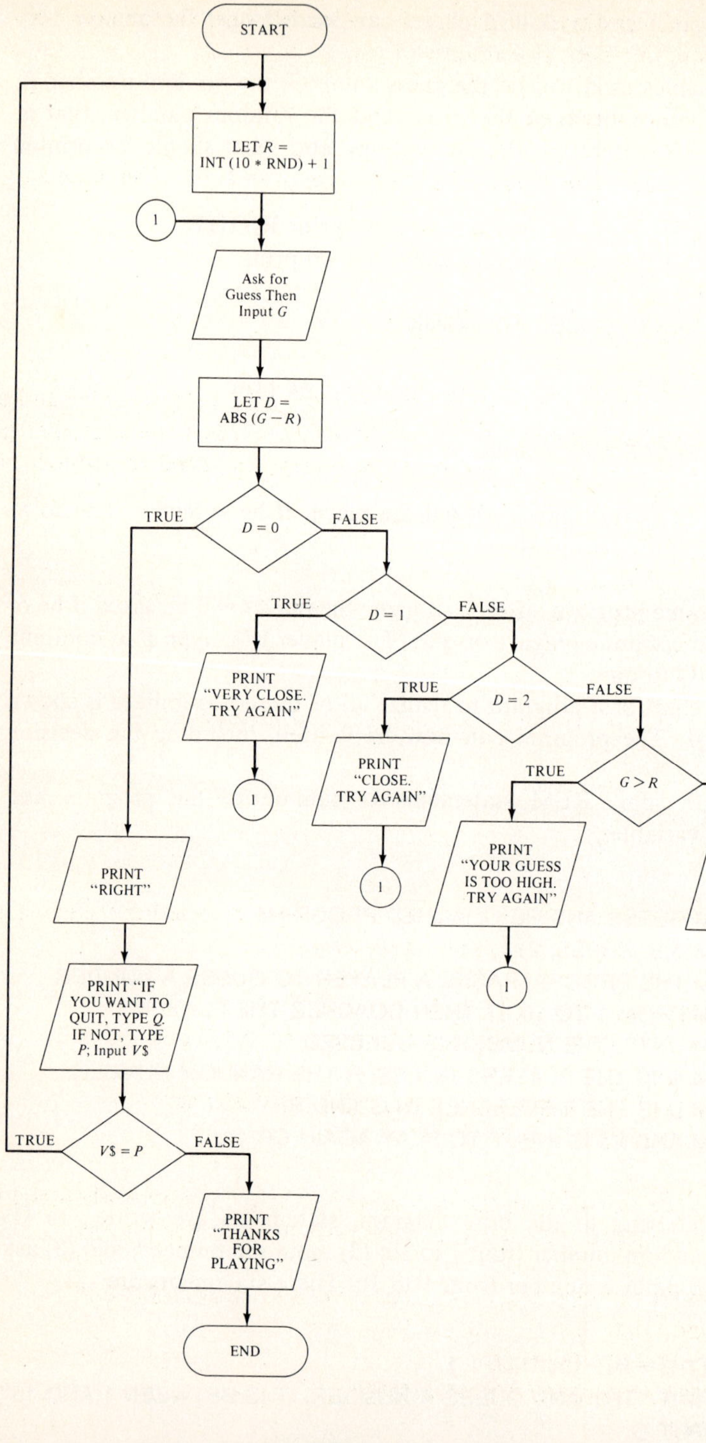

Fig. 8-1 Flow Diagram of Coaching Program

Now, it is necessary to find the difference between G, the guess, and R, the random number. This requires a single statement.

```
120 LET D = ABS(G − R)
```

First, if D = 0 the player should be congratulated. The necessary statements are:

```
130 IF D = 0 THEN 600

600 PRINT "RIGHT"
```

The statement number 600 is made large enough so that more code can be fitted in before it. The next jump will be to a statement number that is smaller, but still large enough to allow room for another section of program.

Now, if D is not 0 then D may be 1, so this is written:

```
140 IF D = 1 THEN 500
500 PRINT "VERY CLOSE, TRY AGAIN"
510 GO TO 110
```

(Statement 110 reads the next guess into G and continues.)

```
150 IF D = 2 THEN 400
400 PRINT "CLOSE, TRY AGAIN"
410 GO TO 110
```

If D is greater than 2, the program is to determine whether the guess is high or low and to print whichever is the case.

```
160 IF G > R THEN 190
170 PRINT "YOUR GUESS IS TOO LOW, TRY AGAIN"
180 GO TO 110
190 PRINT "YOUR GUESS IS TOO HIGH, TRY AGAIN"
200 GO TO 110
```

This takes care of coaching the player and telling the player when right. The following section asks if the player wishes to continue playing.

```
610 PRINT "IF YOU WANT TO QUIT, TYPE Q, IF NOT TYPE P"
620 INPUT V$
630 IF V$ = "P" THEN 90
640 PRINT "THANKS FOR PLAYING"
650 END
```

```
 10 REM GUESS AND BE COACHED PROGRAM
 20 REM A. B. PRESS, 2/4/81
 30 REM THE PROGRAM ASKS A PLAYER TO GUESS A NUMBER
 40 REM FROM 1 TO 10. IT THEN COACHES THE PLAYER
 50 REM UNTIL THE NUMBER IS GUESSED, G IS THE
 60 REM THE PLAYER'S GUESS, R THE RANDOM NUMBER,
 70 REM D IS THE DIFFERENCE IN G AND R, AND
 80 REM V$ IS INPUT TO PLAY AGAIN OR QUIT
 90 LET R = INT(10*RND) + 1
100 PRINT "TRY AND GUESS A NUMBER. IT IS BETWEEN 1 AND 10"
110 INPUT G
120 LET D = ABS(G - R)
130 IF D = 0 THEN 600
140    IF D = 1 THEN 500
150       IF D = 2 THEN 400
160          IF G > R THEN 190
170             PRINT "YOUR GUESS IS TOO LOW, TRY AGAIN"
180             GO TO 110
190          PRINT "YOUR GUESS IS TOO HIGH, TRY AGAIN"
200          GO TO 110
400       PRINT "CLOSE, TRY AGAIN."
410       GO TO 110
500    PRINT "VERY CLOSE, TRY AGAIN"
510    GO TO 110
600 PRINT "RIGHT"
610 PRINT "IF YOU WANT TO QUIT, TYPE Q, IF NOT TYPE P"
620 INPUT V$
630 IF V$ = "P" THEN 90
640 PRINT "THANKS FOR PLAYING"
650 END
```

Fig. 8-2 Program to Generate a Random Number and Coach a Player Attempting to Guess It

The above asks the player to input P or Q, stores his input in a character variable V$, and sees if V$ is a P. If V$ is not a P the PRINT statement prints THANKS FOR PLAYING and the program ends.

Some important techniques for making decisions can be found in the above. A complete program is shown in Figure 8-2 and a resequenced program with more comments is shown in Figure 8-3.

8-5 MAKING A SELECTION

Random numbers can also be useful in making decisions. We now consider a case from business. Suppose we have a number of sales personnel

```
100 REM GUESS AND BE COACHED PROGRAM
110 REM A. B. PRESS, 2/4/81
120 REM
130 REM THIS PROGRAM ASKS A PLAYER TO GUESS A NUMBER
140 REM FROM 1 TO 10. IT THEN COACHES THE PLAYER
150 REM UNTIL THE NUMBER IS GUESSED. G IS THE
160 REM PLAYER'S GUESS, R IS THE RANDOM NUMBER,
170 REM D IS THE DIFFERENCE BETWEEN G AND R, AND
180 REM V$ IS INPUT TO PLAY AGAIN OR QUIT.
190 REM
200 LET R = INT(10*RND) + 1
210 PRINT "TRY AND GUESS A NUMBER. IT IS BETWEEN 1 AND 10."
220 INPUT G
230 LET D = ABS(G - R)
240 REM
250 REM IS GUESS RIGHT?
260 REM
270 IF D = 0 THEN 480
280   REM
290   REM IS GUESS VERY CLOSE?
300   REM
310   IF D = 1 THEN 460
320     REM
330     REM IS GUESS CLOSE?
340     REM
350     IF D = 2 THEN 440
360       REM
370       REM IS GUESS HIGH OR LOW?
380       REM
390       IF G > R THEN 420
400         PRINT "YOUR GUESS IS TOO LOW, TRY AGAIN."
410         GO TO 220
420       PRINT "YOUR GUESS IS TOO HIGH, TRY AGAIN."
430       GO TO 220
440     PRINT "CLOSE. TRY AGAIN."
450     GO TO 220
460   PRINT "VERY CLOSE. TRY AGAIN."
470   GO TO 220
480 PRINT "RIGHT"
490 REM
500 REM SEE IF PLAYER WANTS TO QUIT
510 REM
520 PRINT "IF YOU WANT TO QUIT TYPE Q, IF NOT TYPE P"
530 INPUT V$
540 IF V$ = "P" THEN 200
550 PRINT "THANKS FOR PLAYING"
560 END
```

Fig. 8-3 Program to Assist Player in Search for Random Number

who work for a company and a new product. The company does not know if the new product will be a success, so it decides to try the product using a few salespeople (not all) to see if it sells. The company managers know the salespeople and their performances so if they choose the test salesperson, the choice will likely be prejudiced in one way or another. Instead, a random selection of the salespeople is to be made by computer and the product given to these salespeople for trial.

This is how selections of viewers are made for television surveys, election polls, and so on. Surveys almost always depend on a random selection from the possibilities at some point.

For our illustrative case we consider a company, Acme Manufacturing, which has just hired a new programmer, John Newton. Acme wishes to select three salespeople from seven in their largest district and to try a new product using these three salespeople. Therefore, the company president gives John his first job writing this program.

To begin programming John identifies the salespeople in the program by assigning numbers to them from 1 to 7. The salespeople's names are Smith, Jones, Able, Falb, Dane, Eagle, and Fix so he calls Smith number 1, Jones number 2, and so on, up to Fix who is number 7. The problem is now to choose three integers from 1 to 7.

To choose a number from 1 to 7, John uses this statement:

```
30 LET M = INT(RND*7) + 1
```

The above statement is then placed in a FOR loop to execute and print each random number generated.

```
10 RANDOMIZE
20 FOR I = 1 TO 3
30 LET M = INT(RND*7) + 1
40 PRINT M,
50 NEXT I
60 END
```

In haste John inputs his program and it prints 2, 3, and 6. He is delighted and rushes into the President's office where he explains the numbering system for the salespeople and how the program will choose them for the company.

John then runs the program and it chooses the numbers 1, 1, and 4. The President looks worried and says he wants three salespeople, not two. John quickly blames the computer for malfunctioning and runs the program again. This time it chooses 3, 3, and 3. The President looks even more worried and John leaves quickly, assuring him the computer room must surely be in flames by now but that the program is perfect.

Back in his room John examines the program and sees the problem; the same integer can be chosen twice or more and three *different* salespeople are needed. He has programmed without thinking the problem through and without enough testing.

The first important thing John notes is that each choice must be recorded. Subsequent choices can then be tested against what has been chosen so far.

He chooses variables R1, R2, and R3 to store the values each time a random number is chosen. Here is the decision process.

1. On first pass through the loop the random number generated will be stored in R1.
2. On second pass through the loop the random number generated will be called R2 and be tested to see if it is the same as R1. If the number is the same as R1, a new number must be generated and tested. This is continued until a different number is found and stored in R2.
3. On third pass through the loop, the random number generated will be stored in R3 and then tested against R1 and R2 until a number different from both is generated.

After three different numbers are generated using the above process, they can be printed. A flow diagram of this process is shown in Figure 8-4.

John is now ready to begin coding. The beginning statements are:

```
10 RANDOMIZE
20 LET R1 = INT(RND*7) + 1
```

To generate the second value, R2, he writes:

```
30 LET R2 = INT(RND*7) + 1
40 IF R1 = R2 THEN 30
```

The next section of program will generate R3, and then print R1, R2, and R3.

```
50 LET R3 = INT(RND*7) + 1
60 IF R3 = R2 THEN 50
70 IF R3 = R1 THEN 50
80 PRINT R1, R2, R3
90 END
```

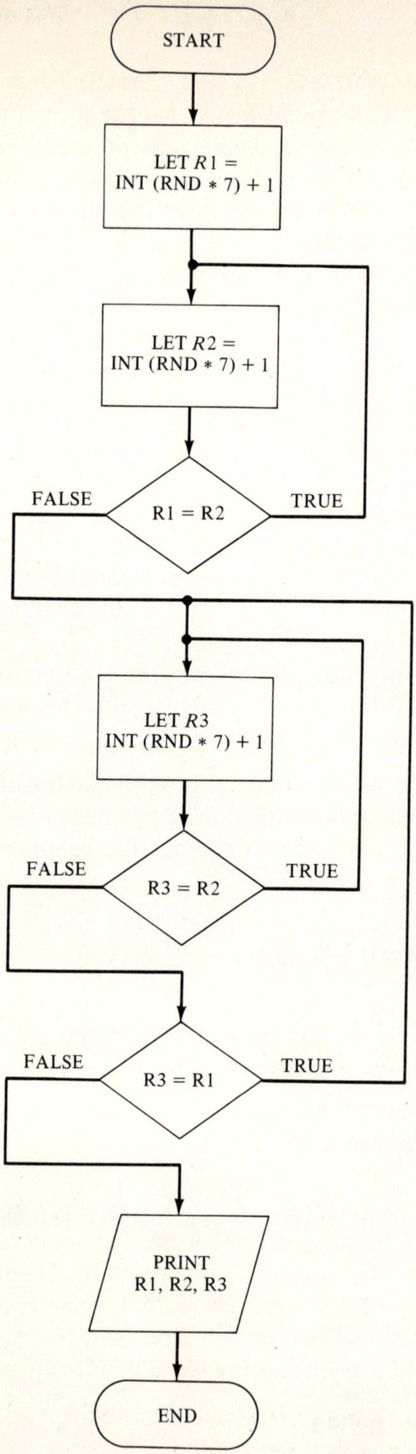

Fig. 8-4 Flow Chart of Selecting Three Different Random Numbers

Here is the complete program:

```
10 RANDOMIZE
20 LET R1 = INT(RND*7) + 1
30 LET R2 = INT(RND*7) + 1
40 IF R1 = R2 THEN 30
50 LET R3 = INT(RND*7) + 1
60 IF R3 = R2 THEN 50
70 IF R3 = R1 THEN 50
80 PRINT R1, R2, R3
90 END
```

John tests this program many times and gets three different numbers each time. To be doubly sure he shows it to another programmer who is very experienced.

Because we have introduced the program a statement at a time, the program is hopefully understandable and the principle of using variables to record values and then testing them has been introduced. However, if this program were given to you with no explanations or REM statements, it would be hard to decipher. The programmer friend thus advises John to add REM statements.

She also shows John the following technique. If R1 is the number, or position, of the salesperson in a list of salespersons, to actually print the selected salesperson's name (and not a number) the following short section of program can be used. The salespersons' names are simply entered in the DATA statement.

```
 90 RESTORE
100 FOR K = 1 TO R1
110       READ A$
120 NEXT K
130 DATA "SMITH", "JONES", "ABLE", "FALB", "DANE", "EAGLE",
140 DATA "FIX"
150 PRINT A$
```

Using this technique John adds a section of program for R1, R2, and R3, then adds REM statements, resequences (renumbers) the program, and tests it many times. The program is in Figure 8-5. Satisfied that it works he again goes to the President and runs it. This time the program prints three different salespersons' names and the President is delighted. His computer has been fixed and he begins testing his new sales program. The moral is:

1. Think things through before programming.
2. Test a new program thoroughly.
3. Use REM statements.
4. Be good to your friends, especially if they are programmers.

```
100 REM SALESPERSONNEL
110 REM J. Y. PRESS, 4/6/81
120 REM
130 REM THIS PROGRAM SELECTS THREE SALESPEOPLE FROM
140 REM SEVEN LISTED IN THE DATA STATEMENT.
150 REM THE SALESPEOPLE SELECTED ARE ASSIGNED VARIABLES
160 REM R1, R2, AND R3, WHICH ARE CONVERTED TO NAMES
170 REM A$, B$, AND C$.
180 REM
190 RANDOMIZE
200 REM
210 REM CHOOSE FIRST SALESPERSON'S NUMBER
220 REM
230 LET R1 = INT(RND*7) + 1
240 REM
250 REM CHOOSE SECOND SALESPERSON'S NUMBER
260 REM
270 LET R2 = INT(RND*7) + 1
280 IF R1 = R2 THEN 270
290 REM
300 REM CHOOSE THIRD SALESPERSON'S NUMBER
310 REM
320 LET R3 = INT(RND*7) + 1
330 IF R3 = R2 THEN 320
340 IF R3 = R1 THEN 320
350 REM
360 REM CONVERT SALESPERSONS' NUMBERS TO NAMES
370 REM
380 RESTORE
390 FOR K = 1 TO R1
400       READ A$
410 NEXT K
420 RESTORE
430 FOR K = 1 TO R2
440       READ B$
450 NEXT K
460 RESTORE
470 FOR K = 1 TO R3
480       READ C$
490 NEXT K
500 REM
510 REM PRINT SALESPERSONS' NAMES
520 REM
530 PRINT "THE THREE SALESPEOPLE ARE ";A$;", ";B$;", AND ";C$
540 DATA "SMITH", "JONES", "ABLE", "FALB", "DANE", "EAGLE"
550 DATA "FIX"
560 END
```

(a)

```
THE THREE SALESPEOPLE ARE EAGLE, ABLE, AND SMITH
```

(b)

Fig. 8-5 Program to Select Three Salespeople from a List of Seven. (a) Program to Select Three Sales Persons' Names; (b) Typical Run from Program (a)

8-6 SIMULATION USING THE RND

In order to introduce the ideas of simulation, we will examine the dice game most played in casinos. In this game the player rolls two dice (which are cubes with six sides numbered from 1 to 6) at each play. The player then loses or wins the game as follows:

1. If a 7 or 11 is thrown on the first roll, the player wins.
2. If a 4, 5, 6, 8, 9, or 10 is thrown on the first roll, the player continues rolling the dice until (1) the player throws the number thrown on the first roll, in which case he wins, or (2) the player throws a 7, in which case he loses.
3. If the player throws 2, 3, or 12 on the first roll, he loses.

This game can be analyzed using probability theory but it is also possible (and easier) to analyze the game using a computer simulation. (This is the essence of simulation. A situation is programmed in which decisions are made in some random manner. The program is then run many times to determine what will happen and how often.) In the case of the dice game we have the computer "play" the game many times and count the wins and losses, thereby determining the player's chances in a real game.

To prepare the simulation, we must first outline our program. The parts of the program are as follows: (1) the player (computer) rolls the dice; (2) if the player wins or loses on the first roll of the dice, we are done, but if not, the player (computer) must continue rolling dice until the game ends.

Clearly, an important part of this program is rolling the two dice and adding the numbers on the uppermost sides. Because the dice have sides numbered from 1 to 6, numbers from 2 to 12 can be generated at each roll. These numbers are not equally probable, because, for example, the number 7 can be made with a 4 and a 3, or a 5 and a 2, or a 6 and a 1; while a 2 can only result from both dice having a 1 up. We can simulate the dice throw as follows: First, to "throw" a single die we write

```
10 LET A = INT(RND*6) + 1
```

The INT(RND*6) generates an integer from 0 to 5; adding 1 to this gives a random integer from 1 to 6.

Now, to roll two dice and add the two numbers generated we write

```
20 LET A = (INT(RND*6) + 1) + (INT(RND*6) + 1)
```

The remainder of the programming process consists of (1) forming a flow chart that details the decision to be made after each roll of the dice and (2) writing a program that realizes this flow chart.

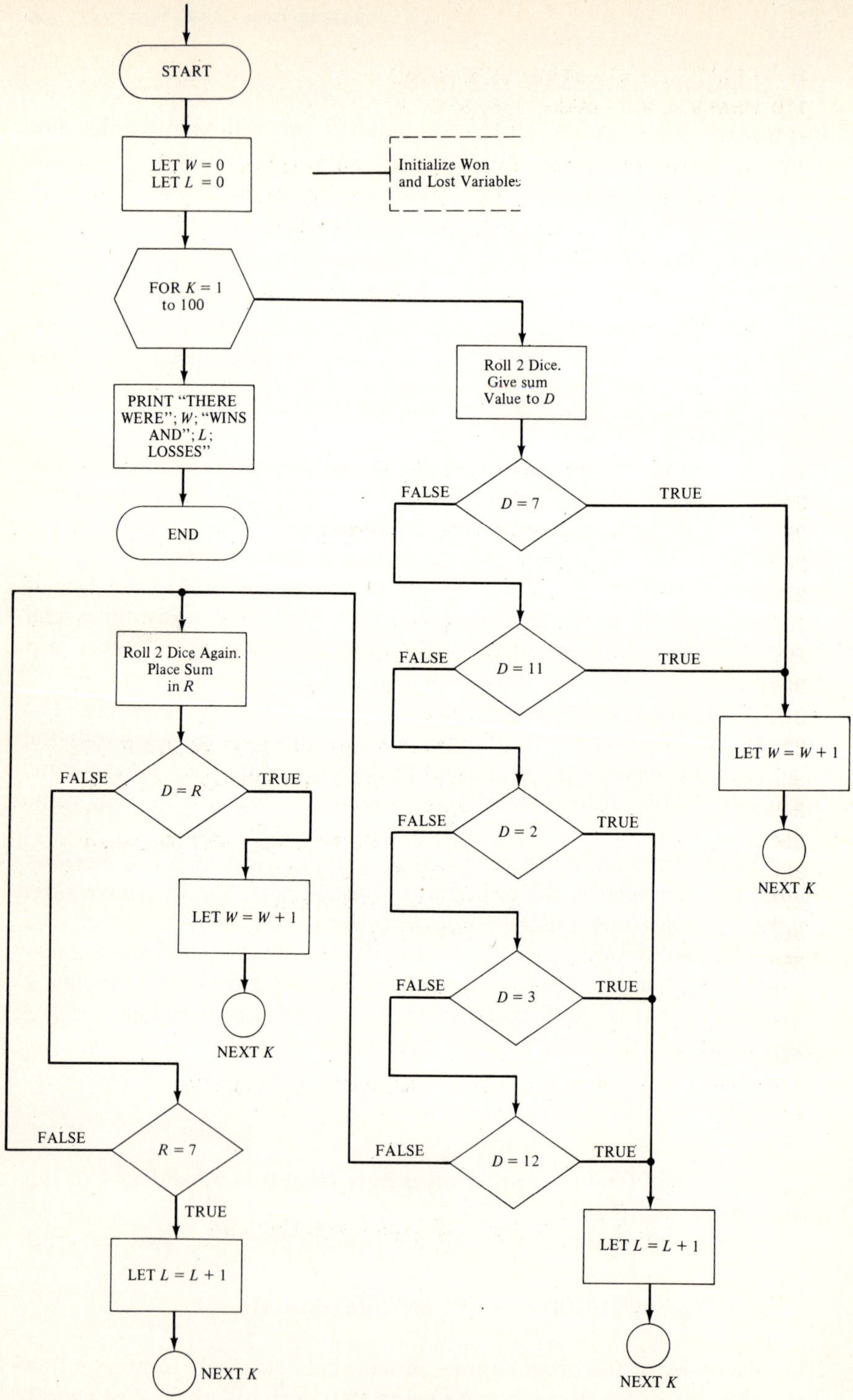

Fig. 8-6 Flow Diagram of Dice Game

```
100 REM SIMULATION OF DICE GAME
110 REM V. I. WILLIAMS, 5/6/81
120 REM
130 REM THIS PROGRAM SIMULATES A DICE GAME.
140 REM A NUMBER OF GAMES ARE PLAYED, AND
150 REM THE WINS AND LOSSES ARE COUNTED
160 REM AND PRINTED.
170 REM
180 LET W = 0
190 LET L = 0
200 FOR K = 1 TO 100
210       RANDOMIZE
220       REM
230       REM THIS STATEMENT ROLLS THE DICE
240       REM
250       LET D = INT(6*RND) + INT(6*RND) + 2
260       IF D = 7 THEN 390
270             IF D = 11 THEN 390
280                   IF D = 2 THEN 410
290                         IF D = 3 THEN 410
300                               IF D = 12 THEN 410
310                                     REM
320                                     REM PLAYER HAS NOT WON OR LOST
330                                     REM MUST TRY AND ROLL A POINT
340                                     REM
350                                     LET R = INT(RND*6) + INT(RND*6) + 2
360                                     IF R = D THEN 390
370                                     IF R = 7 THEN 410
380                                     GO TO 350
390       LET W = W + 1
400       GO TO 420
410       LET L = L + 1
420 NEXT K
430 PRINT "THERE WERE"; W; "WINS AND"; L; "LOSSES"
440 END
```

Fig. 8-7 Simulation of Dice Game Program

```
DICEM.B        09:10        26-APR-80

THERE WERE 42 WINS AND 58 LOSSES

TIME: 2.07 SECS.

READY
RUN

DICEM.B        09:11        26-APR-80

THERE WERE 48 WINS AND 52 LOSSES

TIME: 2.16 SECS.

READY
RUN

DICEM.B        09:11        26-APR-80

THERE WERE 54 WINS AND 46 LOSSES

TIME: 2.10 SECS.

READY
RUN

DICEM.B        09:11        26-APR-80

THERE WERE 52 WINS AND 48 LOSSES

TIME: 2.08 SECS.

READY
```

Fig. 8-8 Runs from Simulation

Figure 8-6 shows the flow chart for the program and Figure 8-7 shows the program itself. Notice the program runs the game a number of times and keeps track of the wins and losses. Several runs are shown in Figure 8-8.

8-7 USER-DEFINED FUNCTIONS

In BASIC a facility is provided for the user to define useful functions. This can shorten the statements in some programs and can lead to a simpler, more obvious development of certain programs.

The function-defining facility is provided through use of a DEF statement. (DEF is short for DEFINE.) Here is an example of a DEF statement.

```
20 DEF FNP = 3.14159
```

In this case the "function" defined is simply the constant value of "pi." The DEF indicates the statement defines a function. The FNP is the name of the function and the number 3.14159 is the function's value. After this statement, we write

```
30 LET A = 6 + FNP
```

When this statement is executed, A will be given value 9.14159.

The names that can be given functions always begin with an FN and end with a letter. Thus there are 26 possible functions that can be defined which are FNA, FNB, FNC, . . . , FNZ. (This includes functions with a parameter, which will be defined next.) The DEF statement defining a function must occur in a lower numbered line than the first reference to the function.

We could write

```
10 DEF FNB = 26.423
20 DEF FNC = 7.968
30 DEF FND = 5/9
40 LET A = FNB + FNC
50 LET B = A*FND
60 END
```

After this program is run, B will have value (26.423 + 7.968)*5/9.

If the functions defined could only be constants, this BASIC facility would have limited value. There is a further DEF statement form, however, which allows for a *parameter*.[5] An example is

```
10 DEF FNF(X) = X^2 - 4*X
```

[5]A parameter or "dummy variable" is simply a variable used to mark positions in a statement. Here are three equivalent statements.

```
10 DEF FNA(X) = 2*X
10 DEF FNA(Y) = 2*Y
10 DEF FNA(A1) = 2*A1
```

The parameter or dummy variable is X in the first statement, Y in the second, and Al in the third. If the second statement above is used in a program and we then write

```
50 LET M = 6*FNA(4)
```

then FNA is evaluated by replacing each instance of Y on the right side of the = sign by 4 giving 2*4; so FNA(4) = 8 and 6 times this will be 48. Thus M will be given value 48.

This defines a function with name FNF which has an input "parameter" or "dummy variable," X.

Now, if after defining the above function we write

```
20 LET A = FNF(3)
```

then A will be given value

$3^2 - (4 \times 3)$

What has happened is the following: The DEF statement defines a function which takes an input value and squares this value and then subtracts 4 times this value from the square. When statement 20 is executed it says "substitute 3 for the parameter or dummy variable in the function." This results in the squaring 3, giving 9, and the subtracting 4 times 3 from this, giving -3.

If, instead of the former statements, we had written

```
10 DEF FNF(X) = X^2 + 4*X
20 LET A = FNF(2)
```

then A will be given value $2^2 + (4 \times 2)$.

A numeric variable can also be used when a call to a user defined function is made. We could write

```
10 DEF FNC(Y) = Y^2 + 3
20 LET A = 10
30 LET B = FNC(A)
```

Here the DEF statement defines a function FNC(Y) where whatever value is substituted for Y will be squared and 3 added to the result. Then A is given value 10 and statement 30 gives B the value $10^2 + 3$ because A with value 10 has been substituted for the parameter Y in statement 10.

The parameter can be any numeric variable; so we can write, for example,

```
10 DEF FNG(K3) = K3*4 - 6
```

Also, systems defined functions such as INT, RND, and so on, can be used in a function definition; so we can write

```
10 DEF FND(A) = INT(A*3 - 0.4)
```

In this case, each time the BASIC translator sees a FND( ) in the program it will multiply whatever is in the parentheses by 3, subtract 0.4, and then cut off the fraction part to form an integer.

Here is another example of how DEF statements are used in a program. Consider the statement

```
10 DEF FNB(W) = 2*W + 3
```

This statement defines FNB as a function which takes an input value and then multiplies it by 2 and adds 3 to give the value of the function. Later[6] in this program, these statements could be used:

```
40 LET A = 4
50 LET B = FNB(A)
```

When statement 50 is executed, the translator needs the value of FNB(A) and therefore looks for and finds the definition statement for FNB. Because the value of FNB(A) is to be given to B, the translator substitutes 4 for each occurrence of the parameter or dummy variable to the right of the = sign in the DEF statement thus getting the value of FNB(4).

The name of a parameter or dummy variable in a function definition can be used in another part of the program for other purposes. For example, we can write

```
10 DEF FNA(Y) = Y^2 + 3
20 DEF FNB(Y) = 2*Y - 6
30 DEF FNC(Y) = INT(SQR(Y))
40 LET A = 16.4
50 LET Y = FNC(A)
```

Here Y has been used as the parameter in all three function definitions. This same variable has also been used in statement 50 which will give it the value 4. The BASIC translator considers the usage of Y in the DEF statements only to indicate how functions are to be evaluated and does not attach any further meaning to use in a DEF statement.

Notice that in the above section of program, systems or implementation-supplied functions were used to define a function. Other user-defined functions can also be used. Here is an example.

```
10 DEF FNA(M) = M^2 - 5
20 DEF FNB(M) = INT(SQR(FNA(M)))
30 LET B = 5
40 LET X = 6
50 LET C = FNA(B)
60 LET D = FNB(X)
```

[6]DEF statements can be placed anywhere in the program but common practice is to place them near the beginning. The DEF statement defining a function must precede any reference to the function. When a DEF statement is encountered during program operation, it is skipped over like a REM statement. There are three classes of statements in BASIC: (1) statements that are actually operated; (2) statements that are used for definitions and to give dimensions (to be covered later); and (3) remark statements.

When this is run C will be given the value FNA(5), which is $5^2 - 5$ or 20. D will be given value INT(SQR(FNA(6))), which is INT(SQR($6^2 - 6$))), or INT(SQR(30)), or 5.

8-8 ROUNDING

We now present an example of some useful functions that can be put in DEF statements. In banking and in business, calculations are often performed using several digits in the fraction part of numbers because calculations need to be as accurate as possible. However, pennies are our smallest coins so all payments must ultimately be rounded to "pennies and dollars." We cannot pay a bill of $2.6912, we can only pay $2.69 or $2.70.

In calculating interest, for example, numbers sometimes result that can have several digits in the fraction part, but on a bank statement all numbers must be rounded to dollars and cents. A function statement can be used to effect this rounding.

The following shows a function that will change a number with several digits in the fraction part to a dollar value with pennies only in the fraction.

```
10 DEF FND(A) = INT(100*A + 0.5)/100
```

To show how this can be used, suppose we have a balance in a savings account and the interest is 6 percent, to update the account we must multiply the balance by 1.06, and then round this to a two-digit fraction.

For example, if the balance is $632.54 and the interest rate is 6 percent, we would have

$$632.54 + 0.6 \times 632.54 = 670.5524$$

or more simply

$$632.54 \times 1.06 = 670.5524$$

If we then use the FND above to round this and print the rounded value, we would have

```
20 LET B = FND(632.54*1.06)
30 PRINT B
```

This will give the updated balance in dollars and cents.

The FND function works as follows. First, the 632.54×1.06 in parentheses is evaluated to give 670.5524. Then FND of this is taken. This gives INT($100 \times 670.5524 + 0.5$)/100. The next step is to take INT(67055.74)/100. The INT fraction cuts off the 0.74 giving 67055/100, which is 670.55, a decimal number correct to two places in the fraction part.

Defining a function using a DEF statement is most useful when the function defined is used several times in a program. It has another advantage, however, because if later versions of the program require changing the function in some way, changing the single DEF statement will change all occurrences of the function in the program.

Rounding can be directly implemented using this function definition.

```
10 DEF FNR(X) = INT(X + 0.5)
```

After this is written we can write, for example,

```
30 LET B = FNR(C)
```

The B will have the value of C rounded to the nearest integer. In order to change the function FNR we simply retype the DEF statement with the new function.

8-9 COMPUTER GRAPHICS—THE TAB FUNCTION

An important area of computer usage is in generating "pictures" or graphical displays of information. In many cases "a picture is worth a thousand words" and some kinds of data are better displayed in graphical form than in numerical form. This becomes particularly true when data are so numerous as to be difficult to examine or where a pattern or trend is looked for.

Computer graphics is a large area where much progress is currently being made. Current research includes three-dimensional systems, color, moving displays, and so on. We write programs here to form conventional two-dimensional graphics displays that can be generated by a conventional printer or CRT display.

Since our graphics will be printed in two dimensions the (first) vertical dimension will be controlled by the "line feed" mechanism which moves print from line to line. The horizontal (second) dimension will be controlled by movement of the print head to the various character print positions in a given line.

A useful BASIC feature in graphics is a PRINT statement with a TAB(N) format. As an example, consider this line:

```
20 PRINT TAB(10); "A"
```

The TAB(10) section of this PRINT statement says "move the print position 10 places to the right of the left margin of the page." As a result, the line will cause an A to be printed in the tenth position in the current line.

In order to understand exactly how the TAB works it is necessary to know how the print positions in a line are numbered on the BASIC system you are using. The ANSI standard recommends that the leftmost position be numbered 1, the next position 2, and so on, to the right so that the tenth position to the right would be numbered 10. However, some BASIC systems have the leftmost print position in a line numbered 0, the next position 1, and so on, so that the tenth position is number 9. You will have to check your system to see what is used. The programs that follow will print in either system except that the BASIC systems with print positions 0, 1, 2, 3,... will print one position to the right of those with print positions 1, 2, 3, 4,... . This will not make any difference in the programs but the user should know how the systems print positions are numbered.[7]

The TAB function always moves the printing position to the position given in the TAB. (It does *not* cause the print position to be moved right the number of positions given by the TAB.) Consider this program:

```
10 PRINT TAB(10); A; TAB(25); B; TAB(40); C
20 END
```

This will cause "A" to be printed in the tenth position, "B" in the twenty-fifth position, and "C" in the fortieth position.

In many systems (and in the ANSI specifications) a numeric expression can be used inside the parentheses of a TAB function. Here is a simple example.

```
10 LET X = 5
20 PRINT TAB(2*X); "A"
30 END
```

This will cause "A" to be printed in the tenth position.

If the expression in parentheses in a TAB does not have an integer value when evaluated, BASIC rounds the value to the nearest integer value. Consider this program:

```
10 LET X = 2.3
20 PRINT TAB(2*X); "A"
30 END
```

This will cause "A" to be printed in the fifth position in the line.

[7]A simple experiment using this program will help you determine this, if necessary.

```
10 PRINT "12345"
20 PRINT TAB(0); "A"
30 PRINT TAB(1); "B"
40 PRINT TAB(2); "C"
50 END
```

8-10 GRAPHICS DISPLAY GENERATION

We can now examine a technique for generating a graphical display of values for a BASIC numeric expression. The expression $X^2/2 - X + 4$ is an example of an algebraic expression. If we would like to know the general slope of the curve for this expression calculated from 0 to 10, a table of values could be made as follows:

X	$X^2/2 - X + 4$
0	4
1	3.5
2	3
3	5.5
4	8
5	11.5
6	16
7	21.5
8	28
9	35.5
10	44

Now we can "see how this expression behaves" by looking at the values in this table. However, the following simple BASIC program will calculate and print the same values, but in graphic form, which is much easier to examine.[8]

```
10 FOR X = 0 TO 10
20       LET Y = X^2/2 - X + 4
30       PRINT TAB(Y); "*"
40 NEXT X
50 END
```

The printout for this is shown in Figure 8-9. This little program works as follows: X is given values from 0 to 10 in the FOR loop. For each value of

[8]If your system does not have a PRINT TAB(X) facility, then the graphics programs in this book can still be run as follows: For every occurrence of a statement such as

```
20 PRINT TAB(X); "*"
```

substitute this section of program

```
20 FOR I = 1 TO X - 1
21 PRINT " ";
22 NEXT I
23 PRINT "*"
```

This little section of program will cause the printer to be advanced X positions across the page just like the TAB(X) and a * to then be printed.

```
    *
   *
    *
     *
        *
           *
                *
                     *
                            *
                                   *
                                            *
```

Fig. 8-9 Printout of Graph for $X^2/2 - X$ for X equals 0 Through 10

X a value of $Y = X^2/2 - X + 4$ is calculated. This is then used to position a * using the TAB function. Notice that when X equals 1, 3, 4, 7, and 9, the value of $X^2/2 - X + 4$ contains a fraction and the TAB function rounds this to the nearest integer value. For instance, if X equals 3 then $X^2/2 - X + 4$ has value 5.5 which results in the * being printed in the sixth print position. As long as we can only use a fixed number of print positions to position the points on a display such "rounding" will occur. This phenomenon is called *quantization* and all digital displays have some quantization[9] effects. The secret of making a really accurate digital display is to have a great many positions in which points can be printed both horizontally and vertically.

8-11 A GRAPHICS PROGRAM WITH LABELED AXES

There are several problems with the graphics program just shown. For instance, the X and Y axes are not labeled. Also, the function values for Y all were positive and less than the number of print positions on the page. Finally, X had only integer values 0, 1, 2, . . . , 10, each corresponding to a new paper position.

We now present a program to cure these problems. The program is shown in Figure 8-10. It allows a user to:

1. Input any desired function.
2. Select maximum and minimum values for the X and Y axes and the number of values for X to be used in the graph.

A printout from this program is shown in Figure 8-11.

[9]Quantization is the breaking up (subdivision) of a range of values of a variable into a number of intervals, each of which is represented by an assigned value within the interval. For instance, a person's age is quantized into intervals (quanta) of a year.

```
100 REM GRAPH PROGRAM
110 REM H. K. NUHN, 8/9/81
120 REM
130 REM THIS PROGRAM INPUTS AND GRAPHS A FUNCTION FNF(X)
140 REM FROM A DEF STATEMENT. IT ALSO READS IN ORDER AN
150 REM UPPER AND LOWER BOUND FOR X, NUMBER OF VALUES
160 REM TO BE CALCULATED, AND THE LOWER AND UPPER
170 REM VALUES FOR Y
180 REM
190 DATA -5, +5, 21, -25, +25
200 DEF FNF(X) = X^2 - 2*X - 12
210 DEF FNG(X) = INT(X*100 + 0.5)/100
220 DEF FNH(X) = (60/(H - L))*(Y - L) + 6
230 READ X1, X2, N, L, H
240 REM
250 REM LABEL Y AXIS
260 REM
270 FOR K = 0 TO 8
280     LET S = K*(60/8) + 6
290     LET T = K*((H - L)/8) + L
300     PRINT TAB(S); FNG(T);
310 NEXT K
320 PRINT
330 REM
340 REM PRINT ROW OF DASHES
350 REM
360 FOR K = 6 TO 66
370     PRINT TAB(K); "-";
380 NEXT K
390 PRINT
400 REM
410 REM LABEL X AXIS
420 REM
430 FOR K = 0 TO N - 1
440     LET X = K*((X2 - X1)/(N - 1)) + X1
450     PRINT FNG(X);
460     REM
470     REM PRINT FUNCTION VALUE
480     REM
490     LET Y = FNF(X)
500     PRINT TAB(FNH(Y)); "*"
510 NEXT K
520 END
```

Fig. 8-10 Program to Graph Function

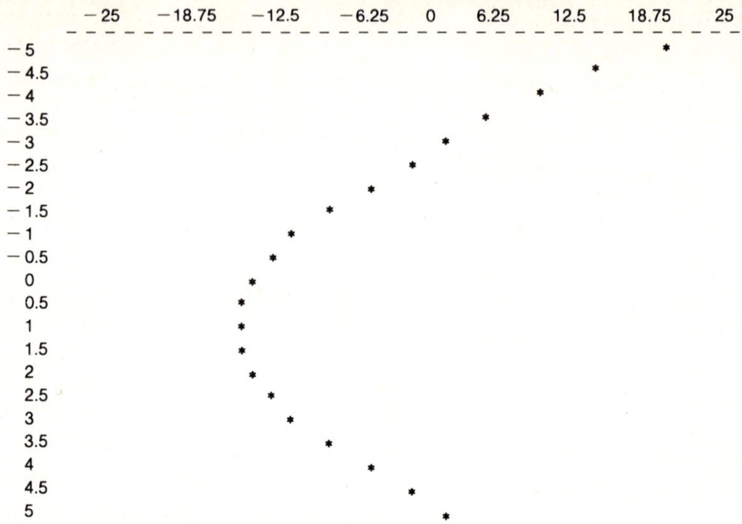

Fig. 8-11 Printout from Program in Figure 8-10

Details of the use of this program are as follows:

1. The function plotted is introduced using a DEF statement. This is statement 200 in the program. To introduce a function of your choice simply retype line 200, typing the new function to the right of the = sign in the DEF statement. As an example, to plot values for the function

   $$Y = X^2 + 4X + 3$$

   this statement is typed:

   ```
   200 DEF FNF(X) = X^2 + 4*X + 3
   ```

2. Maximum and minimum values for the X and Y axes and the number of points to be plotted can be introduced using the DATA statement with statement number 190. The X axis runs vertically on the page as printed and the Y axis horizontally. As an example suppose we wish to use −5 as the lower maximum value for X and + 5 as the maximum value and to plot 21 points. We also wish the lowest (minimum) value for Y to be −25 and the maximum value + 25. This statement will cause the values to be plotted:

   ```
   190 DATA -5, +5, 21, -25, +25
   ```

−5	+5	21	−25	+25
Minimum value in *X* axis	Maximum value in *X* axis	Number of points along *X* axis	Minimum *Y* value	Maximum *Y* value

It is a good idea to enter this program and run it for one or two functions and for several choices of X and Y limits. The Questions also explore the use of this program.

Here are some notes on the operation of the program in Figure 8-7.

1. The Y axis used consists of the print positions from +6 to 66 so that most printers can be used. The minimum and maximum values for Y input from the DATA statement are "scaled" into the value from +6 to +66 and nine values of Y are printed by statements 270 through 310. These values label the Y axis. Each value is rounded to two decimal fraction places by the FNG function in statement 210.
2. A row of dashes starting at print position 6 and extending through print position 66 are printed under the Y axis values by statements 360 through 380. The first of these dashes corresponds to the minimum Y value used (the value of L in the program) and the rightmost dash corresponds to the highest value of Y used (the value of H in the program). The dashes give more precise values of Y because several print positions are used for each written number. (The leftmost digit of each number is generally over the dash it is associated with.)
3. The first and last values X is to take are input into variables X1 and X2 and the number of different values X is to take is input into N. Statements 430 through 510 cause values of the function to be "scaled" into the 60 print positions available and a * printed at the correct position. To facilitate use of the graph, each value of X is rounded to two decimal fraction positions by the FNG statement and the X axis is labeled by statement 450.

The program shown in Figure 8-10 illustrates several important parts of a graphic display program, including the labeling and scaling of the X and Y axes. Notice that the program can be used to plot functions without an understanding of the details of the program operation. Only how to introduce minimum and maximum values for the X and Y axes and how to introduce functions using the DEF statement needs be known to use the program. Even longer and more complicated programs can be used in a similar way; only the operating instructions and program characteristics need be known to use the program.

If the program requires modification or improvement or if additional features need to be added, the program operation must be delved into, however. This is, however, a good example of a "canned" program and should be tested and used.

8-12 SUMMARY

The RND function generates a random number each time it is encountered in a program. The number generated is from 0 up to (and not

Table 8-1 THE RND FUNCTION AND RANDOMIZE STATEMENT

The randomize function has form RND (or RND(N) with N an integer in some systems)

The value of RND is from 0 to 1 with the value 1 not included.

The RANDOMIZE statement has form

line number RANDOMIZE

In the absence of a RANDOMIZE statement, the RND generates the same sequence of numbers each time a program is run; the RANDOMIZE statement causes the RND to generate a sequence with an unpredictable start each time.

In some systems (HP, for example) no RANDOMIZE statement is used, however, if a RND(−1) is used on the first occurrence of the RND and a RND(0) used thereafter, the same sequence will be generated each run. Use of RND(N) with N an integer greater than 0 gives a different sequence each time. The values of RND are uniformly distributed from 0 to 1.

---

including) 1. The same sequence of numbers will be generated each time a program is run unless a RANDOMIZE statement is placed before the first occurrence of an RND in the program. Table 8-1 gives some details of the RND function.

RND statements were used in programs to simulate a dice game and to determine the player's chance of winning. A RND statement was also used in a program to choose several names from a list. This type of program is used in surveys, scientific studies, business market testing, and many other areas.

The user-defined function in a DEF statement provides the BASIC programmer with a facility that can sometimes be used to shorten programs and to make them better organized. This function definition feature was used in the graphics program to make changing the function plotted straightforward. A DEF statement to round a number to two decimal digits (dollars and cents) in the fraction part was shown and this will be used in following chapters. Table 8-2 gives details of the DEF statement.

The TAB function can be used in PRINT statements to position characters in a line. This function is very useful in graphic programs (a FOR loop can be used for the same purposes). Table 8-3 gives details of the TAB function.

Graphic programs can be used to plot values in a two-dimensional graph which displays some kinds of data better than tables or lists. A simple graphics program to show the principle of graphics printing was shown followed by a more useful program. The final graphics program introduced plots function values on a labeled graph and allows the user to introduce his own function using a function definition statement and to

Table 8-2 USER-DEFINED FUNCTIONS

The general forms for defining functions are

line number DEF FN*x* = constant

or

line number DEF FN*x*(parameter) = expression

Here *x* is a single letter and a parameter is a simple numeric variable.

Examples:

```
2 DEF FNA = 16.4            8 DEF FNC(X) = SQR(X) + 6
6 DEF FNB(X) = X*2 + 4     10 DEF FND(A) = A - FNA(A)
```

The function definition specifies the rules for evaluating the function in terms of the value of an expression that can include the parameter as well as other expressions or constants.

When the function is referenced (called) the expression to the right of the = sign in the function definition statement is evaluated and this value is given to the function. The value inside the parentheses to the left of the = sign in the call is substituted into the right side of the = sign as indicated by the appearance of the parameter.

The parameter in the function definition statement is local to the definition and the same variable can be used in other parts of the program. Variables in the expression (the right of the = sign, not the parameter) are assigned their current values.

A function definition must occur in a lower numbered line than the first reference to the function.

A function definition can refer to other defined functions but not to the function being defined. A function can only be defined once in a program.

Table 8-3 THE TAB FUNCTION

The general form is TAB(n) where *n* is a numeric expression.
Examples:

```
TAB(14)     TAB(N + 16)
TAB (N)     TAN(2*N + 4)
```

The *n* in TAB(n) is evaluated and rounded to the nearest integer.

TAB(*n*) positions the print head at the number given by the value of *n* after rounding.

If the TAB function is called and should position the print head to position *N* but already more than *N* + 1 characters have been printed, printing resumes at position *N* on the next line.

choose upper and lower values for the graph along both the X and Y axes through the use of a DATA statement.

Questions

1. Write a BASIC statement that will generate a random number which is an integer with value from 10 to 20, including 10 and 20. Assign this value to a variable A.
2. Write a BASIC statement that will generate a random number, including numbers with a fraction part (such as 6.1973), in the interval from 6 up to but not including 12. Store the number in variable X.
3. Write a BASIC statement to generate a random integer in each interval listed, assigning the value to a variable B.
   (a) 5 to 15 (c) -5 to $+5$
   (b) -5 to -10 (d) -16 to $+32$
4. Write a BASIC statement to generate a random number (including fractions) for each interval listed. Assign the value to a variable X.
   (a) $0 \leqslant X < 2$ (c) $-5 \leqslant X < +5$
   (b) $0 \leqslant X < 22.5$ (d) $-10 \leqslant X < +20$
5. Modify the program in Section 8-3 so that the random integer generated is in the interval 1 to 25.
6. Modify the program in Figure 8-3 so that the player guesses a number from 0 to 20 and the program prints "NOT BAD" if D is equal to 3.
7. Modify the program in Figure 8-2 so the player quits by typing QUIT and continues playing by typing PLAY.
8. Modify the program in Figure 8-5 so it chooses only two salespeople from seven.
9. Modify the program in Figure 8-5 so it chooses three salespeople from six by dropping Jones from the list.
10. Modify the program in Figure 8-5 so it chooses four names instead of three.
11. Write a program that picks out a random homecoming queen and two princesses from a list of ten seniors.
12. Write a program to choose at random three viewers from a list of ten to survey television watching habits.
13. Modify the dice game in Figure 8-7 so the player wins when a 3 is thrown on the first roll. Run the program to see how this changes the odds.
14. Write a single BASIC statement to roll three dice and assign a value to variable D.
15. Write a user-defined function to assign the value 0.24639 to the function FNC.
16. Write a section of program to round a value X to three places in the fraction part of the number (so that three digits appear to the right of the decimal point).
17. Write a user-defined function FNX(Y) which squares an input value and then rounds the result to the nearest integer.
18. Using the TAB function, write a BASIC statement to print JOHN MARTIN with the J at the twentieth position in a line and MARY KAY with the M at the thirty-fifth position in the same line.
19. Write a program like that in Section 8-9 that will plot the function $X^2/3 - X + 6$ for each integer in the interval from 0 to 10.

20. Operate the program in Figure 8-10 plotting values as shown in Figure 8-11.
21. Change the DATA statement in Figure 8-10 so that a graph will be made with thirty X values from 0 to +10 and Y values from 0 to 100.
22. Use the program in Figure 8-10 to plot values for $\frac{1}{3}X^2 - 4X + 2$ for thirty values of X from −5 to +5 and for Y from −10 to +50.
23. Explain how the Y axis values are scaled and printed in the program in Figure 8-10.
24. Explain how the program labels the X axis in the program in Figure 8-10.
25. Make up your own function and intervals and graph the function using the program in Figure 8-10.
26. Modify the program in Figure 8-10 so only five values are used to label the Y axis.
27. Explain the purpose of FNG and FNH in the program in Figure 8-10.
28. Write a statement defining a function FNG which takes an input A into $\sqrt{3 \times A^2 + 2 \times A - 5}$ and then takes the integer part of this.
29. Let us label the axes of a plane with X and Y axes as follows:

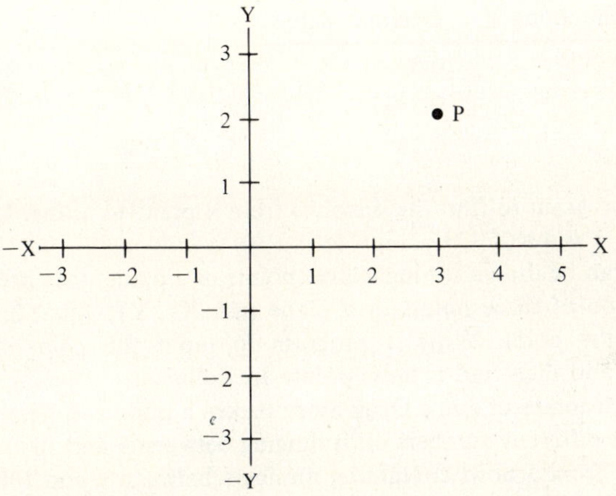

The point P here lies at $X = 3$ and $Y = 2$. An equation for a line in this plane is

$$AX + BX + C = 0$$

Now, if we have two lines in this plane $A1{*}X + B1{*}X + C = 0$ and $A2{*}X + B2{*}X + C = 0$ they will intersect at a point where X has this value.

$$X = \frac{B1{*}C2 - B2{*}C1}{B2{*}A1 - B1{*}A2}$$

Write a program to input the values of A1, B1, C1, A2, B2, C2 and find the point of intersection.

30. Write a program to find if two lines intersect in a plane. Use inputs as in the above question. Write a program to find if two lines are at right angles (perpendicular) in a plane. Use the input in the above question.
31. A *geometric sequence* is a sequence of numbers $s_1, s_2, \ldots, s_n$, where $s_n = s_1C^{n-1}$ and C and s_1 are constants. For example, if $s_1 = 1$ and $C = \frac{1}{2}$ then the geometric sequence is $1, \frac{1}{2}, \frac{1}{4}, \frac{1}{8}, \frac{1}{16}, \ldots$. Write a program to print a geometric sequence after it inputs a starting value and constant value.

32. For the first 10 Fibonacci numbers, find the greatest common divisor of adjacent numbers in the sequence.
33. How long will it take to get one foot from a wall if you start 200 feet away and every minute you walk $\frac{1}{3}$ of the remaining distance to the wall? How long will it take to get 4 inches from the wall?
34. If we have a ball that bounces to 1/2 times the height from which it is dropped, how high will it be after 20 bounces if it is dropped from a height of 10 feet? (On the first bounce the ball bounces to 5 feet.)
35. Suppose the ball in the preceding question bounces to $\frac{2}{3}$ of the height from which it is dropped. Write a program to simulate the balls bounces, printing the height after each bounce for 20 bounces.
36. Write a program to input a number of grades from a test and print the number of As, Bs, Cs, Ds, and Fs. The grade range for A is 90–100; for B, 80–89; for C, 70–79; for D, 60–69; and an F is below 60.
37. Write a program to convert the fractions $\frac{1}{2}, \frac{1}{3}, \frac{1}{4}, \ldots$ up to $\frac{1}{20}$ to decimal form and print the converted values. Here are the first few lines of a possible tabular output format:

Fraction	Decimal Value
$\frac{1}{2}$	0.5
$\frac{1}{3}$	0.333333
$\frac{1}{4}$	0.25

38. Write a program to find the distance from a point to a line. Use the equation for a line $Y = 4 \times X + 3$.
39. If a line can be drawn through three points in a plane, they are *collinear*. Input the location of three points in a plane (use X1, Y1; X2, Y2; and X3, Y3 to describe the point. Write a program to input the point values from the terminal) and then find if these points are collinear.
40. When a customer of Jim's Drug Store makes a purchase, he or she gets a card with three different numbers on it ranging between 1 and 1000. Jim then draws a number from a bowl containing numbers between 1 and 1000. If any of the customer's numbers matches the one drawn, the customer gets $50. Write a program to issue 50 customer cards, each with three random numbers, and to make 50 draws from the bowl. By running the program several times, determine the dollar amount lost by Jim so he can estimate what this scheme will cost him.

Chapter 9
Arrays, Subroutines, and More Functions

There is an important feature in almost all programming languages which makes it possible for programmers to use sets of variables. These are called *subscripted variables* and permit the writing of powerful programs in a very compact form. In BASIC, a set of superscripted variables with the same name is called an *array*. In mathematics, arrays are called *vectors* and *matrices* and are widely studied and used. In science, engineering, and business, lists and tables of data are widely used and these are generally handled in programs using array techniques.

An important programming tool involves the use of *subroutines*—parts of programs which form independent modules in program operation. The use of subroutines facilitates modular program organization and can sometimes shorten and help better organize a program.

There are systems supplied functions in addition to those presented in Chapter 7. These are primarily mathematical functions (such as log, sine, and tangent) and a description of these functions is presented along with some examples of their usage.

9-1 OBJECTIVES

Arrays and Subscripted Variables

The subject of arrays and subscripted variables is introduced and the corresponding ideas of vectors and matrices in mathematics and lists and tables in other areas are discussed. Several examples where arrays can be used to advantage are explained and the details of array usage are presented.

Subroutines—The GOSUB and RETURN Statements

The BASIC language uses two statements called a GOSUB statement and a RETURN statement to set up subroutines in programs. These statements and ideas for using subroutines in a modular program organization are introduced. Examples of subroutine usage are also presented.

Systems Supplied Functions

There are several mathematical functions that are very useful and that the BASIC system supplies through function notation. These functions are listed and examples of their usage are shown. A program to find the area under a curve using a technique called *numerical integration* is also presented and explained as an example of the subject of numerical analysis.

9-2 ARRAYS

In processing sets of data, a problem sometimes arises in naming the data. This problem is solved by the use of what are called *subscripted variables* and *arrays*. The use of subscripted variables and arrays also makes it possible to organize problems efficiently and to write short powerful programs to process large quantities of data.

As an example, suppose we wish to process grades for several classes. The number of students in each class will vary, but we wish to write a program that will calculate the average grade and then find the number of grades less than the average grade in the class. We might try writing a program using a number of variables greater than the number of students in the largest class but this would lead to a long repetitious program. Fortunately, BASIC makes a solution to this problem straightforward through the use of subscripted variables.

In mathematics, subscripted variables are widely used. As an example, if we need four variables, we can use A_1, A_2, A_3, and A_4 to designate them. The 1, 2, 3, and 4 are called *subscripts* and A_1 is read as "A sub one." In BASIC, because terminals and printers do not generally have subscript capabilities (half-line spacing) a subscript is indicated by placing the subscript number in parentheses. As a result, in BASIC A_1, A_2, A_3, and A_4 become A(1), A(2), A(3), and A(4).

A set of subscripted variables with the same name is called an *array*.[1] When the BASIC translator reads an array variable, it sets aside several locations in memory for the values that the array variables will take.

As an example of array usage in BASIC, we could write a program to input values A(1), A(2), A(3), and A(4) and then sum these values, as follows:

```
10 PRINT "INPUT A(1), A(2), A(3), and A(4)"
20 INPUT A(1), A(2), A(3), A(4)
30 LET S = A(1) + A(2) + A(3) + A(4)
40 PRINT "THE SUM IS"; S
50 END
```

If we input 5, 6, 7, and 8, in that order, then A(1) will have value 5, A(2) value 6, A(3) value 7, A(4) value 8, and S will have value 26. The use of subscripted variables in this program has no advantage over using variables A, B, C, D. However, it is possible to use a variable (or numeric expression) as a subscript in BASIC. We can therefore write A(N) in a program, and if N has value 2, when the statement containing A(N) is reached the variable A(2) will be used. This makes it possible to write a program that will accept a number of values that can be input when the program is run.

Here is a program that uses this capability.

```
 10 REM READ THE NUMBER OF GRADES"
 20 READ N
 30 REM READ THE GRADES"
 40 LET S = 0
 50 FOR I = 1 TO N
 60 READ A(I)
 70       LET S = S + A(I)
 80       NEXT I
 90 PRINT "THE SUM IS"; S
100 DATA 4
110 DATA 6, 14, 7, 9
120 END
```

When this program is run, N is given value 4 in the READ statement. Then 6 is read into A(1), 14 into A(2), 7 into A(3), and 9 into A(4). The

[1]The array B might consist of the subscripted variables B(1), B(2), and B(3), for example. B is then the *array name* and B(1) is a "subscripted variable in the array B."

variable S accumulates these values and will have value 36 after the fourth pass through the loop.

The simplicity of a loop like the above, which very simply processes N variables, is the primary reason for the widespread usage of arrays. If N was made 10 in the DATA statement, then 10 values could be read into A and summed by the same program. Similarly, N could be 50 or 100 using the same program.

9-3 THE DIMENSION STATEMENT

As has been mentioned, the use of arrays, each consisting of a number of subscripted variables, is an important feature in BASIC. We now give some details on array usage.

Each array variable consists of a single letter followed by a subscript. Therefore A(1), B(1), C(2), F(3), and Z(5) are all subscripted variables and there are 26 different arrays that can be used in a program, one for each different subscripted variable.

Numeric expressions can be used inside the parentheses in a subscripted variable. This means we can write B(N), A(N + 1), C(N*2 + 6), and so on. This section of program sums the elements B(1), B(2), B(3) in an array B, placing the sum in a variable S.

```
10 LET S = 0
20 FOR I = 1 TO 3
30        LET S = B(I) + S
40 NEXT I
```

This section of program sums the elements C(6), C(9), and C(12) in an array C placing the sum in a variable S.

```
10 LET S = 0
20 FOR I = 1 TO 3
30        LET S = C(I*3 + 3)
40 NEXT I
```

How many subscripts can be used in an array? When the BASIC translator first reads a subscripted variable it automatically sets aside a number of locations in memory for an array with that name. In ANSI Standard BASIC, locations for eleven variables are set aside and the subscripts that can be used are 0, 1, 2, 3, . . . , 10. As a result, if you write a program using an array named B, then as long as you use only subscripted variables with subscripts having values from 0 to 10 [the array variables B(0), B(1), B(2), . . . , B(10)] there will be no problem.[2] If larger subscript values are required, however, these can be called for by using a DIMEN-

[2]Some systems provide more (or less) subscript values for undimensioned arrays. Also, many systems do not allow the value 0 as a subscript, and we will avoid using it.

SION (DIM) statement. To increase the subscript range for any array B to 25 we simply write

```
10 DIM B(25)
```

Then values for B(1), B(2), . . . , B(25) can be used in a program.

Several arrays can be dimensioned in the same statement. If we write

```
10 DIM A(15), B(35), G(19)
```

then the array A can have subscripts up to 15, B can have subscripts up to 35, and G can have subscripts up to 19.

There will be some upper limit in your system for how large the subscripts can be in an array and if you are going to write programs with large arrays you should find what this limit is.

You can dimension an array only once in a program (that is, you can not change the dimension in the middle of the program). Also, only constants can be used in DIM statements; the following is *not allowed*, even if N is given a value in a prior statement.

```
10 DIM A(N)
```

Now, let us develop a program that will accept the grades for a class and then calculate the average grade for the class. Also, the school's principal is worried that some teachers are grading too high and some are grading too low, and so the program is to find the lowest grade in the class if the class average is below 80 and the highest grade in the class if the class average is 80 or above. The program sections will be as follows:

1. Input the grades.
2. Find the sum and average of the grades and print the average.
3. If the average is below 80, find the lowest grade and print it; if it is 80 or above, find the highest grade and print it.

A flow diagram is shown in Figure 9-1(a).

The next step is to decide what variables are needed. The array will be called G, N will be the number of grades, S the sum of the grades, A the average grade, H the highest grade, and L the lowest grade.

The input section of the BASIC program to input the grades is as follows. A flow chart is shown in Figure 9-1(b).

```
10 DIM G(50)
20 PRINT "INPUT THE NUMBER OF GRADES"
30 INPUT N
40 PRINT "NOW INPUT THE GRADES"
50 FOR I = 1 TO N
60      INPUT G(I)
70 NEXT I
```

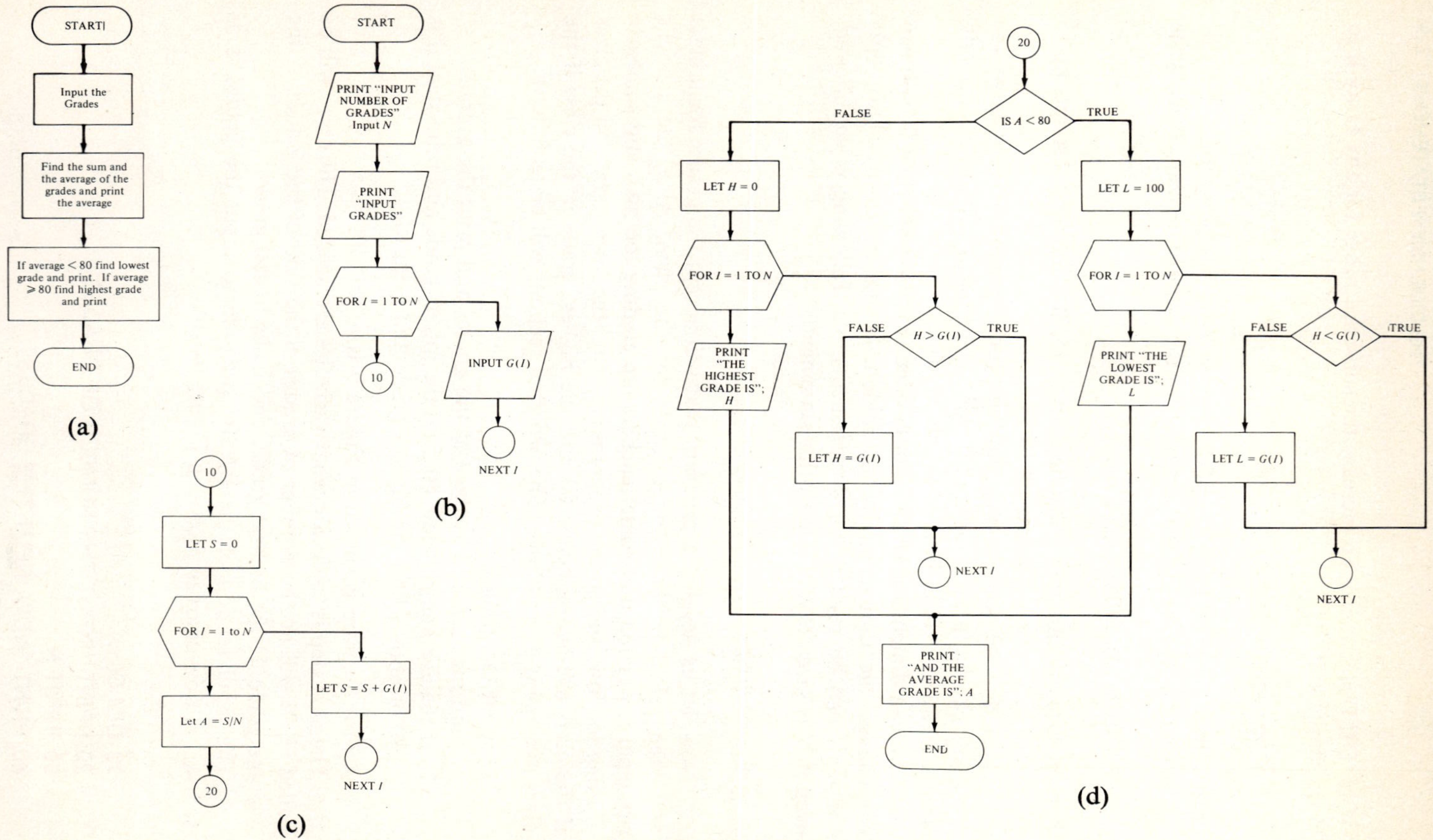

Fig. 9-1 Grades Program

```
100 REM GRADES, AVERAGE AND HIGHEST OR LOWEST
110 REM A. K. JOHNSON, 15/3/81
120 REM
130 REM THIS PROGRAM LISTS AVERAGE AND HIGHEST GRADE
140 REM IF THE AVERAGE IS 80 OR ABOVE AND THE LOWEST IF
150 REM AVERAGE IS BELOW 80.
160 REM
170 DIM G(50)
180 PRINT "INPUT THE NUMBER OF GRADES"
190 INPUT N
200 PRINT "NOW INPUT THE GRADES"
210 FOR I = 1 TO N
220      INPUT G(I)
230 NEXT I
240 REM
250 REM CALCULATE THE AVERAGE
260 REM
270 LET S = 0
280 FOR I = 1 TO N
290      LET S = S + G(I)
300 NEXT I
310 LET A = S/N
320 REM
330 REM SEE IF AVERAGE IS BELOW 80
340 REM
350 IF A < 80 THEN 490
360   REM
370   REM FIND THE HIGHEST GRADE
380   REM
390   LET H = 0
400   FOR I = 1 TO N
410        IF H > G(I) THEN 430
420             LET H = G(I)
430   NEXT I
440   PRINT "THE HIGHEST GRADE IS"; H;
450   GO TO 550
460   REM
470   REM FIND THE LOWEST GRADE
480   REM
490 LET L = 100
500 FOR I = 1 TO N
510      IF L < G(I) THEN 530
520           LET L = G(I)
530 NEXT I
540 PRINT "THE LOWEST GRADE IS"; L;
550 PRINT "AND THE AVERAGE GRADE IS"; A
560 END
```

(a)

Fig. 9-1(a) First (Lowest Level) Flow Diagram for Grade Processing Program; (b) Flow Diagram of Input Section; (c) Flow Diagram of Average Finding; (d) Finding and Printing Lowest or Highest Grade; (e) Program to FInd Average and Select and Find Highest or Lowest Grade in List

This program will input the number of grades and then the actual grades, placing them in an array G. The number of grades can be up to 50 because G can have subscript values of up to 50, the number given in the DIM statement.

The next step is to sum the grades and form the average by dividing the sum S, by the number of grades N, and to put the result in a variable A.

```
 80 LET S = 0
 90 FOR I = 1 TO N
100      LET S = S + G(I)
110 NEXT I
120 LET A = S/N
```

Figure 9-1(c) shows the flow chart for this.

Now, if A is less than 80, we want to find the lowest grade in the class and if A is 80 or above, we want to find the highest grade. We therefore test using an IF THEN statement.

```
130 IF A < 80 THEN 210
```

If the average is less than 80, we jump to a section of BASIC program that will find the lowest grade; if not, we use this to find the highest grade in the class and print it.

```
140 LET H = 0
150 FOR I = 1 TO N
160 IF H > G(I) THEN 180
170    LET H = G(I)
180 NEXT I
190 PRINT "THE HIGHEST GRADE IS"; H;
200 GO TO 270
```

If the average grade is below 80, we use this to find the lowest grade in the class and print it.

```
210 LET L = 100
220 FOR I = 1 TO N
230      IF L < G(I) THEN 250
240      LET L = G(I)
250 NEXT I
260 PRINT "THE LOWEST GRADE IS"; L;
```

The flow chart for the above section of the program is shown in Figure 9-1(d).

Now, what remains is to print the average and end.

```
270 PRINT "AND THE AVERAGE GRADE IS"; A
280 END
```

The above has developed a workable program which is shown, with remarks, and resequenced, in Figure 9-1(e). To show how straightforward it is to add features to a program like this, we add a section that prints the number of grades below the average if the average is below 80 and the number of grades above the average if the average is 80 or greater (Figure 9-2). (It is, incidentally, very difficult to develop this program without using an array.)

```
100 REM GRADES, AVERAGE AND DISTRIBUTION
110 REM A. K. JOHNSON, 15/3/81
120 REM
130 REM THIS PROGRAM TAKES GRADES INPUT BY THE USER
140 REM AND LISTS THE AVERAGE. IF THE AVERAGE IS
150 REM ABOVE 80, IT WILL GIVE THE HIGHEST GRADE AND THE
160 REM NUMBER OF GPADES ABOVE 80. IF THE AVERAGE
170 REM BELOW 80, IT WILL LIST LOWEST GRADE AND NUMBER
180 REM OF GRADES BELOW 80.
190 REM
200 DIM G(50)
210 PRINT "INPUT THE NUMBER OF GRADES"
220 INPUT N
230 PRINT "NOW INPUT THE GRADES"
240 FOR I = 1 TO N
250       INPUT G(I)
260 NEXT I
270 REM
280 REM CALCULATE THE AVERAGE
290 REM
300 LET S = 0
310 FOR I = 1 TO N
320       LET S = S + G(I)
330 NEXT I
340 LET A = S/N
350 REM
360 REM SEE IF AVERAGE IS BELOW 80
370 REM
```

Fig. 9-2 Program to Process Grades

```
380 IF A < 80 THEN 580
390   REM
400   REM FIND THE HIGHEST GRADE
410   REM
420   LET H = 0
430   FOR I = 1 TO N
440       IF H > G(I) THEN 460
450           LET H = G(I)
460   NEXT I
470   PRINT "THE HIGHEST GRADE IS"; H
480   REM
490   REM FIND THE NUMBER OF GRADES 80 OR MORE
500   REM
510   LET K = 0
520   FOR I = 1 TO N
530       IF G(I) < 80 THEN 550
540       LET K = K + 1
550   NEXT I
560   PRINT "THE NUMBER OF GRADES 80 OR ABOVE IS"; K
570   GO TO 760
580 REM
590 REM FIND THE LOWEST GRADE
600 REM
610 LET L = 100
620 FOR I = 1 TO N
630 IF L < G(I) THEN 650
640 LET L = G(I)
650 NEXT I
660 PRINT "THE LOWEST GRADE IS"; L
670 REM
680 REM FIND THE NUMBER OF GRADES BELOW 80
690 REM
700 LET K = 0
710 FOR I = 1 TO N
720     IF G(I) > = 80 THEN 740
730     LET K = K + 1
740 NEXT I
750 PRINT "THE NUMBER OF GRADES BELOW 80 IS"; K
760 PRINT "THE AVERAGE GRADE IS"; A
770 END
```

Fig. 9-2 *cont.*

9-4 A STATISTICS PROGRAM USING ARRAYS

An important statistical value that gives an indication of the deviation or variation in a set of data values is the *standard deviation*. The standard deviation is often used in statistics and is an important measure in biological studies, economic analyses, and in determining the meaning of experiments in physics, chemistry, and so on. The standard deviation measures variations around the mean (or average) of a set of values giving an indication of how much variation is present.

In statistics the standard deviation is measured as follows. Suppose we have N values $X(1)$, $X(2)$, . . . , $X(N)$. We assume each of these is a number. Now, first the mean (average) M is found. This is equal to

$$M = \frac{X(1) + X(2) + \cdots + X(N)}{N}$$

(Simply add all the values and divide by N.)

To find the standard deviation we then form

$$\frac{(X(1) - M)^2 + (X(2) - M)^2 + \cdots + (X(N) - M)^2}{N - 1}$$

The square root of this value is the standard deviation.

Let us do this for a simple case. Let N equal 4 so our variables are $X(1)$, $X(2)$, $X(3)$, and $X(4)$. We have four values (they might be meter readings from a physics experiment) and these are 5, 10, 15, and 2 so $X(1) = 5$, $X(2) = 10$, $X(3) = 15$, and $X(4) = 2$. The mean is then

$$\frac{X(1) + X(2) + X(3) + X(4)}{4}$$

which is

$$\frac{5 + 10 + 15 + 2}{4}$$

Therefore the mean is 8.

The standard deviation has value

$$\sqrt{\frac{(X(1) - M)^2 + (X(2) - M)^2 + (X(3) - M)^2 + (X(4) - M)^2}{N - 1}}$$

which is, for our case,

$$\sqrt{\frac{(5 - 8)^2 + (10 - 8)^2 + (15 - 8)^2 + (2 - 8)^2}{3}} = 5.715476$$

As can be seen, calculating the standard deviation for very many points is a considerable task. Therefore we develop a program to calculate the standard deviation given a set of input values.

The first step is to input the data values. We will input the number of values and then the values themselves and will use the four values given as an example.

```
100 REM STANDARD DEVIATION PROGRAM
110 REM T. M. MONROE, 7/4/81
120 REM
130 REM THIS PROGRAM FINDS THE STANDARD DEVIATION IN
140 REM A LIST OF NUMBERS. N IS THE NUMBER OF POINTS,
150 REM X IS THE ARRAY OF POINTS, M IS THE MEAN, AND S
160 REM IS THE STANDARD DEVIATION. THE MAXIMUM NUMBER
170 REM IS 20.
180 REM
190 DIM X(20)
200 DATA 4
210 DATA 5, 10, 15, 2
```

We combine the reading of values into the array X with finding the mean.

```
220 LET S = 0
230 READ N
240 REM
250 REM FIND THE AVERAGE
260 REM
270 FOR J = 1 TO N
280       READ X(J)
290       LET S = S + X(J)
300 NEXT J
310 LET M = S/N
```

The value of the standard deviation is found by subtracting the mean from each element in the array X, squaring this value, forming the sum of these values, and dividing by N − 1. Finally, the square root of this value is found and this is the standard deviation. The complete program is shown in Figure 9-3.

A standard library of programs of this type which find statistical values can be written and kept for usage by social scientists. Several such packages of programs are available commercially that have been developed by schools and programming concerns.

```
100 REM STANDARD DEVIATION PROGRAM
110 REM T. M. MONROE, 7/4/81
120 REM
130 REM THIS PROGRAM FINDS THE STANDARD DEVIATION IN
140 REM A LIST OF NUMBERS. N IS THE NUMBER OF POINTS,
150 REM X IS THE ARRAY OF POINTS, M IS THE MEAN, AND S
160 REM IS THE STANDARD DEVIATION. THE MAXIMUM NUMBER
170 REM IS 20.
180 REM
190 DIM X(20)
200 DATA 4
210 DATA 5, 10, 15, 2
220 LET S = 0
230 READ N
240 REM
250 REM FIND THE AVERAGE
260 REM
270 FOR J = 1 TO N
280       READ X(J)
290       LET S = S + X(J)
300 NEXT J
310 LET M = S/N
320 LET D = 0
330 REM
340 REM FIND THE STANDARD DEVIATION
350 REM
360 FOR J = 1 TO N
370       LET D = D + (X(J) - M)^2
380 NEXT J
390 LET S = SQR(D/(N - 1))
400 PRINT "THE STANDARD DEVIATION IS"; S
410 END
```

Fig. 9-3 Program to Find the Standard Deviation

9-5 TWO-DIMENSIONAL ARRAYS

The arrays so far have all had subscripted variables with form A(n), where A is a letter and n is a numeric expression. For instance, A(2), B(M), G(I + 2*M) are all examples of subscripted variables and the expression in parentheses always has a single numeric value when evaluated. These are variables for *one-dimensional* arrays.

BASIC has a provision for *two-dimensional arrays*. In this case, a subscripted variable again consists of a letter followed by parentheses, but inside the parentheses are two numeric expressions separated by a comma (remember that a numeric expression can be a number or a single variable as well as more complicated numeric expressions). For example, A(1, 2) is an element in a two-dimensional array, as are B(I, J), H(3, 4 + M), and Z(2*I, 6).

The two-dimensional arrays in BASIC correspond to what are called *matrices* in mathematics. For example, a matrix A with two rows and three columns is the following:

$$\begin{vmatrix} A_{1,1} & A_{1,2} & A_{1,3} \\ A_{2,1} & A_{2,2} & A_{2,3} \end{vmatrix}$$

It is easy to know the position of an element in this matrix. The element in the second row and third column is $A_{2,3}$, the element in the first row and second column is $A_{1,2}$, and the element in the second row and first column is $A_{2,1}$. The row number appears first and the column number second inside the brackets (mathematicians call this the Royal Crown or RC rule).

In BASIC, the matrix shown above would be subscripted as follows:

```
A(1, 1)    A(1, 2)    A(1, 3)
A(2, 1)    A(2, 2)    A(2, 3)
```

When the BASIC translator sees a subscripted variable with two values inside the parentheses, it immediately sets aside locations in memory for 121 subscripted variables. This allows use of variables with subscripts ranging from 0 to 10. Thus, if the translator reads the line

```
20 LET S = D(6, 7)
```

it immediately puts aside 121 locations for the two-dimensional array D and values of D(R, C) from D(0, 0) to D(10, 10) can be used in the program. (Do not forget that many systems do not allow the value 0 as a subscript, so only 100 locations are put aside in these systems.)

If a larger array than what is automatically assigned is desired, or if you want to conserve space by not having such a large array, then a DIM statement can be used to declare the size desired.

Consider the statement

```
30 DIM G(20, 30)
```

This sets aside space for a two-dimensional array with subscript values of up to 20 in the first (left) subscript inside the parentheses and up to 30 for the second (right) subscript inside the parentheses.

The statement

```
40 DIM A(6, 7)
```

will only allow for subscript values of up to 6 in the left subscript and up to 7 in the right subscript.

As in the case for one-dimensional arrays, if a subscript is not an integer, then 0.5 is added to the subscript, truncated to the integer part.[3] Therefore A(1.6, 2.7), A(1.9, 3.1), A(2.4, 3.4), and A(2, 2.98) will all be given the value A(2, 3) and so will A(C + 0.4, D − 1.5) if C has value 1.5 and D has value 4.6 when the subscripted variable is read by the translator.

To firm up the BASIC nomenclature on two-dimensional arrays, here is an example of an array named Q.

Q(1, 1) = 6	Q(1, 2) = 9	Q(1, 3) = 8.5
Q(2, 1) = 7	Q(2, 2) = 4	Q(2, 3) = 4.5
Q(3, 1) = 4.2	Q(3, 2) = 5	Q(3, 3) = 7.1

The array has nine elements which are the numbers 6, 9, 8.5, 7, ..., 7.1. The subscripted variable Q(2, 3) has value 4.5. Written in matrix form the values in the array (elements) would be

$$\begin{vmatrix} 6 & 9 & 8.5 \\ 7 & 4 & 4.5 \\ 4.2 & 5 & 7.1 \end{vmatrix}$$

We could assign these values to the array Q as follows:

```
10 DATA 6, 9, 8.5, 7, 4, 4.5, 4.2, 5, 7.1
20 READ Q(1, 1), Q(1, 2), Q(1, 3), Q(2, 1), Q(2, 2)
30 READ Q(2, 3), Q(3, 1), Q(3, 2), Q(3, 3)
```

Another way is the following:

```
10 DATA 6, 9. 8.5, 7, 4, 4.5, 4.2, 5, 7.1
20 FOR I = 1 TO 3
30      FOR J = 1 TO 3
40           READ Q(I, J)
50      NEXT J
60 NEXT I
```

The above has the virtue that the size of the array could be read in along with the values in the array by making the following changes:

```
10 DATA 3, 3, 6, 9, 8.5, 7, 4, 4.5, 4.2, 5, 7.1
20 READ M, N
30 FOR I = 1 TO M
40      FOR J = 1 TO N
50           READ Q(I, J)
60      NEXT J
70 NEXT I
```

[3] That is, the value is rounded.

Whatever the input scheme used, if we write

```
90 LET S = Q(1, 2) + Q(2, 3)
```

then S will have value 13.5.

9-6 APPLICATION OF A TWO-DIMENSIONAL ARRAY

The use of arrays can help organize many business applications. For example, we now examine a problem in inventory control for a warehouse. The warehouse has four rooms and we number them 1, 2, 3, and 4. Our inventory list will contain only three different items, chairs, tables, and beds, to keep the example to a reasonable size.

First, we form a table (or two-dimensional array, or matrix) that lists the rooms as rows and the items as columns:

	ITEM 1 CHAIRS	ITEM 2 TABLES	ITEM 3 BEDS
ROOM 1	0	1	4
ROOM 2	2	2	0
ROOM 3	6	3	2
ROOM 4	4	2	0

In the above, the number of items in each room has been listed so that the number of chairs (ITEM 1) in Room 1 is 0, the number of chairs in Room 2 is 2, the number of tables in Room 1 is 1, the number of tables in Room 3 is 3, and so on. If we call this array A and use subscripts as before in our table, then A(1, 1) will have value 0, A(1, 2) will have value 1, A(1, 3) will have value 4, A(2, 1) will have value 2, and so on.

First, let us input the values in the table into the array A. The number of rows will be 4 and the number of columns will be 3; therefore we write

```
10 REM INPUT TABLE INTO A
20 REM TABLE HAS 4 ROWS AND 3 COLUMNS
30 FOR I = 1 TO 4
40       FOR J = 1 TO 3
50             READ A(I, J)
60       NEXT J
70 NEXT I
80 DATA 0, 1, 4, 2, 2, 0, 6, 3, 2, 4, 2, 0
```

The above lines will input the values in our example table into the array A.

To find the number of chairs (ITEM 1) in Room 2 we note that A(2, 1) has that value. Further, the number of tables (ITEM 2) in Room 3 is A(3, 2). The rule is simple. The room number is the first subscript and the item number is the second subscript:

We can now answer, using a simple section of program, questions such as: How many chairs (ITEM 1) do we have? This section of program will find that number.

```
 90 LET S = 0
100 FOR P = 1 TO 4
110       LET S = S + A(P, 1)
120 NEXT P
```

How many tables?

```
130 LET T = 0
140 FOR R = 1 TO 4
150       LET T = T + A(R, 2)
160 NEXT R
```

How many pieces of furniture are in Room 3?

```
170 LET P = 0
180 FOR F = 1 TO 3
190       LET S = S + A(3, F)
200 NEXT F
```

Notice that these are small sections of BASIC but could be used for a warehouse with many rooms and many different items by simply changing the final value in the FOR statements. That is the great value of organizing inventory control programs in this way.

Let us now introduce price into the warehouse control problem. Suppose the price of a chair (ITEM 1) is \$55.00, the price of a table (ITEM 2) is \$105.00, and the price of a bed (ITEM 3) is \$250.00. We form a price array P as follows:

```
210 DATA 55.00, 105.00, 250.00
220 READ P(1), P(2), P(3)
```

The value of the items in Room 2, for example, can be found by simply multiplying the number of chairs times the chair price P(1), multiplying the table price P(2) by the number of tables, multiplying the number of beds by the bed price, P(3), and then adding the three numbers. In BASIC language this is as follows:

```
230 LET C = A(2, 1)*P(1) + A(2, 2)*P(2) + A(2, 3)*P(3)
```

Notice how straightforward it would be to make this scheme for organizing an inventory work if we have many items, for instance, 215 and as a result

```
100 REM INVENTORY PROGRAM USING AN ARRAY
110 REM T. S. BARTH, 4/24/81
120 REM
130 REM THIS PROGRAM PERFORMS SEVERAL STEPS IN A
140 REM TYPICAL INVENTORY SYSTEM. THE NUMBER OF
150 REM PIECES OF FURNITURE IN VARIOUS LOCATIONS,
160 REM TOTAL VALUES OF THOSE PIECES, AND SO ON, ARE
170 REM FOUND AND PRINTED.
180 REM
190 READ M, N
200 FOR I = 1 TO M
210       FOR J = 1 TO N
220             READ A(I, J)
230       NEXT J
240 NEXT I
250 REM
260 REM FIND THE NUMBER OF CHAIRS
270 REM
280 LET S = 0
290 FOR P = 1 TO M
300       LET S = S + A(P, 1)
310 NEXT P
320 PRINT "THE NUMBER OF CHAIRS IS"; S
330 REM
340 REM FIND THE NUMBER OF TABLES
350 REM
360 LET T = 0
370 FOR R = 1 TO M
380       LET T = T + A(R, 2)
390 NEXT R
400 PRINT "THE NUMBER OF TABLES IS"; T
410 REM
420 REM FIND THE NUMBER OF PIECES OF FURNITURE IN ROOM 3
430 REM
440 LET S = 0
450 FOR F = 1 TO N
460 LET S = S + A(3, F)
470 NEXT F
480 PRINT "THE NUMBER OF PIECES IN ROOM 3 IS"; S
490 REM
500 REM READ NUMBER OF PRICES AND THEN PRICES
510 REM
520 READ W
```

Fig. 9-4 Inventory Program

```
530 FOR K = 1 TO W
540     READ P(K)
550 NEXT K
560 REM
570 REM FIND VALUE OF ALL PIECES IN ROOM 2
580 REM
590 LET C = 0
600 FOR S = 1 TO W
610     LET C = C + P(S)*A(2, S)
620 NEXT S
630 PRINT "THE VALUE OF THE PIECES IN ROOM 2 IS $"; C
640 REM
650 REM FIND TOTAL VALUE OF ENTIRE INVENTORY
660 REM
670 LET T = 0
680 FOR D = 1 TO M
690     FOR H = 1 TO N
700         LET T = T + P(H)*A(D, H)
710     NEXT H
720 NEXT D
730 PRINT "THE TOTAL VALUE OF THE INVENTORY IS $"; T
740 DATA 4, 3
750 DATA 0, 1, 4, 2, 2, 0, 6, 3, 2, 4, 2, 0
760 DATA 3, 55, 00, 105, 00, 250, 00
770 END
```

Fig. 9-4 *cont.*

215 prices. We simply make a table with 215 columns and a price array with 215 values, and this program section will find the value of all items in Room 2.

```
240 LET C = 0
250 FOR S = 1 TO 215
260     LET C = C + P(S)*A(2, S)
270 NEXT S
```

For our small example with 4 rooms and 3 items, let us calculate the value of the entire inventory.

```
280 LET T = 0
290 FOR D = 1 TO 4
300     FOR H = 1 TO 3
310         LET T = T + P(H)*A(D, H)
320     NEXT H
330 NEXT D
```

After the section of program is run, T will have a value equal to the total value of all the items (the inventory) in the warehouse.

Figure 9-4 shows an entire program with comments and with the table values used in the example. Notice how direct and straightforward the program is. Notice also that numeric variables have been substituted for integers in the FOR statements. Making the table larger by increasing the number of rows and columns can be accomplished using the DATA statements. This greatly increases the number of calculations performed with no increase in the number of program statements. This shows the power of arrays in this kind of problem.

9-7 SUBROUTINES

In writing programs, sometimes a particular set of statements must be repeated in different places in the program. BASIC makes it possible to write such sections of program only once and to "call" the section from various points in the program and have the BASIC translator provide the duplication.

For example, we may write a program where at several points it is necessary to find the larger of two numbers. Let us call these numbers A and B. A section of program to find the larger of A and B and give this value to C is

```
500 IF A > B THEN 530
510 LET C = B
520 GO TO 540
530 LET C = A
540
```

In BASIC it is possible to make this section of code into a *subroutine* by simply adding a RETURN statement at the end. The section of program then becomes

```
500 IF A > B THEN 530
510 LET C = B
520 GO TO 540
530 LET C = A
540 RETURN
```

Now, anywhere in a program, when we wish to call this section of program we simply write

```
GOSUB 500
```

A line number must precede the GOSUB. Each time this GOSUB 500 is read by the translator it causes the four statements beginning with statement 500 to be executed. After this the statement following the GOSUB is executed. As an example, consider this outline of a program.

```
100 GOSUB 500
110 (more program)
. . . . . . . . . . . . . . . . . . . . .
210 GOSUB 500
220 (more program)
. . . . . . . . . . . . . . . . . . . . .
300 GOSUB 500
320 (more program)
. . . . . . . . . . . . . . . . . . . . .
500 IF A = B THEN GO TO 530
510 LET C = B
520 GO TO 540
530 LET C = A
540 RETURN
```

When this is run, the subroutine consisting of lines 500 through 540 will be performed three times: once when statement 100 is reached, again when 210 is reached and finally when 300 is reached. Each time the statement after the GOSUB will be performed after statement 530. The RETURN says "go back to the statement after the GOSUB statement which called this subroutine."

To be more specific, when statement 100 is reached the GOSUB 500 causes statement 500 to be performed next followed by 510, 520, and 530; then 540 RETURN causes statement 110 to be performed next. The RETURN statement always causes a return to the statement following the GOSUB which "called" the subroutine.

There is one problem in the use of such subroutines that should be briefly noted. Subroutines are usually placed at the end of the program. A program must always end with an END statement because the BASIC translator uses this statement to stop the translation. Because the subroutine is at the end, however, some way must be found to stop program operation before it is reached. A STOP statement can be used for this purpose. A STOP statement causes a jump to the END statement and has exactly the same effect as a GO TO statement which causes a jump to the END statement. For our subroutine, the following sets of statements are the same:

```
490 STOP
500 IF A > B THEN 530
510 LET C = B
520 GO TO 540
530 LET C = A
540 RETURN
550 END
```

```
490 GO TO 550
500 IF A > B THEN 530
510 LET C = 13
520 GO TO 540
530 LET C = A
540 RETURN
550 END
```

Subroutines are sometimes very useful in organizing and preparing a program. Subroutine usage makes a program modular and can add to understandability of a program and its debugging.

We now organize a program around a subprogram made from an original program which can be independently tested. The original program is immediately following. This program inputs two integers A and B and finds the largest positive integer which divides both. This integer is called the *greatest common divisor*, or GCD, of the two integers. The GCD of 6 and 8 is 2; the GCD of 6 and 9 is 3; the GCD of 27 and 18 is 9; the GCD of 7 and 5 is 1; and so on. Here is the program.

```
100 REM EUCLID'S ALGORITHM
110 REM E. F. GAUSS, 6/23/81
120 REM
130 REM THE INPUT NUMBERS ARE A AND B AND THE
140 REM GCD IS B AFTER THE PROGRAM IS RUN.
150 REM
160 READ A, B
170 LET Q = INT(A/B)
180 LET R = A - Q*B
190 IF R = 0 THEN 230
200      LET A = B
210      LET B = R
220      GO TO 170
230 PRINT "THE GREATEST COMMON DIVISOR IS"; B
240 DATA 27, 30
250 END
```

This program uses an algorithm discovered by Euclid to find the GCD of two number. This algorithm is discussed in detail in the Questions. The program inputs the two integers using a DATA statement and prints the GCD using an appropriate PRINT statement. The above DATA statement yields a GCD of 3.

After testing this program we decide it is correct and decide to make a larger program that will find the GCD of three integers. (Our knowledge of math assures us that if D is the GCD of A and B and if E is the GCD of C and D, then E is the GCD of A, B, and C.) The larger program to be developed will use a modified version of the preceding program as a module or *subroutine*. To effect this we remove the REM statements at the beginning, and the PRINT statement. We then replace the END statement with a RETURN statement and write a REM statement to mark the beginning of the subroutine.

```
250 REM SUBROUTINE TO RETURN GCD OF A AND B IN B
260 REM
270 LET Q = INT(A/B)
280 LET R = A - Q*B
290 IF R = 0 THEN 330
300    LET A = B
310    LET B = R
320    GO TO 270
330 RETURN
340 END
```

When the subroutine is called it will find the GCD of A and B and place that value in B.

We now write the main body of the program. This section of program uses the fact that if we wish to find the GCD of three numbers X, Y, and Z, then we can proceed by finding the GCD of X and Y. Call this number G and then the GCD of G and Z will be the GCD of X, Y, and Z.

The program first reads values for X, Y, and Z from a DATA statement. It then gives A the value of X, B the value of Y, and calls the subroutine just developed at statement 170. This subroutine finds the value of the GCD and places it in B. The main program then places the value of Z in A and calls the subroutine again, then finding the GCD of A and B which will also be the GCD of the original values of X, Y, and Z. Here is the main body of the program.

```
100 REM FIND GCD
110 REM I. L. GALOIS, 6/22/81
120 REM
130 REM THIS PROGRAM FINDS THE GCD
```

```
140 REM OF THREE NUMBERS. INPUT NUMBERS ARE X, Y, AND Z.
150 REM
160 READ X, Y, Z
170 DATA 81, 72, 18
180 LET A = X
190 LET B = Y
200 GOSUB 260
210 LET A = Z
220 GOSUB 260
230 PRINT "THE GCD OF"; X; ","; Y; "AND"; Z; "IS"; B
240 STOP
```

The complete program is shown in Figure 9-5. A typical printout is as follows:

```
THE GCD OF 81, 72, AND 18 IS 9
```

```
100 REM FIND GCD
110 REM I. L. GALOIS, 6/22/81
120 REM
130 REM THIS PROGRAM FINDS THE GCD
140 REM OF THREE NUMBERS. INPUT NUMBERS ARE X, Y, AND Z.
150 REM
160 READ X, Y, Z
170 DATA 81, 72, 18
180 LET A = X
190 LET B = Y
200 GOSUB 260
210 LET A = Z
220 GOSUB 260
230 PRINT "THE GCD OF"; X; ","; Y; "AND"; Z; "IS"; B
240 STOP
250 REM
260 REM SUBROUTINE TO RETURN GCD OF A AND B IN B
270 REM
280 LET Q = INT(A/B)
290 LET R = A - Q*B
300 IF R = 0 THEN 340
310    LET A = B
320    LET B = R
330    GO TO 280
340 RETURN
350 END
```

Fig. 9-5 Program to Find GCD of Three Numbers

9-8 FUNCTIONS—SYSTEM SUPPLIED

In addition to the INT, ABS, and SQR functions described in Chapter 7, the BASIC system provides several other mathematical functions. A complete list of the functions in ANSI standard BASIC is presented in Table 9-1.

The SIN, COS, and TAN functions are trigonometric functions; the input values X in SIN(X) and other trigonometric functions is in radians (not degrees). A table of values for these functions is shown in Table 9-2. This table was generated by the program in Figure 9-6. As an example of the use of these functions, consider this statement.

```
10 LET X = SIN(0.523598)
```

After this statement is run, X will have value 0.5 (refer to Table 9-2). Consider the following:

```
10 LET A = 0.785398
20 LET B = COS(A)
```

After this is run B will have value 0.707107 (again refer to Table 9-2).

Table 9-1 ANSI SYSTEMS SUPPLIED FUNCTIONS

FUNCTION	FUNCTION VALUE
ABS(X)	The absolute value of X.
ATN(X)	The arctangent of X in radians (the angle whose tangent is X). The range of the function is $-(\pi/2) < \text{ATN}(x) < (\pi/2)$ where π is the ratio of the circumference of a circle to its diameter.
COS(X)	The cosine of X, where X is in radians.
EXP(X)	The exponential of X, that is, the value of the base of natural logarithm (e = 2.71828...) raised to the power X.
INT(X)	The largest integer not greater than X; for example, INT(1.3) = 1 and INT(−1.3) = −2.
LOG(X)	The natural logarithm of X; X must be greater than zero.
RND	The next pseudorandom number in an implementation-supplied sequence of pseudorandom numbers uniformly distributed in the range 0 < = RND < 1 (see Chapter 8).
SGN(X)	The algebraic "sign" of X: −1 if X < 0, 0 if X = 0, and +1 if X > 0.
SIN(X)	The sine of X, where X is in radians.
SQR(X)	The nonnegative square root of X; X must be nonnegative.
TAN(X)	The tangent of X, where X is in radians.

Table 9-2 SELECTED TRIGONOMETRIC VALUES

SINE	COSINE	TANGENT	RADIANS	DEGREES
0	1	0	0	0
0.258819	0.965926	0.267949	0.261799	15
0.5	0.866026	0.57735	0.523598	30
0.707106	0.707107	0.999999	0.785398	45
0.866025	0.500001	1.73205	1.0472	60
0.965926	0.25882	3.73203	1.309	75
1.	1.31077E-6	756156.	1.5708	90
0.965926	− 0.258818	− 3.73207	1.83259	105
0.866026	− 0.499998	− 1.73206	2.09439	120
0.707108	− 0.707105	− 1.	2.35619	135
0.500002	− 0.866024	− 0.577353	2.61799	150
0.258821	− 0.965925	− 0.267952	2.87979	165
2.64496E-6	− 1	− 2.64496E-6	3.14159	180
− 0.258816	− 0.965927	0.267946	3.40339	195
− 0.499997	− 0.866027	0.577346	3.66519	210
− 0.707104	− 0.707109	0.999993	3.92699	225
− 0.866024	− 0.500003	1.73204	4.18879	240
− 0.965925	− 0.258823	3.732	4.45059	255
− 1	− 3.97914E-6	251311.	4.71239	270
− 0.965927	0.258815	− 3.73211	4.97418	285
− 0.866028	0.499996	− 1.73207	5.23598	300
− 0.70711	0.707103	− 1.00001	5.49778	315
− 0.500004	0.866023	− 0.577357	5.75958	330
− 0.258824	0.965925	− 0.267955	6.02138	345
− 5.28991E-6	1	− 5.28991E-6	6.28318	360

The effects of doing mathematics with numbers with a fixed number of significant digits can be seen in this table.[4] The value of SIN(3.14159), which is as close as the number system can come to $\pi/2$, should be 0 but is 2.64496E-6 or about 2.6/1000000 which is small but not quite 0. Testing for zero using an IF statement such as

```
40 IF SIN(3.14159) = 0 THEN 100
```

will not cause a jump to statement 100. The accepted procedure is

```
40 IF ABS(SIN(3.14159)) < 0.0001 THEN 100
```

This will cause a jump to 100. The ABS is necessary because the number being tested may be negative and if we are testing for 0, then we would not want to jump on SIN(3.40339) or any other number that is negative but not small enough in magnitude to constitute a "zero." Also, remember that calculations in general are performed using numbers such as those in Table 9-2 and must be rounded if only a few significant digits are desired.

[4] This table was printed by a DEC PDP-10.

```
 10 REM PRINT TRIG VALUES PROGRAM
 20 REM A. L. GRANT, 3/21/81
 30 REM THIS PROGRAM PRINTS VALUES OF TRIG FUNCTIONS
 40 REM A IS ANGLE IN DEGREES AND R IS ANGLE IN RADIANS
 50 LET K = 3.14159/180
 60 PRINT "SINE", "COSINE", "TANGENT", "RADIANS", "DEGREES"
 70 FOR A = 0 TO 360 STEP 15
 80      LET R = A*K
 90      PRINT SIN(R), COS(R), TAN(R), R, A
100 NEXT A
110 END
```

Fig. 9-6 Program to Test Trig Functions

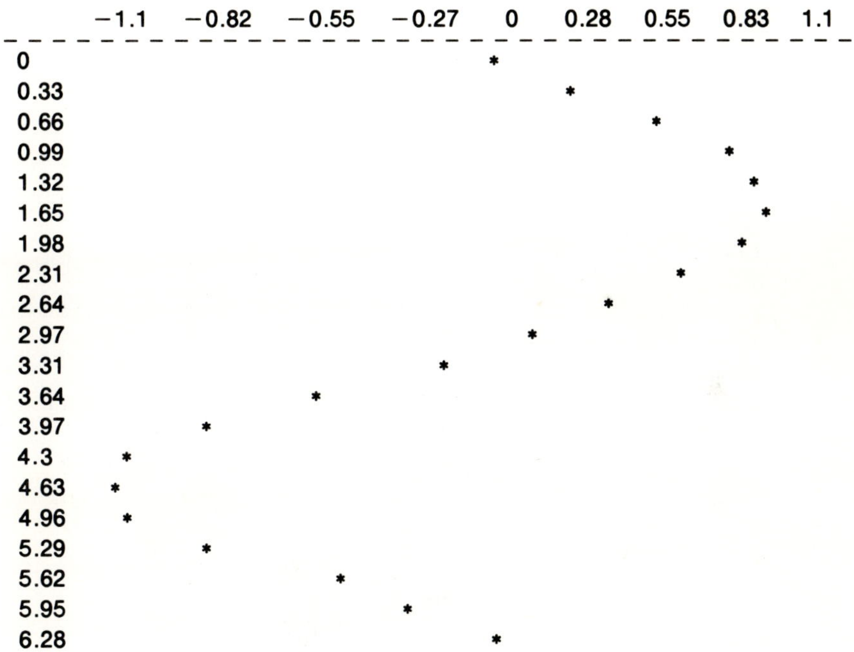

(a)

Fig. 9-7 Graphs of User-Supplied Functions. (a) Sine Function; (b) Trig Function Graph

```
70 DATA 0, 6.28, 35, -2, 2
80 DEF FNF(X) = SIN(X) - COS(2*X)
```

```
GRAPH.H       13:59       01-MAR-80
        -2   -1.5     -1     -0.5    0   0.5  1    1.5    2
- - - - - - - - - - - - - - - - - - - - - - - - - - - - - - -
                     *
 0.18                  *
 0.37                          *
 0.55                                *
 0.74                                     *
 0.92                                          *
 1.11                                             *
 1.29                                                 *
 1.48                                                   *
 1.66                                                   *
 1.85                                                 *
 2.03                                             *
 2.22                                          *
 2.4                                      *
 2.59                                *
 2.77                         *
 2.96                  *
 3.14              *
 3.32          *
 3.51          *
 3.69              *
 3.88                  *
 4.06                       *
 4.25                          *
 4.43                           *
 4.62                            *
 4.8                             *
 4.99                           *
 5.17                          *
 5.36                       *
 5.54                   *
 5.73               *
 5.91          *
 6.1           *
```

Fig. 9-7(b)

```
SINES.B      15:04      17-FEB-80

                              QUENTIN'S SINE
                                   QUENTIN'S SINE
                                        QUENTIN'S SINE
                                            QUENTIN'S SINE
                                               QUENTIN'S SINE
                                                QUENTIN'S SINE
                                                QUENTIN'S SINE
                                            QUENTIN'S SINE
                                          QUENTIN'S SINE
                                     QUENTIN'S SINE
                                QUENTIN'S SINE
                           QUENTIN'S SINE
                      QUENTIN'S SINE
                 QUENTIN'S SINE
             QUENTIN'S SINE
            QUENTIN'S SINE
            QUENTIN'S SINE
             QUENTIN'S SINE
                QUENTIN'S SINE
                    QUENTIN'S SINE
                         QUENTIN'S SINE
                               QUENTIN'S SINE
```

(a)

```
10 FOR I = 0 TO 6.4 STEP 0.3
20     LET A = 15*SIN(I)
30     PRINT TAB(A + 20); "QUENTIN'S SINE"
40 NEXT I
50 END
```

(b)

Fig. 9-8 Graph of a Design Using a User Supplied = Function. (a) Design Using Sine Function; (b) Program to Print (a)

The LOG, EXP, and other mathematical functions operate just as in conventional mathematics.

It is possible to examine the functions using the graphical display techniques described in Chapter 8. A simple graph of SIN(X) is shown in Figure 9-7(a). The program in Figure 9-7(a) is formed by making the function definition statement in the graph program (Figure 8-10) read

```
80 DEF FNF(X) = SIN(X)
```

and by placing appropriate values in the DATA statement.

Figure 9-7(b) shows a graph of a more complicated function and the statements used to generate this graph using the graph program in Chapter 8 are shown above the graph.

A "design" graph and the program that generated it are shown in Figure 9-8. Interesting artistic patterns can be generated using similar programs.

9-9 FINDING THE AREA UNDER A CURVE

An important problem in mathematics concerns finding the area under a curve. The problem is often set up as shown in Figure 9-9. First, a curve is given by a function, in this case

$$Y = \frac{X^2}{5} + 2$$

A drawing of this curve in two dimensions is shown in the figure. The area under this curve is to be found between two points on the X axis; in this case the points are +1 and +6. There are calculus techniques for finding this area if the function is in a certain class (which includes this function) but there are many cases where a computer solution is either necessary or more direct than classical analysis.

An approximation to this area can be made in the following way. First, divide the line along the X axis into some number of subintervals of equal length which we will call D. Figure 9-9 shows the X axis from 1 to 6 divided into five subintervals each of length 1. Second, find the midpoint of each of these intervals; this will be at 1.5 for the first subinterval, 2.5 for the second subinterval, and so on, as shown in Figure 9-9. Third, find the value of the function at each of these midpoints and multiply this value by the width D of each subinterval. For example, in Figure 9-9 the first subinterval is from +1 to +2 on the X axis, the midpoint is at 1.5, the value of $X^2/5+2$ for $X = 1.5$ is $1.5^2/5+2$, which is $2.25/5+2$, or 2.45. Multiplying this by 1, the length of the subinterval, simply gives 2.45. This value is the area of the leftmost rectangle drawn in the Figure 9-9. (The next rectangle has area 3.25.)

The final step is to add the areas of the rectangles and this will approximate the area under the curve.

Performing the above algorithm using pencil and paper can be time consuming if the number of subintervals is very large. However, to get a good approximation the number of subintervals should be large because as the number of subintervals goes up the accuracy or "goodness" of the approximation gets better, particularly if the curve "bends" on the graph.

We can program this approximation directly and then test to see how the approximation improves as the number of intervals increases.

First, let us develop the program. We will define the function using a function definition statement. Here the function is $X^2/5+2$. (We can

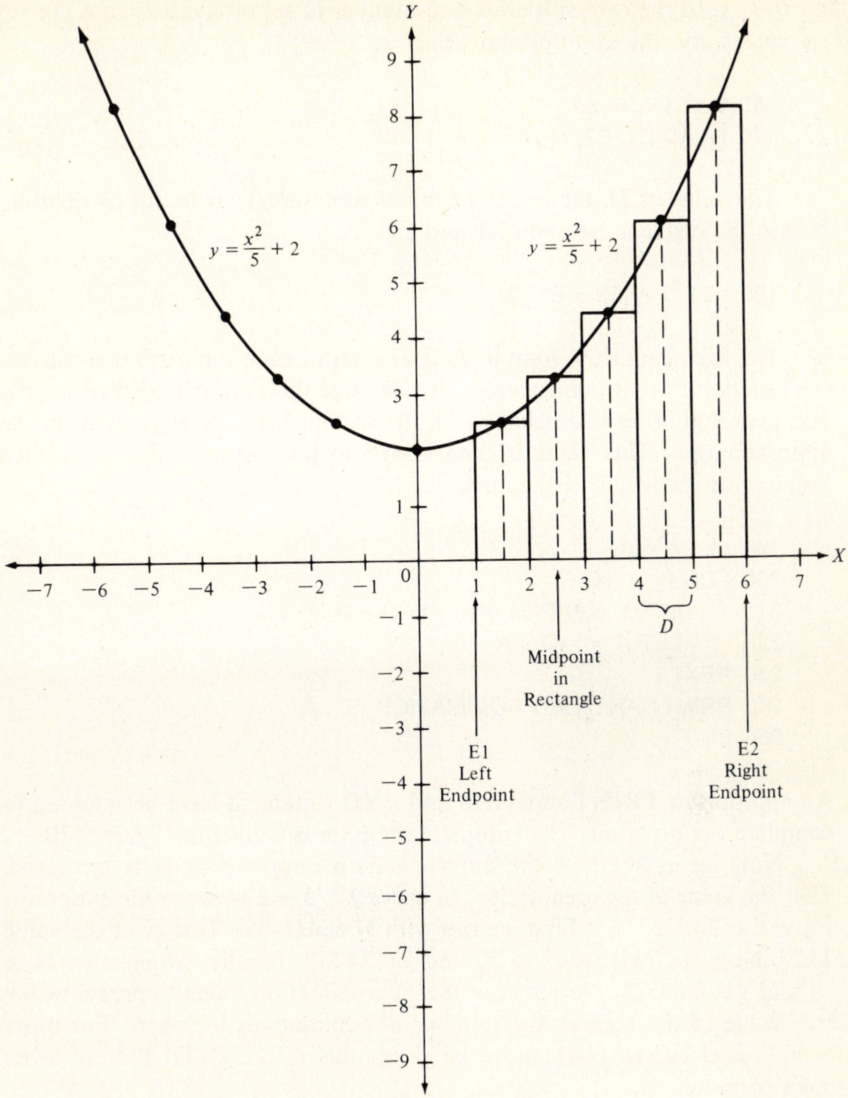

Fig. 9-9 Finding the Area Under a Curve

change the function by simply retyping statement 150.)

```
100 REM FINDING AN AREA
110 REM J. LOVRE, 4/15/81
120 REM A IS AREA, D IS SUBINTERVAL WIDTH, N IS NO OF
130 REM SUBINTERVALS, FNF IS FUNCTION E1 IS LEFT ENDPOINT,
140 REM E2 IS RIGHT ENDPOINT
150 DEF FNF(X) = X^2/5+2
```

Next we read the two endpoints and number of subintervals from a DATA statement into the appropriate variables.

```
160 DATA 1, 6, 50
170 READ E1, E2, N
```

The value of D, the length of the N subintervals, is found by dividing N into the distance between E1 and E2.

```
180 LET D = (E2 - E1)/N
```

The following FOR loop finds the center of each subinterval, evaluates the function at that point giving the height of the approximated rectangle, and then multiplies this value by D, the width of the rectangle used in the approximation. This value is then added to the current value of A thus building up the value of the area.

```
190 LET A = 0
200 FOR I = 1 TO N
210        LET Y = FNF(E1 + (I - 1)*D + D/2)
220        LET A = Y*D + A
230 NEXT I
240 PRINT "AREA APPROXIMATION IS"; A
250 END
```

An appropriate PRINT statement and END statement have been added to complete the program. The complete program is shown in Figure 9-10.

Now let us see how the approximation improves as N is increased. The true value of the area under the curve $X^2/5 + 2$ between the endpoints 1 and 6 is 24.3333. . . . First we run with N equal to 6. This gives the value 24.25. Now we increase N to 10 and get 24.312. Finally, we increase N to 50 and get 24.3325. Notice how the approximation value approaches the true value of the area as the number of subintervals increases. For more complicated curves (with more bending) this effect would become even more pronounced.

Notice the flexibility of the program. The function can be changed by simply retyping the function definition statement and the endpoints and number of subintervals can be changed by retyping the DATA statement. The Questions develop this in more detail.

The above program performs what is called *numerical integration*. There are more refined numerical integration techniques and several of them are developed in the Questions.

Numerical integration is part of the subject matter called *numerical analysis*. This topic includes evaluating differential equations, solving simultaneous equations, and many other mathematical topics involving numerical techniques and algorithms.

```
100 REM FINDING AN AREA
110 REM J. LOVRE, 4/15/81
120 REM A IS AREA, D IS SUBINTERVAL WIDTH, N IS NO OF
130 REM SUBINTERVALS, FNF IS FUNCTION E1 IS LEFT ENDPOINT,
140 REM E2 IS RIGHT ENDPOINT
150 DEF FNF(X) = X^2/5 + 2
160 DATA 1, 6, 50
170 READ E1, E2, N
180 LET D = (E2 - E1)/N
190 LET A = 0
200 FOR I = 1 TO N
210     LET Y = FNF(E1 + (I - 1)*D + D/2)
220     LET A = Y*D + A
230 NEXT I
240 PRINT "AREA APPROXIMATION IS"; A
250 END
```

Fig. 9-10 Program to Find the Area Under a Curve

9-10 SUMMARY

The preceding sections have introduced arrays and subscripted variables and have presented several examples of their usage. The DIMENSION (DIM) statement was explained. Details of the DIM statement are shown in Table 9-3 and some facts concerning arrays can be found in Table 9-4.

Arrays make possible the writing of compact programs which perform long sequences of computations. The subscripts in arrays can be used in loops that are repeatedly performed, thus providing a powerful computational tool. Examples from statistics and business were used to point up the advantages of arrays in program usage.

Subroutines are organized in BASIC using GOSUB, RETURN, and STOP statements. Some facts concerning these statements can be found in Table 9-5. The use of subroutines shortens a program and also helps to organize a program and make it more understandable. An example of subroutine usage was shown where a complete program was written and tested and then incorporated in another program as a subroutine.

The systems supplied functions in BASIC include several mathematical functions and these were introduced and their usage explained. Some graphs and tables of these functions values were presented.

A program to perform numerical integration was explained and its usage demonstrated. This program can be used to find the area under a curve described by a continuous function within specified endpoints.

Table 9-3 ARRAY DECLARATIONS

The general form of the DIM statement is

line number DIM *declaration*, . . . , *declaration*

Each *declaration* has the form

letter(*integer*)

or

letter(*integer*, *integer*)

The integers are *called "bounds."*
Examples:

```
20 DIM A(15)
30 DIM A(6), B(23), M(15)
40 DIM A(6, 3), B(3, 3), C(15)
```

Each array declaration in a DIM statement declares the array to be one- or two-dimensional according to whether one or two bounds are listed for the array. The bounds specify the maximum value the subscripts can have in the array.

Note: ANSI BASIC has subscripts with values 0, 1, . . . , B up to the bound (B) given in the DIM statement. For instance, DIM A(15) says the array A consists of variables A(0), A(1), . . . , A(15). Many commercial systems have no subscript value of 0, subscripts have values 1, 2, . . . , B. A DIM A(15) statement means the array A consists of A(1), A(2), . . . , A(15). The ANSI specification has a statement called OPTION BASE 1 which, when inserted in a program, causes subscripts to not have 0 values.

Table 9-4 ARRAYS

An array is a set of subscripted variables.

A subscripted variable has the forms:

$X(n)$ $\quad X\$(n)$ $\quad X(n,n)$ $\quad X\$(n,n)$

Here X is a letter and each n is a numeric expression.The first two forms are for *one-dimensional arrays* and the last for *two-dimensional arrays*.
The n in the above is called the *subscript*. *Examples*:

A(1)	B(N + 1)	D$(1)
A(N)	C(N*2 + 3)	A$(N + 16)

A(2, 3)	C(N*2, M + 1)
B(N, 2 + 3)	C$(8, N + 1)

Array variables with a $ sign in the name are for strings and the single letter names are for numeric values.
The expression(s) in the parentheses in a subscripted variable have their values rounded to the nearest integer when the variable is used.
If a subscripted variable does not appear in a DIMENSION statement, the subscript can have values of from 0 to 10 in ANSI BASIC. Other systems have other limits.
In ANSI BASIC subscripts of value 0 are allowed but many other systems do not allow 0, starting subscript values at 1.
In most systems the same letter cannot be used as both a single variable and as an array. (In HP systems they can.) The same letter cannot be used for both a two-dimensional and one-dimensional array.

Questions

1. Write BASIC statements to assign the values 4, 6, and 9 to the subscripted variables A(1), A(2), and A(3) and sum these values.
2. Write a BASIC program to input five numbers typed into the terminal for the five subscripted variables B(1), B(2), B(3), B(4), and B(5) and then to subtract the sum of the first three numbers from the second two and print the result.
3. Write a section of a program using a FOR loop to sum 20 values stored in an array C with subscripts from 1 to 20.
4. Write a DIM statement to allow for 20 subscripted variables in an array A, 30 subscripted variables in an array B, and 6 subscripted variables in an array C.
5. What is wrong with this DIM statement?

```
20 DIM A(5), B(N), C(25)
```

6. Modify the program in Figure 9-1(e) so that it also finds the *median* grade in the class.
7. Show how to modify the program in Figure 9-2 so that all decisions are based on the grade 75 instead of 80.
8. Alter the program in Figure 9-2 so that if a grade higher than 100 or lower than 0 is input, the program will reject the grade and print an error statement.
9. Operate the standard deviation program in Figure 9-3 using these data values:
   9, 15, 20, 18, 24
10. Operate the standard deviation program in Figure 9-3 using these data values:
    (a) 9, 23, 15, 4, 12
    (b) 23, 15, 16, 29, 3
    (c) 18, 19, 21, 15, 17, 18
11. From the results in the preceding question, discuss the deviation from the mean for the values and any conclusions that might be drawn.
12. The program in Figure 9-3 can be shortened by using the following statement. Show how by writing a new program.

```
LET S = S + X(J)/N
LET D = D + (S(J) - M)^2/N
```

13. Write statements to read these values into a two-dimensional array D:

6	4	3
5	2	1
7	3	9
6	6	2

14. Write a section of program that will find the number of beds in the warehouse for the warehouse program in Section 9-6.
15. Given a price matrix and warehouse as in Section 9-6, write a section of program to find all rooms with total inventory value more than $1000.00.
16. Modify the program in Figure 9-4 so it finds all inventory items of a single type (tables, for example) for which the total inventory value exceeds $400.00.
17. Explain the function of the STOP statement. Show how the STOP statement in Figure 9-5 can be replaced with a GO TO statement.
18. Write a program to find the greatest common divisor of four numbers input from a terminal.

19. We ran this section of code in two computers and the jump to 120 was not taken for either. Explain how this could happen and try this on your system.

```
60 LET X = 27
70 LET Y = X^(1/3)
80 IF Y = INT(Y) THEN 120
```

20. On some computer the jumps to 120 will not be taken; explain how this can happen and try it on your computer.

```
60 LET X = 27
70 LET Y = X^(1/3)
80 IF (Y - INT(Y)) < 0.001 THEN 120
```

21. Explain how to fix the section of program in Question 20 so that the jump will be taken when X has a cube root which is an integer.
22. Plot values for EXP from 0 to 10 using the graph program and choosing an appropriate interval. Plot 30 points.
23. Plot COS(EXP(X)) for X from 0 to 5 and Y from −1 to +1. Plot 30 points.
24. Operate the program in Figure 9-10 running it for N = 3, then for N = 7, and finally for N = 25.
25. Change the program in Figure 9-10 so it finds the area under a curve $Y = X^3 + 3$ for endpoints E1 = 2 and E2 = 7. Make N equal to 5, 10, and then 20.
26. Operate the program in Figure 9-10 for Y = SIN(X) + 3 for endpoints E1 = 2 and E2 = 7. Make N equal to 5, 10, and then 20.
27. Operate the program in Figure 9-10 for Y = LOG(X*3) + SIN(X) + 4 for X from 3 to 7 and for N = 4, 10, and 20.
28. Operate the program in Figure 9-10 for Y = LOG(X*2) + COS(X) + 2 with endpoints E1 = 2 and E2 = 5. Let N equal 4, 10, and then 40.
29. Write a program to read a set of numbers into an array with 20 subscripts. The program is to find the largest and smallest number and print the two subscripts of the array variables storing these values.
30. Write a program to input a set of student names and grades from DATA statements. Then find the average grade and list the names of all students making within 10 points of this grade as *Average*. The program should then list all students making more than 10 points above average as *Outstanding* and those making 10 points or more below average as *Unsatisfactory*.
31. The following formula is useful in estimating the duration of a loan

$$T = -\frac{\log\left(1 - \frac{P \cdot I}{N \cdot R}\right)}{\log\left(1 + \frac{I}{N}\right)} \cdot \frac{1}{N}$$

T = duration of payments (in years)

P = principal

I = interest rate

N = number of payments per year

R = amount of payments

Write a program to input the principal, interest rate, number of payments, and amount and to output the loan's duration.

32. Two integers X and Y are *relatively prime* if no integer greater than 1 divides both of them. Write a program to input two integers and determine and print whether they are relatively prime.
33. Write a program to find and print the greatest common divisor of four integers W, X, Y, and Z input from the terminal.
34. Using a subprogram to compute N!, write a program to find and print C(N, R) the number of N items taken R at a time. The formula is

$$C(N,R) = \frac{N!}{R!(N-R)!}$$

35. Another and often better way to determine the area under a curve is by using the trapezoid rule. When this is done, the value of the distance between the endpoints of the curve is divided into equal intervals; but instead of finding the function value at the midpoint of each interval, the value at the leftmost and rightmost point in each interval is found. Calling these F1 and F2, we then form $\frac{F1 + F2}{2} \times W$, where W is the width of the interval and this approximates the area under this section of curve. Modify the area-finding program so it uses this approach.
36. Run the trapezoid curve-finding program and the midpoint program in the chapter and compare the results for a curve for which you know the area. See which one approaches the area's value better for small numbers of intervals.
37. A method that is even better than the rectangular and trapezoid methods for finding the area under a curve uses Simpson's rule. Simpson's rule involves labeling the points in the curve as follows:

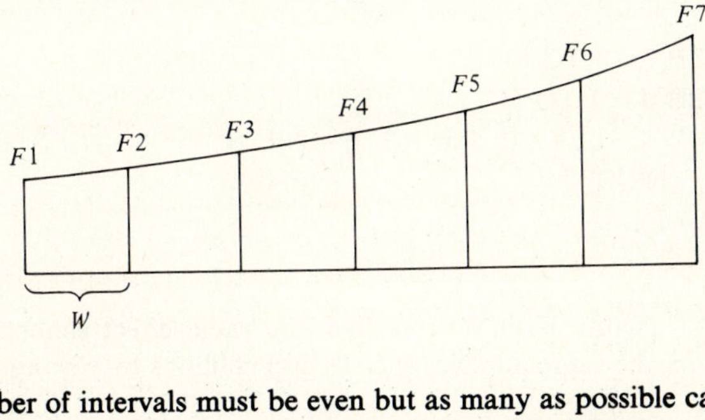

The number of intervals must be even but as many as possible can be used; we show six intervals. The value of the area is found as follows:

$$A = \frac{W}{3}(F1 + 4 \times F2 + 2 \times F3 + 4 \times F4 + 2 \times F5 + 4 \times F6 + F7)$$

For more intervals, the F's are simply increased in number and the *weights* of 2 and 4 continue as above. Write a program to find areas using Simpson's rule.

38. Many BASIC systems supply a set of system supplied matrix operations called MAT. ANSI BASIC does not cover these operations directly (they can be programmed). As a first example, the READing of a matrix from DATA statements was described in this chapter. In BASIC systems with the MAT

facility a matrix A can be *loaded* into A by simply writing

```
20 MAT READ A
```

The matrix A must be dimensioned before this statement occurs in the program. In some systems it is possible to dimension the matrix using the MAT READ statement as follows:

```
20 MAT READ A(3, 4)
```

This will read values into a 3-row 4-column matrix. (To the authors knowledge all systems with the MAT facility number rows and columns beginning with 1 not 0.)
Here are INPUT statements in MAT form.

```
20 DIM A(3, 4)        30 MAT INPUT A(3, 4)
30 MAT INPUT A
```

To print, we write

```
40 MAT PRINT A
```

Write a program to input a 3-row 4-column matrix from DATA statements and a 2-row 4-column matrix from the terminal and then print both matrices.

39. It is possible to add two matrices if they have the same number of rows and columns. The BASIC statements to add an M-row N-column matrix A to an M-row N-column matrix B placing the sum in a matrix C are as follows:

```
10 FOR I = 1 TO M
20 FOR J = 1 TO N
30          LET C(I, J) = A(I, J) + B(I, J)
40      NEXT J
50 NEXT I
```

If the MAT facility is in your system, the same effect can be had for two matrices with the same number of rows and columns by writing

```
MAT C = A + B
```

Write a program to read in and add two 3-row 4-column matrices and to print the sum using both the FOR loops and the MAT statements and compare the sum.

40. Two matrices can be multiplied together if the number of columns in the first matrix is equal to the number of rows in the second matrix. If we multiply an M-row N-column matrix by an N-row K-column matrix, the product will be an

M-row K-column matrix. These statements will perform such a multiplication.

```
10 FOR I = 1 TO M
20        FOR J = 1 TO K
30        LET X = 0
40        FOR L = 1 TO M
50        LET X = X + A(I, L) * B(L, J)
60 NEXT L
70        LET C(I, J) = X
80        NEXT J
90 NEXT I
```

For two properly dimensioned matrices the same effect can be had by writing

```
20 MAT C = A*B
```

Write a program to input two matrices A and B and to multiply them using both the program shown above and the MAT statement and then to print the resulting product matrices so they can be compared.

41. There are many rules or theories in matrix algebra. Here is an example of a rule:

$$A*(B + C) = A*B + A*C$$

This is called the *distributive law* and it can be proved. Write a program to read in three 3-row 3-column matrices A, B, and C. Then find $A*(B + C)$ and $A*B + A*C$. Print both values and compare the results for several sets of matrices.

42. The rule $A*B = B*A$ is called the *commutative law*. It does not necessarily hold for matrix calculations. Write a program to read in 3-row 3-column matrices A and B. Then find $A*B$ and $B*A$ and print each product matrix. Using this program, find two different matrices that do not commute, that is, $A*B \neq B*A$ and two different matrices that do commute: that is, $A*B = B*A$.

43. The *inverse* of a matrix A which has the same number of rows and columns is an inverse matrix A^{-1} such that $A*A^{-1} = I$. I looks like this:

$$\begin{matrix} 1 & 0 & 0 \\ 0 & 1 & 0 \\ 0 & 0 & 1 \end{matrix}$$

if A has 3 rows and 3 columns and similar to this if A is larger. I is the unique matrix such that $I*B = B$ for all matrices B. The MAT command

```
50 MAT B = INV(A)
```

places the inverse of A in B. Both matrices must have the same number of rows and columns. Write a program to input a 3-row 3-column matrix A, find the inverse of A, and then print A, its inverse, and the product of A and its inverse.

44. There are some matrices that have no inverse. Find one using the program prepared in the preceding question.

45. It is possible to solve sets of linear simultaneous equations using the inverse of a matrix. Using an algebra book for a reference, write a program to solve a set of linear simultaneous equations using the MAT INV statements.
46. The first element in the array (X) gives the number of pieces of data that follow. Write a subroutine to search the array for the largest value and assign this value to the variable L.
47. As part of a printout we frequently need N "-" characters printed in a straight line across the page. Write a subroutine to do this. The subroutine inputs N and prints N -'s.
48. The first element in each array X gives the number of elements to follow. Write a subroutine to calculate the mean and standard deviation of the numbers in the array which follow the first element.
49. The table below represents sales made by salespersons:

SALESPERSON	MON	TUE	WED	THU	FRI
Jim Andre	35	81	71	64	95
Sean Jones	76	92	81	71	96
Edna Smith	59	67	83	75	23
Roy Bacon	91	54	54	85	64

Write a program that will store the above data in a matrix and then calculate and print:
(a) Total daily sales.
(b) Total weekly sales for each salesperson.
(c) Total weekly sales.

50. Assume that the first number in the DATA statements gives the number of pieces of data to follow. Also, the data are all integers between 1 and 10. Write a program that will print the number of 1's, number of 2's, and so on in the data. To count the numbers, increase the elements of an array.
51. The following is a set of two simultaneous linear equations.

$$A_1x + B_1y = C_1$$

$$A_2x + B_2y = C_2$$

These can be solved using *Cramer's rule.*

$$X = \frac{\det\begin{vmatrix} C_1 & B_1 \\ C_2 & B_2 \end{vmatrix}}{\det\begin{vmatrix} A_1 & B_1 \\ A_2 & B_2 \end{vmatrix}}$$

$$Y = \frac{\det\begin{vmatrix} A_1 & C_1 \\ A_2 & C_2 \end{vmatrix}}{\det\begin{vmatrix} A_1 & B_1 \\ A_2 & A_2 \end{vmatrix}}$$

where

$$\det\begin{vmatrix} A & B \\ C & D \end{vmatrix} = A \cdot D - C \cdot B \qquad \text{(det is short for determinant)}$$

This is called the *determinant* of the matrix. Write a program to read a set of values for A_1, B_1, C_1, A_2, B_2, C_2 and then solve the simultaneous equations using GOSUB to calculate each determinant.

52. A matrix X with 5 rows and 6 columns is to be read from DATA statements.
    (a) Read in the array and write it out in row form (one row per line).
    (b) Calculate the sum of the elements in the fourth row and print it.
    (c) Find the largest value in column 2.
    (d) Interchange column 3 and column 4.
    (e) Print the smallest element of the array A and its position in the array (column, row).
53. Draw a flow chart of the program in Figure 9-5.
54. Explain the operation of the subroutine in Figure 9-5.
55. Discuss why it is possible to use the Euclid algorithm and subroutine in Figure 9-5 without understanding the Euclid algorithm. Would you ever be really sure of a program that used such a subroutine if you did not completely understand it?
56. Write a program that selects M names from a list of N names. This program will resemble the program to choose three salespeople from seven (developed in Chapter 8) except the terminal operator is to input:
    (a) The number of names to be considered.
    (b) The number of names to be selected.
    (c) The names to be used.
    Use an array to develop your program and notice the great advantage in using this approach.

Chapter 10 Data Processing Using Files

When quantities of information are to be processed, the data are generally organized into *files*, each of which contain data of a similar type. Maintaining files of data, processing, and searching files for specific data is an important part of computer usage.

In order to process data, they must be organized in some systematic way and the terms *record*, *item*, *field*, and *key*, which will be introduced, play important roles in understanding file organization.

After an introduction to data processing concepts, BASIC programs to perform several major operations on data are developed, including sorting, searching, and merging. The efficiency of the algorithms used in programs is also discussed.

Many BASIC systems offer file handling operations and the file modes of operation and general principles involved are presented.

10-1 OBJECTIVES

File Organization

Files must be structured and the data organized in some consistent way in order for the data to be processed by a computer. Some principles of file organization, and the terms *record*, *key*, *item*, and *field* are introduced.

Sorting, Searching, and Merging

Important data processing operations include sorting, searching, and merging data. Algorithms and programs to perform these operations are explained and illustrated.

Efficiency

When large quantities of data must be processed, the programs should be efficient in terms of computer time or operations performed in order to minimize data processing costs. This important subject is introduced and the efficiency of sorting and searching algorithms is examined.

BASIC File Operations

Many BASIC systems provide the ability to maintain data in named files. The concepts involved are introduced, an example given, and the most used operations explained.

10-2 IMPORTANCE OF FILES AND DATA STRUCTURES

Maintaining files of data on transactions is an important part of running a business and one of the largest areas of computer usage is in business file maintenance. In science, files are equally important with scientists maintaining records of experimental data, statistics for analyses, and so on. In business, computers commonly perform such functions as inventory control in factories and warehouses, processing checks, calculating balances in banks, and managing airline and train reservations. In science, computers take part in just about every aspect of data collection and file maintenance. In cancer research, for example, records of cancer patients' habits (smoking, diet, drugs taken, and so on) are recorded for analysis to determine cancer causing factors.

Important applications in science include work in psychology, biology, and medicine, as well as the social sciences in general. In industrial work, the long-term effects of chemicals are often studied by keeping records on working personnel exposed to these chemicals. In hospitals computers monitor patients after surgery and process blood tests. Probably no other part of the computer business is growing as fast as the work in these areas, and the potential gain for humanity is truly staggering.

Just as business management finds it advantageous to be able to process data and gather statistics in business transactions, medical researchers find an important application in gathering statistics on the effects of drugs when used in treating patients. Similarly, biologists and chemists now use the data processing capabilities of computers to gather statistics for their work. All this requires keeping records in computer maintained files.

10-3 MAINTAINING DATA FILES

Because businesses have large files to maintain, sophisticated filing techniques are called for. Similarly, many scientists who gather data establish large files of data. For another example, consider the work in automated libraries and information retrieval systems which maintain bibliographic files containing hundreds of millions of items. In these systems it is possible to search millions of abstracts for key items in minutes. It was, in fact, a need for special types of files with extraordinary maintenance procedures that led researchers to some of the most interesting data structures.

It is useful to define certain file maintenance terms more carefully. An *item* is an individual piece of information.[1] A *record* is composed of all the items in a file relating to the same object or individual. A collection of related records is called a *file*.

Examples will help clarify these definitions. An item might be a name, such as "John M. Jones," an age, such as "29," a marital status, such as "M" or "S," or an address, such as "39 Rhodes Avenue, Newton, Iowa." A *record* would then be the set of all items for John M. Jones, which would be John M. Jones, 29, M. 39 Rhodes Avenue, Newton, Iowa. A collection of records such as the above would constitute a file. Table 10-1 shows a small portion of a typical file for a department of motor vehicles.

Files can consist of from a few to millions of records, each record containing several items. As examples, consider the files of the Bureau of Census or Internal Revenue Service or the files of any major insurance company. Because of the size of these files, they must be maintained on such storage media as magnetic disks or tape. The maintenance of files requires considerable work, since they must be continually updated. Further, in order for the files to be really useful, it must be possible to acquire data of a specified class from the files with minimal search time.

The files for small businesses are similar in construction and in operation, but the need for mass storage is not present. Nevertheless, for reasons of economy disks and tapes are generally used.

In order to maintain large files and to search them effectively for specified records or items in a particular class, the files must be carefully designed with regard to their organization.

[1] Here are two related definitions from the American National Standards Committee X3, "American National Dictionary for Information Processing."

Item. (1) One member of a group. A file may consist of a number of items such as records which in turn may consist of other items.
(2) A collection of characters treated as a unit.

Field. (1) In a record, a specified area used for a particular category of data, for example, a group of card columns in which a wage rate is recorded.

Both the words *item* and *field* are often used for what we are calling an item. Strictly speaking a field is where you store an item, but the words are often loosely used.

Table 10-1 A SECTION OF A FILE

	AUTOMOBILE			OWNER			
	LICENSE	MAKE	YEAR	NAME	STREET ADDRESS	TOWN	STATE
Entries in file	219–606	Mercury	1969	F. R. Jackson	18 Knoll St.	Concord	Mass.
	219–607	Plymouth	1975	J. F. Jones	163 Kernel St.	Belmont	Mass.
	219–609	Cadillac	1978	F. M. Mayo	19 Carey Ave.	Woburn	Mass.
	219–611	Corvair	1978	J. P. French	462 April Ave.	Bedford	Mass.
	...	...	...	...	...	...	...

Note: Each row is a complete *record* consisting of seven *items*: (1) the license number, (2) the make of the car, (3) the year of manufacture, (4) the name of the owner, (5) the owner's street address, (6) the town in which the owner resides, and (7) the state in which the owner resides.

The term *data structure* refers to the method used for organizing data and the resulting interrelations between the data items and their locations in computer memory so that an efficient computer implementation results. Data structures form an important study area in computer science, as do the algorithms for maintaining and using them.

10-4 FILE MAINTENANCE

Files must be continually maintained. This primarily consists of adding new records to the file, deleting old records, and modifying records already in the file. In performing these operations and in locating and processing data in the files, it is generally efficient to maintain the records in the file in some prescribed order rather than simply adding new items at the end, closing up "holes" when items are deleted, and so on.

To see the need for ordering the items in a file, consider the way we find a name in a telephone book. If the names in a telephone book were not ordered, to find a name we would have to start on page 1 and search the book a name at a time. However, because we know last names are arranged in alphabetic order, we can guess at the location of a name, open the book to that point, and see if we have made a good guess or if we need to move forward or backward in the book. Contrast the small amount of hunting necessary to locate a name in a telephone book with the effort required to find a name in a novel or some other book where it is necessary to search at random.

Arranging a given file in a prescribed order is called *sorting* the file. Generally some particular item in each record is chosen (such as last name, social security number, or part number) and the file is sorted by arranging the records in the file so that the selected items are in the prescribed order. The selected item is called a *key*, and the file is said to be *sorted on the key*. The records in Table 10-1 are sorted on the key "License."

Sorting in a computer generally consists of arranging the records by ordering the keys in ascending (or sometimes descending) numerical order. When alphanumeric characters are used in the key, these characters must be ordered just as numbers are ordered. Most ordering is simple; for instance, A comes before B, B before C, and so on. However, commas and periods must be considered and rules for comparing strings of differing lengths made up. The order in which the characters in an alphanumeric code are arranged when they are in ascending order is called the *collating sequence* for the characters and the collating sequence for your terminal can be determined by the procedure in Question 3 of Chapter 5.

Sorting is such an important function in file maintenance that many algorithms have been invented for sorting and several are examined in the following sections.

When a particular record or set of records with some specific characteristic in a file is required, *searching* the file is necessary. The simplest form of a search is the *linear search* where the records are examined one at a time in order. This is time-consuming for most memories (but is natural for tape memories). If a file has been sorted, the very efficient *binary search* can be used. Some aspects of the search problem are examined in following sections.

10-5 SORTING

An important operation in maintaining files consists of sorting a file on a selected key. As was mentioned previously, sorting places the records in the file in an order so that the key items in the records are in ascending order. (If no two records in the file have the same value for the key, for instance, if the key is a social security number in a personnel file, the records can be arranged with the keys in ascending order. If the item used has duplication, the sorting simply places the items in nondescending order.)

In an actual file consisting of many records each containing several items, sorting the file can involve moving entire records around.[2] The actual sorting is generally done on an array of the values of the key, however, as this is more efficient, and, if necessary, the records can be moved only after the new arrangement for the keys has been found. In fact, for most large files it is necessary to keep the file on some mass storage device such as magnetic tape or disks, and to sort the file in stages, moving portions of the file (or key file) from and into the mass storage devices. Our concern here will be with the sorting process only; excellent descriptions of file maintenance procedures for mass storage devices will be found in several of the references.

As can be seen, an important, often performed operation in computer file systems is that of *sorting* a table or list of items. There are many sorting techniques, but, for now, we consider a table or list of numbers that are

[2] In many cases a file consisting only of keys and the corresponding addresses of each record in memory is used. Then only this small "key file" need be sorted.

stored in an array L(1), L(2), L(3), . . . , L(N). Each of the array variables L(1), L(2), and so on, has a numeric value, and the problem is to rearrange the numbers in ascending order and to print this reordered array. (If two or more "items" or numbers have the same value, they are listed one after the other.) After the array has been sorted, the smallest number will be at the head of the table and the largest number at the end of the table. That is, L(1) will be the least and L(N) the largest number.

Perhaps the most natural or intuitive way to sort an array is to search through the set of values in the array and find the smallest value. Call this value L(K) and place this value in L(1) by exchanging this L(K) with L(1). Next examine L(2), L(3), . . . , L(N) and find the smallest value. Call this value L(J) and place this element in L(2) by exchanging L(2) and L(J). These steps are repeated for L(3), L(4), and so on, until L(N − 1) and L(N) are finally compared and arranged.

The above description details the procedure generally used by people when arranging a bridge hand or when sorting a deck of index cards into order.

To implement this using a program we need more detail. For instance, the smallest number in the array can only be found by examining each number in turn. Here is a more detailed procedure. The first number in the list, L(1), is compared with each of the N − 1 numbers which follow it, and if any number is less than the number currently in the first position, the two are swapped; that is, the number presently in L(1) is replaced by the smaller number and the number in L(1) is given the position previously occupied by the smaller number. The second number in the list, L(2), is then considered, and the number in that position is compared with the N − 2 numbers beneath it in the list. (Notice that the number in the first position need not be again considered, for it is certainly smaller than (or equal to) the number currently in the second position.) Again, smaller numbers are "swapped" into the second position until the second-least number resides in the second position. This process continues until the next-to-the-bottom position is reached. (The final position need not be considered because it will have been compared with the number in the next-to-the-last position and the lesser number placed in the next-to-the-last position.) The flow chart for this algorithm is shown in Figure 10-1 and a program for the algorithm is shown in Figure 10-2.

We now discuss an important subject: the efficiency of this algorithm. For large files efficiency is very important and good sort programs are even sold by program concerns.

Examination of the flow chart in Figure 10-1 and the program in Figure 10-2 indicates that there is an outer and inner loop in the algorithm. For an array with N elements, the outer loop is performed N − 1 times; the first time the smallest of L(1), L(2), . . . , L(N) is found and moved into L(1), the final time the smaller of L(N − 1) and L(N) is found and moved into L(N − 1). The inner loop in the algorithm sequences through

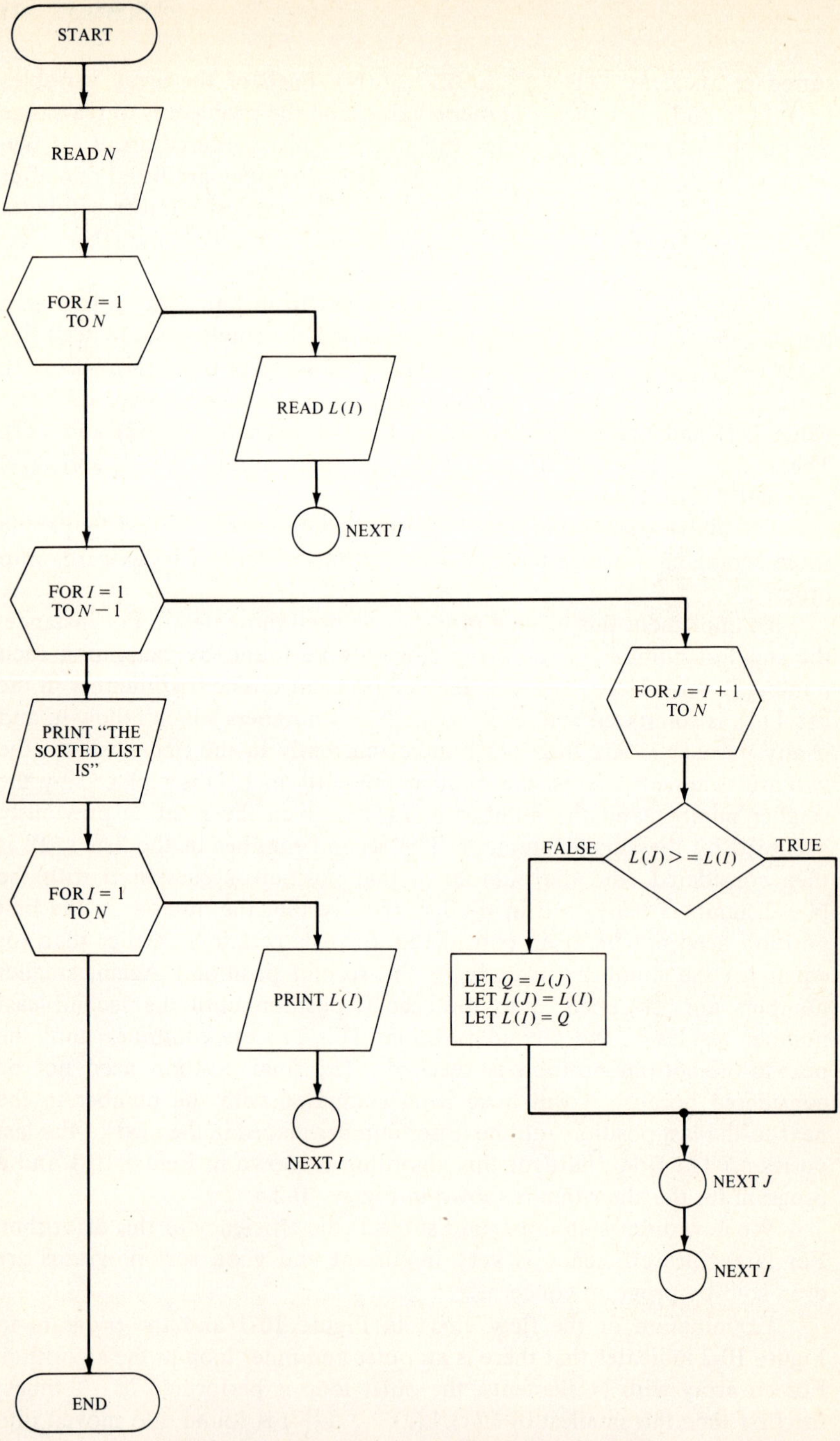

Fig. 10-1 Flow Chart for Replacement Sort

```
100 REM REPLACEMENT SORT
110 REM I. L. FOSTER
120 REM
130 REM THIS PROGRAM SORTS A LIST L OF N NUMBERS
140 REM INTO ASCENDING ORDER. THE NUMBERS ARE
150 REM INPUT THROUGH THE USE OF A DATA STATEMENT.
160 DIM L(50)
170 REM
180 REM READ LIST
190 REM
200 READ N
210 FOR I = 1 TO N
220       READ L(I)
230 NEXT I
240 REM
250 REM PERFORM REPLACEMENT SORT
260 REM
270 FOR I = 1 TO N - 1
280       FOR J = I + 1 TO N
290             IF L(J) > = L(I) THEN 330
300             LET Q = L(J)
310             LET L(J) = L(I)
320             LET L(I) = Q
330       NEXT J
340 NEXT I
350 REM
360 REM STATEMENTS 300-320 SWAP VALUES
370 REM PRINT SORTED LIST
380 REM
390 PRINT "THE SORTED LIST IS";
400 FOR I = 1 TO N
410       PRINT L(I); ",";
420 NEXT I
430 DATA 6
440 DATA 7, 8, 4, 2, 9, 1
450 END
```

(a)

```
THE SORTED LIST IS 1, 2, 4, 7, 8, 9,
```

(b)

Fig. 10-2 Replacement Sort Program. (a) Program; (b) Run from (a)

the set of elements under consideration, determining the smallest of them, and moving this element into the correct position.

In order to evaluate the efficiency of this algorithm, we first count the number of passes that are made through the inner loop. Let us set N equal to 10 so we have an array of 10 elements. First the algorithm examines L(1), L(2), . . . , L(10), finding the smallest and placing it in position L(1). This requires nine passes through the inner "comparison" loop. Then the algorithm examines L(2), L(3), . . . , L(10), finding the smallest element, which involves eight passes through the inner loop. We now see the basic pattern: on the third pass through the outer loop seven passes will be made through the inner loop; on the fourth pass through the outer loop, six passes will be made through the inner loop; and on the final ninth pass through the outer loop one pass will be made through the inner loop. Thus the algorithm requires $9 + 8 + 7 + 6 + \cdots + 2 + 1$ passes through the inner loop, that is, 45 passes.

The general case is as follows: To sort an array of N elements, the algorithm makes $N - 1$ passes through the outer loop. The first pass requires $N - 1$ passes through the inner loop; the second pass through the outer loop requires $N - 2$ passes through the inner loop; and this pattern continues until the final or $(N - 1)$st pass through the outer loop, when one pass is required through the inner loop. Thus we arrive at the following sum for the number of passes through the inner loop: $(N - 1) + (N - 2) + \cdots + 2 + 1$.

Then let us call P the value of the above sum. Now, $P = N(N - 1)/2$ or, written another way,[3]

$$P = \frac{N^2 - N}{2}$$

This number grows very quickly as N becomes larger. For instance, for $N = 100$ the value of P is 4950, but for $N = 1000$ the value of P is 499,500.

10-6 THE BUBBLE SORT—CHARACTER STRING SORTING

Another sorting algorithm which resembles the above but which can be more efficient in many cases is the "bubble sort." When the bubble sort is used, comparisons are made only between *adjacent* elements in the array, and the elements are exchanged if they are out of order. In the first pass of a bubble sort to sort an array L of N elements, L(1) is compared with L(2) and if L(2) is smaller, they are exchanged. Then L(2) is compared with L(3) and the elements are swapped if L(3) is smaller. This is continued until

[3] This can be shown as follows: The average value in the sum $(N - 1) + (N - 2) + \cdots + 1$ is $[(N - 1) + 1]/2$, which is also $N/2$, and there are $N - 1$ terms, so the sum has value $N/2 * (N - 1)$ or $[N(N - 1)]/2$.

L(N – 1) is finally compared with L(N), and an exchange made if necessary. During the second pass the same general procedure is followed except only adjacent items from L(1) to L(N – 1) are considered [this is because the largest element must now be in L(N)]. This process continues until on the final pass only L(1) and L(2) are compared. When this sort is used, larger items float down and small items "bubble up"; hence the name.

It is possible to add a feature to this sort procedure that will generally improve its efficiency. Each time a pass is made through the section of the array being examined by the outer loop, a test is made, and if no exchanges are made, the program discontinues its sort, for the array is already in ascending order. The test is made by setting a variable or "flag" to NO each time the inner loop is entered and by setting the flag equal to YES if an exchange is made in the inner loop. A test at the beginning of the outer loop determines if an exchange has been made; and if no exchange has been made, the program exits from the sort procedure. If an exchange is made, the program continues. Figure 10-3 shows a block diagram of this program and Figure 10-4 shows a program to implement this procedure. Notice the SORT procedure has been placed in a subroutine.

We now examine the efficiency of this program. In the worst case (when the array is originally in descending order) it can be shown that this program requires N(N – 1)/2 passes through the inner loop. However, in the best case (if the array is already in the correct order), the program requires only N – 1 passes through the inner loop. In general, this program exploits the tendency of lists to be already somewhat ordered; thus, as a result, for large values of N, the program tends to be more efficient than the previous algorithm.

Many studies have been made of sorting algorithms and many algorithms have been invented. A comprehensive treatment of sorting techniques can be found in volume 3 in the series of books by Knuth (see the References at the end of the text) which devotes nearly 400 pages to this subject. It is very difficult to evaluate mathematically many of the more complicated sorting techniques, and so quite often algorithms are programmed, sample arrays (or lists) are sorted, and the results evaluated.[4] The book by Rich analyzes a number of the best sorting techniques by programming and evaluating the time required, storage required, and other factors for a number of sample problems.

Studies of file-sorting techniques show that the number of operations required grows approximately as N^2 divided by some constant for "interchange sorting algorithms" such as those mentioned. More sophisticated sorting techniques such as "radix sorts" and "merge sorts" require NK

[4] Day's book describes such sorts (giving FORTRAN programs) as the "monkey puzzle sort" and the "tournament sort."

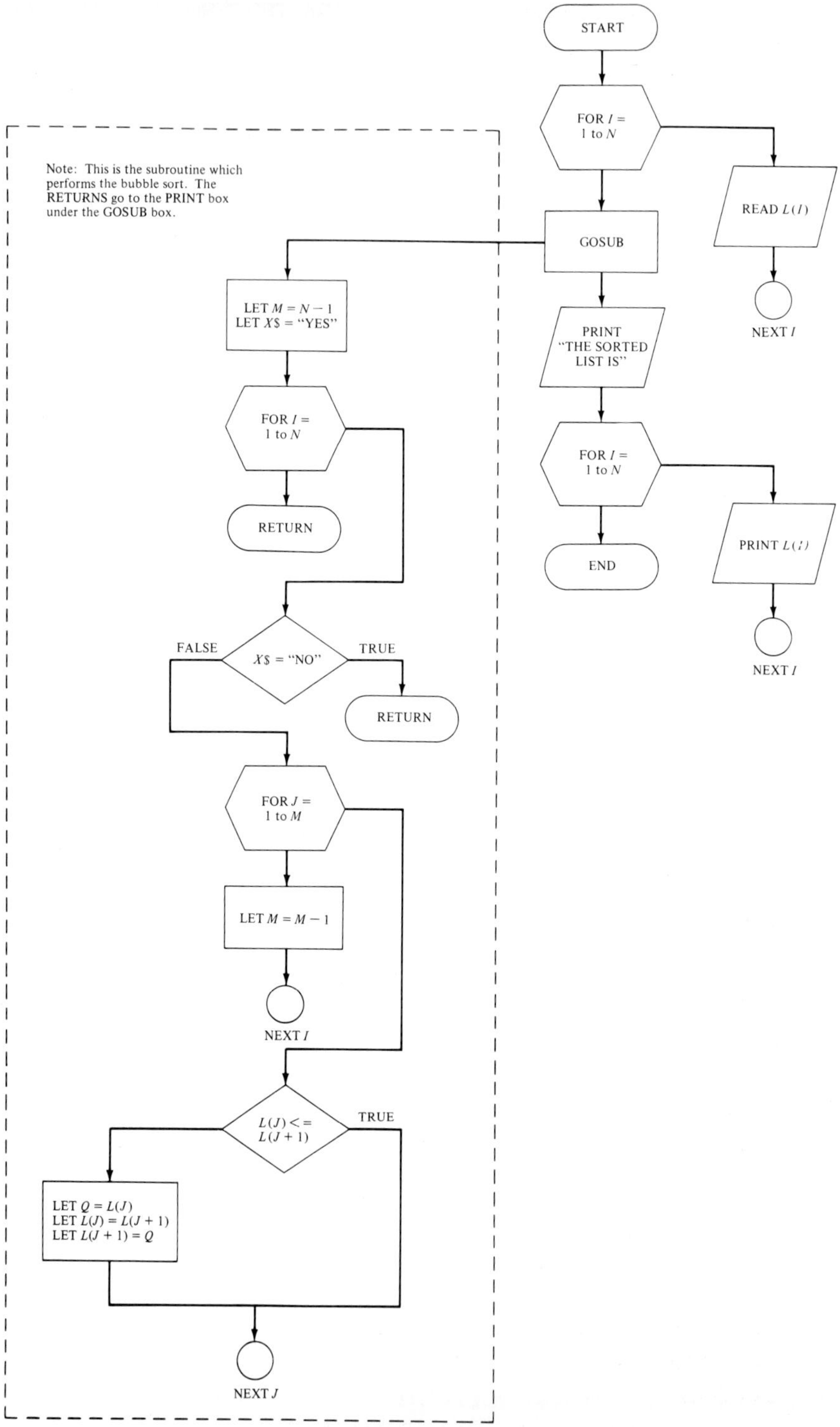

Fig. 10-3 Flow Chart of Bubble Sort

```
100 REM BUBBLE SORT
110 REM F. K. WILLIAMS, 4/18/81
120 REM
130 REM THIS PROGRAM SORTS A LIST OF NUMBERS IN A
140 REM DATA STATEMENT INTO ASCENDING ORDER USING THE
150 REM BUBBLE SORT TECHNIQUE
160 REM
170 DIM L(50)
180 READ N
190 REM READ IN LIST
200 REM
210 FOR I = 1 TO N
220     READ L(I)
230 NEXT I
240 REM
250 GOSUB 350
260 REM
270 PRINT “THE SORTED LIST IS”;
280 FOR I = 1 TO N
290     PRINT L(I); “,”;
300 NEXT I
310 STOP
320 REM
330 REM SORT CODE FOLLOWS
340 REM
350     LET M = N − 1
360     LET X$ = “YES”
370     FOR I = 1 TO N
380     IF X$ = “NO” THEN 520
390         LET X$ = “NO”
400         FOR J + 1 TO M
410             IF L(J) < = L(J + 1) THEN 490
420                 REM
430                 REM SWAP VALUES
440                 REM
450                 LET Q = L(J)
460                 LET L(J) = L(J + 1)
470                 LET L(J + 1) = Q
480                 LET X$ = “YES”
490         NEXT J
500         LET M = M − 1
510     NEXT I
520     RETURN
530 DATA 6, 9, 5, 4, 10, 12, 9
540 END
```

Fig. 10-4 Bubble Sort

```
100 REM ALPHANUMERIC SORT
110 REM I. L. FOSTER
120 REM
130 REM THIS PROGRAM SORTS A LIST OF CHARACTER
140 REM STRINGS L$ INTO ASCENDING ORDER. THE
150 REM STRINGS ARE INPUT USING A DATA STATEMENT.
150 REM
170 DIM L$(50)
180 REM
190 REM READ LIST
200 REM
210 READ N
220 FOR I = 1 TO N
230       READ L$(I)
240 NEXT I
250 REM
260 REM PERFORM REPLACEMENT SORT
270 REM
280 FOR I = 1 TO N − 1
290       FOR J = I + 1 TO N
300             IF L$(J) > = L$(I) THEN 340
310                   LET Q$ = L$(J)
320                   LET L$(J) = L$(I)
330                   LET L$(I) = Q$
340       NEXT J
350 NEXT I
360 REM
370 REM STATEMENTS 310–330 SWAP VALUES
380 REM PRINT SORTED LIST
390 REM
400 PRINT "THE SORTED LIST IS:";
410 FOR I = 1 TO N
420       PRINT L$(I); ",";
430 NEXT I
440 DATA 6
450 DATA "JOHN", "ABLE", "BILL", "JANE", "JAN", "JANET"
460 END
```

(a)

```
THE SORTED LIST IS: ABLE, BILL, JAN, JANE, JANET, JOHN
```

(b)

Fig. 10-5 Program to Sort a List of Character Strings. (a) Program; (b) Run from (a)

times some constant number of operations, or $N^{1.5}$ times some constant operations, where N is the number of elements and K is the number of bits in each element. These sorting techniques require more complicated programs, with the result that they are generally not used for small numbers of elements.

It is possible to sort lists of names or other character strings in much the same fashion as numbers. Figure 10-5 shows a program to sort a list of character strings input using a DATA statement. The program is similar to that in Figure 10-2 except that the character string array L$ replaces the numeric array L, X becomes X$, and Y becomes Y$. A run of this program is also shown in Figure 10-5.

10-7 MERGING

An important operation in maintaining files is that of *merging*. Two lists of items are merged when they are combined into a single set; however, if the two lists have been ordered by sorting in ascending order, the resulting list of items must also be sorted in ascending order.

In order to study merging, let us first consider two arrays of character strings L$ and M$, with L$ having M elements and M$ having N elements. The arrays L$ and M$ are assumed to be sorted in ascending order, and we wish to develop an array N$ with M + N elements that are sorted in ascending order.

The first step in the algorithm is to compare L$(1) with M$(1) and place the smaller of the two in N$(1). If item L$(1) is selected, we then consider L$(2) and M$(1), placing the smaller in N$(2); if M$(1) was selected in the preceding step, we consider L$(1) and M$(2), placing the smaller in N$(2). This basic process continues with L$ being compared with M$ at each step until we reach the end of either L$ or M$ [that is, we select either L$(M) or M$(N)]. When this occurs, the remaining elements in the other array are simply copied into the remainder of N$. Figure 10-6 shows a flow chart for this algorithm, and Figure 10-7 shows a BASIC subprogram to merge two arrays. (Languages such as COBOL provide SORT and MERGE subprograms in their basic library, and a programmer can simply write MERGE A AND B or SORT A rather than writing his own subprogram.)

A *merge sort* is a sorting algorithm that breaks sets of elements into subsets, sorts the subsets, and then merges these sorted subsets. By dividing the original set of elements into an appropriate number of subsets, so that the sorting is efficient, and then depending on the natural efficiency of merging, an efficient sorting algorithm can be obtained. The Exercises develop this procedure. Knuth's book as well as several of the others in the References also treat this sorting procedure in detail.

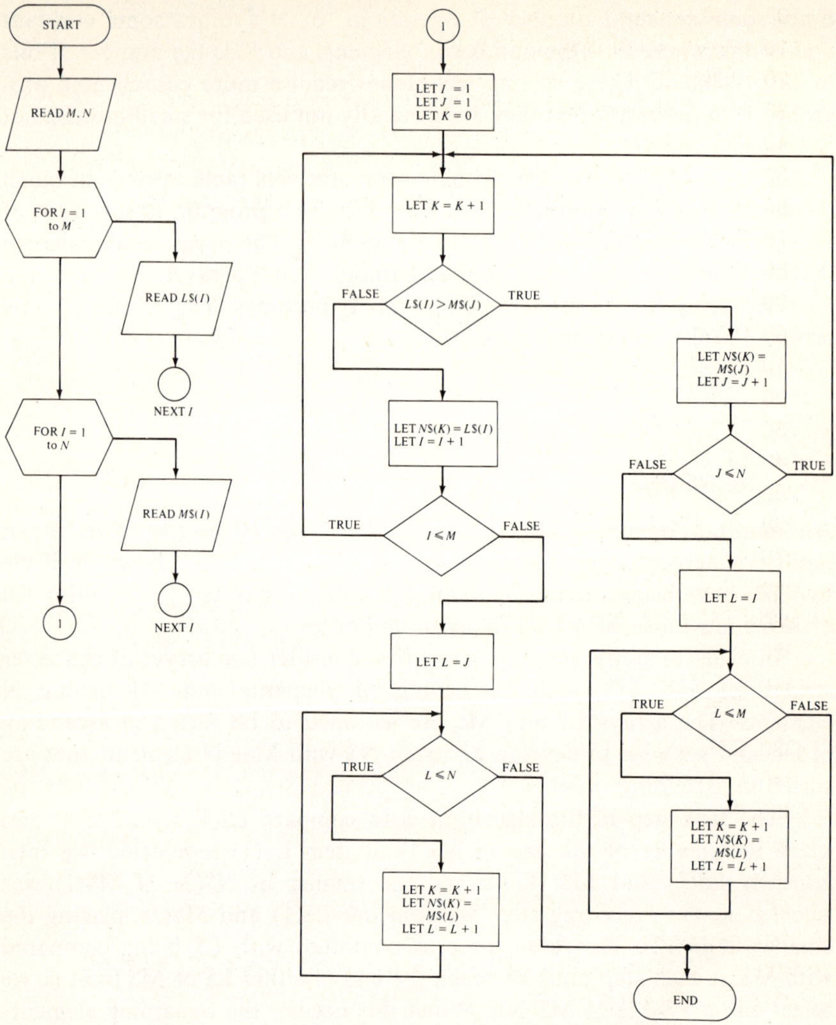

Fig. 10-6 Flow Diagram for Merge Algorithm

10-8 SEARCHING

The most frequently performed operation in business or information systems is that of searching the files for elements that satisfy some specified condition. The condition specified ranges from equality—for instance, "find the record of the person with social security number 872-95-5236,"—to "Produce a list of the parts in our inventory that cost more than $35." In each case, a file must be searched, and it is important that the file be organized so that it can be efficiently searched. It is also

```
100 REM MERGE TWO LISTS
110 REM L. H. BENSON, 4/6/81
120 REM
130 REM THIS PROGRAM MERGES TWO SORTED LISTS
140 REM A$ AND M$ INPUT USING DATA STATEMENTS.
150 REM THE FIRST TWO ENTRIES IN THE DATA STATEMENTS
160 REM GIVE THE NUMBER OF ELEMENTS IN L$ AND M$,
170 REM RESPECTIVELY.
180 REM
190 REM INPUTS LIST
200 REM
210 READ M, N
220 FOR I = 1 TO M
230       READ L$(I)
240 NEXT I
250 FOR I = 1 TO N
260       READ M$(I)
270 NEXT I
280 REM
290 REM NOW BEGIN HERE
300 REM
310 LET I = 1
320 LET J = 1
330 LET K = 0
340 LET K = K + 1
350 IF L$(I) > M$(J) THEN 470
360       LET N$(K) = L$(I)
370       LET I = I + 1
380       IF I < = M THEN 340
390       REM
400       REM ARRAY L$ IS EXHAUSTED SO LOAD REST OF M$
410       REM
420       FOR L = J TO N
430             LET K = K + 1
440             LET N$(K) = M$(L)
450       NEXT L
460       GO TO 570
470 LET N$(K) = M$(J)
480 LET J = J + 1
490 IF J < = N THEN 340
500 REM
510 REM ARRAY M$ IS EXHAUSTED SO LOAD REST OF L$
```

Fig. 10-7 Program to Merge Two Lists. (a) Program; (b) Run from (a)

```
520 REM
530 FOR L = I TO M
540       LET K = K + 1
550       LET N$(K) = L$(L)
560 NEXT L
570 PRINT "HERE IS THE MERGED LIST;"
580 PRINT "_ _ _ _ _ _ _ _ _ _ _ _ _ _ _ _ _ _ _ _ _ _ _ _ _ _ _ _ _"
590 FOR I = 1 TO M + N
600       PRINT N$(I)
610 NEXT I
620 DATA 3, 4
630 DATA ABLE, BAKER, MONA
640 DATA CHARLIE, DAN, WILLIAM, ZED
650 END
```

(a)

```
HERE IS THE MERGED LIST;

_ _ _ _ _ _ _ _ _ _ _ _ _ _ _ _ _ _ _ _ _ _ _ _ _ _
ABLE
BAKER
CHARLIE
DAN
MONA
WILLIAM
ZED
```

(b)

Fig. 10-7 *continued*

important to have an efficient search algorithm so that too much computer time is not expended on searching.

Organizing files and search procedures are important topics in systems design for data processing systems. If files must be regularly maintained (updated) by adding, modifying, and then deleting old records, and if it is further necessary to search the files frequently for records that satisfy some specified criteria, then a file organization must be found that is not too expensive to update, that does not require too much storage space, and that can be conveniently searched. Designing a good data structure for the file and programming efficient file maintenance and search algorithms are interesting and are still developing aspects of data processing systems design.

A particular aspect of file searching and maintenance, that of finding a specified element in an array, will be explained. This will include showing how the search algorithm can be greatly speeded up if the array is sorted.

If a table or array is searched for a given item, the search *succeeds* if the item is found and *fails* if it is not found. We store our table in an array called L with N elements. If these elements are not ordered, in order to find a given item in the array, the most natural search algorithm is to examine L(1), L(2), L(3), and so on, up to L(N), each time seeing if the value is the desired one.

In order to convert this procedure to flow chart form, we let the values in L be integers and call the value to be found B. A flow chart of the resulting search algorithm is shown in Figure 10-8. A BASIC program implementing this algorithm is shown in Figure 10-9. A natural question is: "How efficient is this algorithm?" It is clear that if the desired value is not in the array, N steps or passes through the search loop will be required. If, however, the item is in the array (and we are not required to find duplicate values in the array), on the average N/2 passes through the array will be required.

Now, assume the array has been sorted so that the elements are in numerically ascending order. We sequence through the array, starting with ITEM(1) and proceeding through ITEM(2), ITEM(3), and so on, in turn as before. However, at each step we also test to see if again the ITEM is greater than B, and if it is, the search is immediately terminated, because the element is not in the array. This will improve the efficiency of the search procedure because an entire pass through the array will not be required in most cases where an element is not in the array. About $\frac{1}{2}$N steps will be required on the average, where N is the number of elements in the array.

A still more efficient algorithm for searching a sorted array is the *binary search algorithm*. It closely follows the procedure used by most people in trying to locate a name in a dictionary, index card file, or other alphabetically ordered file.[5] The file is opened to the middle, and an examination then indicates in which half the item lies; this process continues until the particular item is located.

In order to clarify the above procedure, assume a table of N items: M(1), M(2), . . . , M(N). If N is even, we can divide the table into two equal sets of N/2 items and then determine in which half the value to be located might lie. If N is odd, the table is "divided" into two sets, one with INT(N/2) and one with INT(N/2) + 1 items. The largest element in the "lower half" of the table (with the lowest values) is now examined to see in which part of the table the desired item lies; this is done by seeing if the desired element has a value greater than the largest element in the "lower

[5] These often involve a "calculated" search where the searcher estimates where the item is in the list and looks there first, then looking higher or lower in the list depending on the result. In a true binary search the section of file being examined is divided in half at each step.

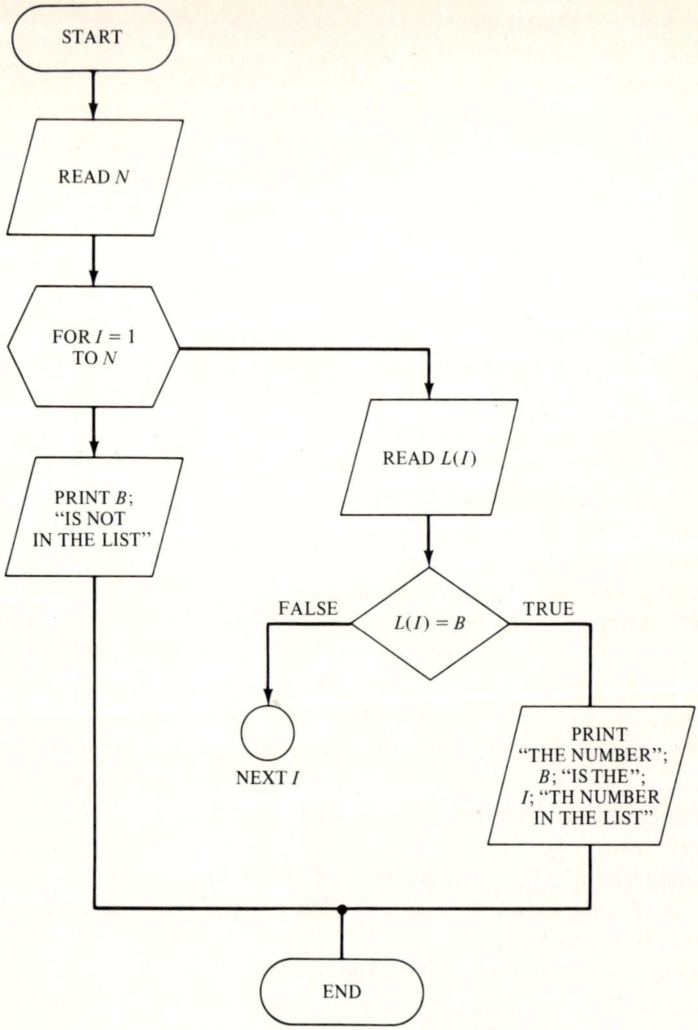

Fig. 10-8 Flow Chart for Linear Search Program

half." If so, the upper half is selected; if not, the lower half is selected. This step is then repeated on the half of the file selected and then on the half of the file selected in this step. Finally, either the item is found or the discovery is made that no such item is in the table. Figure 10-10 shows a flow chart of this algorithm and Figure 10-11 shows a BASIC program implementing the procedure.

In both the flow chart and the program, an array called L$ containing N elements is searched for an item called M$. The variable I is set so that L$(I) = M$ if M$ is in the array.

The efficiency of the binary search algorithm is most easily evaluated for lists with N entries, where $N = 2^I$ for some I (that is, lists with 2, 4, 8,

```
100 REM LINEAR SEARCH PROGRAM
110 REM F. L. MANN, 8/4/81
120 REM
130 REM THIS PROGRAM FINDS A NUMBER B (WHICH IS INPUT
140 REM FROM THE TERMINAL) IN A LIST OF NUMBERS IN A
150 REM DATA STATEMENT.
160 REM
170 PRINT "INPUT A NUMBER"
180 INPUT B
190 READ N
200 FOR I = 1 TO N
210       READ L(I)
220       IF L(I) = B THEN 260
230 NEXT I
240 PRINT B; "IS NOT IN THE LIST"
250 GO TO 290
260 PRINT B; "IS ELEMENT NUMBER"; I; "IN THE ARRAY"
270 DATA 5
280 DATA 7, 8, 15, 45, 2
290 END
```

(a)

```
INPUT A NUMBER
 ?15
 15 IS ELEMENT NUMBER 3 IN THE ARRAY

INPUT A NUMBER
 ?99
 99 IS NOT IN THE LIST
```

(b)

Fig. 10-9 Linear Search Program. (a) Program; (b) Two Runs from (a)

16, 32, and so on, entries), for then the list is reduced to one-half its original size the first step, one-fourth its original size the second step, and so on, until it is reduced to a single element, which either is or is not the item desired. Because our rule is that after J steps the list has been reduced to a "sublist" with size $2^{-J} \times N$, and since $N = 2^{I}$ for some I, then when $2^{-J} \times 2^{I} = 1$, each of the two parts will contain a single element and one of these must be the desired element. Thus, for a table with N elements, where $N = 2^{I}$ for some integer I, exactly I passes through the basic loop are required to find an element using the program or flow chart which has been shown. This value is less than N for N greater than 2 and is much less than N for large N. This shows the great advantage of keeping lists sorted.

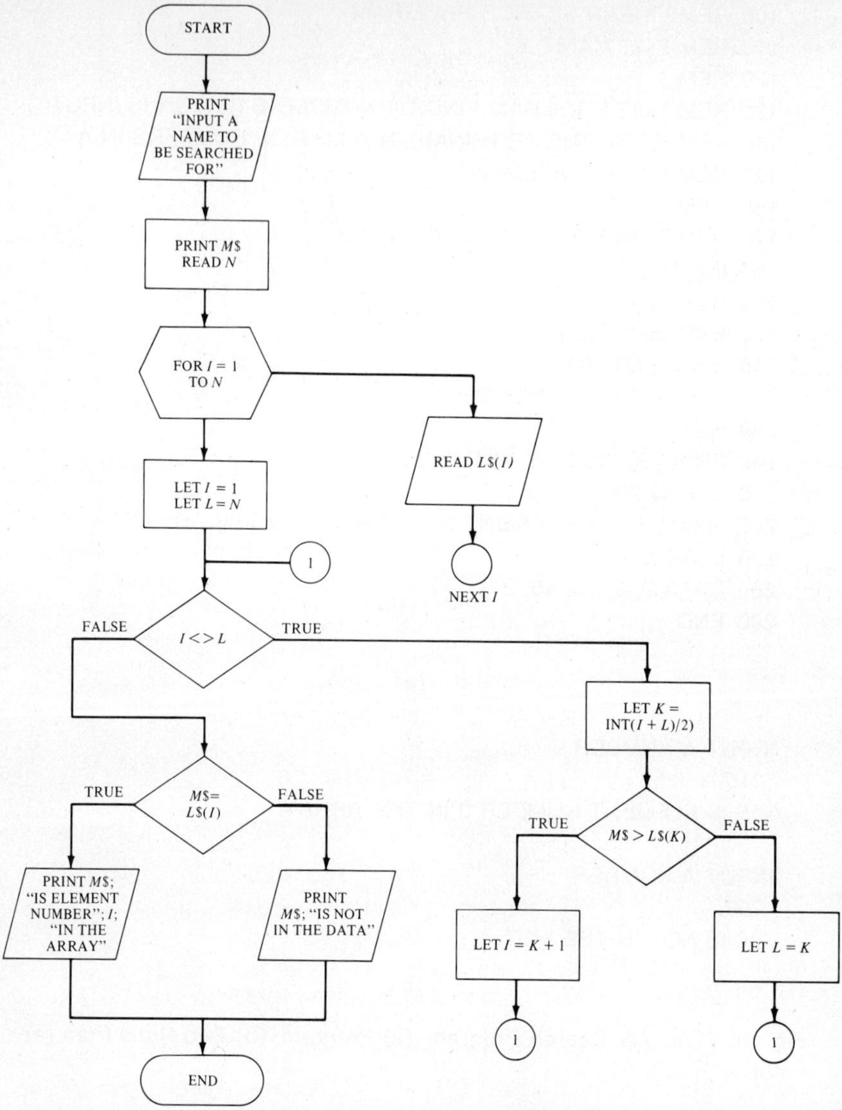

Fig. 10-10 Flow Diagram for Binary Search

For any N that is not a power of 2 (that is, not equal to 2^I for some I), we can determine the number of passes through the loop as follows: Let K be the smallest integer such that $2^K \geqslant N$; then K passes through the loop are required.[6]

[6]In general, if we define $\log_2(N)$ to be a function with value X such that $2^X = N$, then $\log_2(N)$ is called the *binary logarithm* of N, and if $X = \log_2(N)$, X will be some positive real number for each positive integer N. Now, in the general case it can be shown that the number of passes required is exactly CEIL($\log_2$(N)), where CEIL has a value the smallest integer larger than or equal to $\log_2(N)$. This shows that the number of passes through the loop increases at a logarithmic rate.

```
100 REM BINARY SEARCH PROGRAM
110 REM W. G. JOHNSON, 6/7/81
120 REM
130 REM THIS PROGRAM FINDS A CHARACTER STRING M$
140 REM IN THE LIST IN THE DATA STATEMENT. THE
150 REM ARRAY L$ STORES THE LIST.
160 REM
170 PRINT "INPUT A NAME TO BE SEARCHED FOR"
180 INPUT M$
190 DIM L$(25)
200 REM
210 REM READ IN LIST TO BE SEARCHED
220 REM
230 READ N
240 FOR I = 1 TO N
250     READ L$(I)
260 NEXT I
270 REM
280 REM PERFORM BINARY SEARCH
290 REM
300 LET I = 1
310 LET L = N
320 IF I = L THEN 420
330     LET K = INT((I + L)/2)
340     IF M$ > L$(K) THEN 400
350         REM
360         REM M$ IS IN LOWER HALF
370         REM
380         LET L = K
390         GO TO 320
400     LET I = K + 1
410     GO TO 320
420 REM
430 REM IS M$ IN ARRAY?
440 REM
450 IF M$ = L$(I) THEN 480
460     PRINT M$; "IS NOT IN THE DATA"
470     STOP
480 PRINT M$; "IS ELEMENT NUMBER"; I; "IN THE ARRAY"
490 DATA 5
500 DATA "AARON", "BILL", "JANE", "KEN", "WILLIAM"
510 END
```

(a)

```
INPUT A NAME TO BE SEARCHED FOR
 ?JANE
JANE IS ELEMENT NUMBER 3 IN THE ARRAY

INPUT A NAME TO BE SEARCHED FOR
 ?JOHN
JOHN IS NOT IN THE DATA
```

(b)

Fig. 10-11 Binary Search Program. (a) Program; (b) Two Runs from (a)

Can this algorithm be improved? It might seem that before each pass through the loop it would be a good idea to test whether the largest element in the lower half is the item desired and to terminate the search if it is. This would mean that sometimes the search could be terminated early. For instance, if we had a table with four elements which were the integers 1, 3, 7, 9 and we search it for the integer 3, then the table is divided into two parts: 1, 3 and 7, 9. The greatest integer in the lower half, 3, is selected, and, instead of seeing if the desired item 3 is greater than 3, we also test to see if it is equal to 3, and stop if it is. In this case it is the desired element, and only one pass through the major loop has been made, whereas the previous algorithm required two.

It can be shown, however, that on the average the number of passes through the major loop is decreased by only 1. That is, if L passes are required on the average for the first binary search algorithm, then $L - 1$ passes are required for the second algorithm. If L is large, the additional time required to test for equality, which lengthens the basic loop, will probably exceed the time required for a single pass through the loop, and the original procedure will run faster on the average.

The above analysis is typical of that performed on algorithms for system use. In many cases, it is impossible to completely and precisely analyze subtle points, and it is either necessary to test the algorithms with a number of test cases and compare results or to generate simulated data, try the algorithms on the simulated data, and compare results.

10-9 FILE PROCESSING

The programs so far shown have input data either from the terminal or through the use of DATA statements. For large files (or tables) there are several advantages to keeping the data in a separate section of memory. The list of data is then called a file and is not a part of a program. The situation is as shown in Figure 10-12. Both files and programs are kept in memory and are given names so they may be called when needed.

Keeping data files in this way makes it possible to run several different programs using the data from the same file. It also makes it possible to run the same program on data from several different files.

In government, business, and science the files can become very large (10^{12} to 10^{14} characters) and the data in the files must continually be updated. Consider, for example, a customer's file in a life insurance company's file system. The file will be large with many customer names and with considerable data on each customer concerning policies carried, payments made, claims processed, and so on. Further, the file must be continually updated as payments are made, policies are added or dropped, claims are filed, and so on.

Keeping a file up to date is called *maintaining* the file and if the file is kept separate from the program, different programs can be written to add customers, delete customers, update payment data, and so on. Programs can also be written to search the file for needed data when management questions arise, to generate payment demands when customers are delinquent, and to print reports for management summarizing overall statistics on the customers and the general business situation.

For BASIC systems, programs that perform file maintenance and search files are written in the same way as the programs earlier in this chapter except that the READ and INPUT statements access the file instead of a DATA statement or a terminal. When the files are separate from the program, in order to read from a specific file it is necessary to name the file. This is done using either a special BASIC statement, called a FILES statement, or in some systems, in the READ statement or INPUT statement (or in both).

Writing into a file is similar; a PRINT or WRITE statement is used and the file to be written into must be named.

Unfortunately, there is no standard file system in BASIC and most systems vary in operational details, although standards committees are now working on the development of a standard system. Because of the considerable difference in detail between systems it is necessary to obtain the operating details of your system before preparing or using file maintenance programs. Most of the processing work will be done in conventional BASIC, however, and it is only the details of writing into and reading from files that must be obtained for your particular system.

One general comment can be made about the BASIC file systems now in existence. All have a sequential mode of operation and some have a random access mode. The sequential mode of operation in BASIC file systems almost exactly mirrors the reading from DATA statements. The values in the file are listed one after the other in order and can only be read or written in order. A READ statement accessing a sequential file reads values into variables in the order in which they occur in the file. As a result, the file can simply be thought of as a long string of values written one after the other. In fact, it is straightforward to enter data from DATA statements into a sequential file; the data can simply be input in order. Similarly, data can be typed into a sequential file from a keyboard by simply typing the values in order.

A random access file is one where values can be obtained out of order. Generally random access files are organized into records and the records are accessed either using the key value for the record or by the position of the record in the file. For files that are stored on disks this can greatly reduce the time it takes to locate data in a large file because the entire file up to the selected item need not be read; the READ head on the disk access system can be moved (more or less) directly to the disk track on which the item lies. This ability to access data directly is the great advantage of random access systems. (If secondary storage on a tape is used, however, values must be read in order and so the sequential system works about as well.)

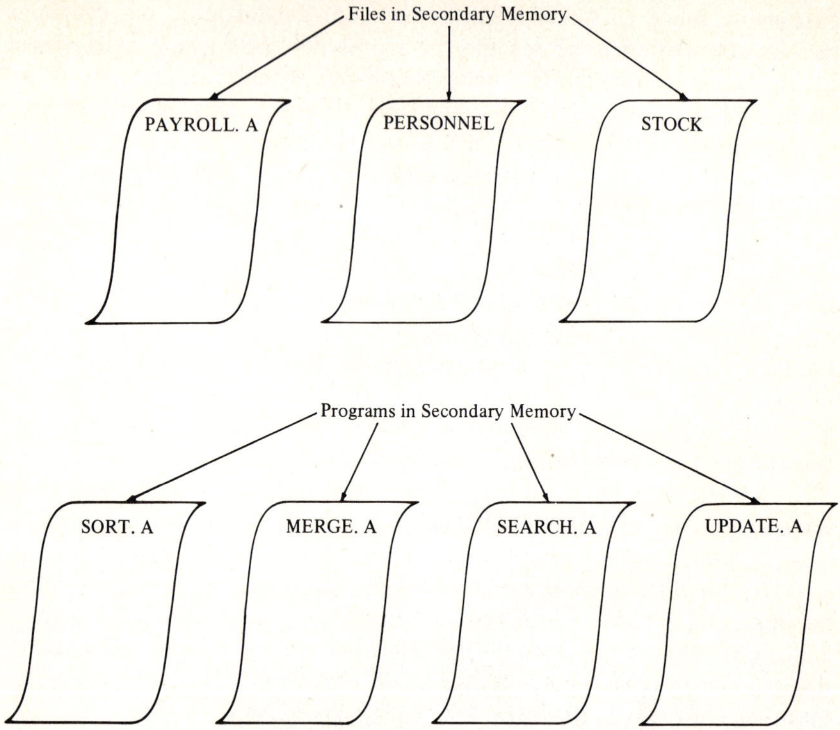

Fig. 10-12 Files and Programs in Memory

There is a considerable difference in the operating details of random access systems and standards will be much harder to arrive at, but there are ANSI committees now considering this subject.

An example of a program to read from a sequential file is shown in Figure 10-13(a). The program is for a DEC System 10. The program reads from a file which is organized as follows:

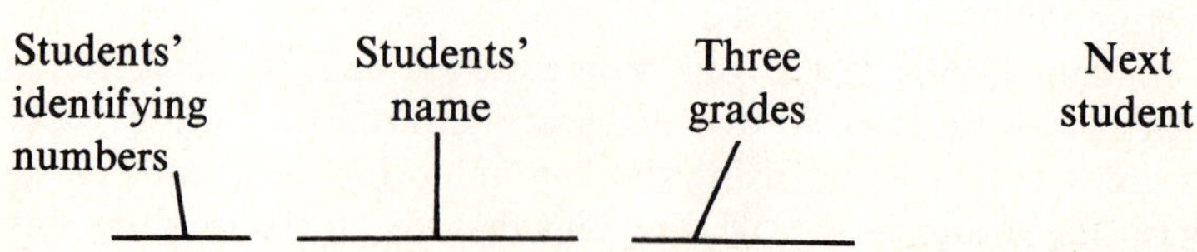

6434, "JOHN JACOBS," 85, 73, 65, "SAM KEEN," 92, 83, 64

The program reads the data on a single student, calculates his or her average grade, then prints the name and average grade in a table.

```
 10 FILES GRADES.A
 20 DEF FNR(X) = INT(10*X + 0.5)/10
 30 PRINT "NAME", "AVERAGE"
 40 INPUT #1: L, N$, S1, S2, S3
 50 LET A = (S1 + S2 + S3)/3
 60 PRINT N$, FNR(A)
 70 IF END #1 THEN 90
 80 GO TO 40
 90 PRINT
100 PRINT "END OF FILE"
110 END
```

(a)

```
GRADES.A

10, "HENRY JONES", 87, 98, 97
20, "JANET EVANS", 88, 78, 89
30, "PETE DANE", 89, 88, 90
40, "MARY KEEN", 93, 90, 89
50, "FRED HENRY", 87, 77, 75
60, "DEAN MORRIS", 96, 89, 78
70, "KATHY MANN", 89, 78, 74
```

(b)

```
NAME              AVERAGE
HENRY JONES        90.7
JANET EVANS        85
PETER DANE         89
MARY KEEN          90.7
FRED HENRY         79.7
DEAN MORRIS        87.7
KATHY MANN         80.3

END OF FILE
```

(c)

Fig. 10-13 Program to Process a File. (a) Program to Read from a File; (b) The GRADES. A File; (c) Run from Program in (a)

The FILES statement names the file to be read from GRADES.A. The (channel) number #1 is also assigned to this file by this statement. A function to round to two decimal places, FNR, is then defined. The table headings "NAME" and "AVERAGE" are then printed.

The INPUT statement names the file to be read from—it is #1 which is GRADES.A. The INPUT statement then reads the first five values from the file into L, N$, S1, S2, and S3. (Notice a READ statement would read from a DATA statement in the same way.) The student's name and his average grade rounded to two digits is then printed. The IF END #1 statement tests to see if the last value in the file has been read. The end of the file is marked and the IF END #1 tests this and goes to the statement number following the THEN if the end of the file has been reached. Otherwise the GO TO is executed and another student's name and grades are read.

The above example gives the essence of the usage of sequential files in BASIC. Unfortunately, details (such as use of the #1) vary from system to system. Despite this, an understanding of the general principles of file processing will greatly facilitate learning a specific system. This subject is an important one and should be pursued whenever possible. (The References contain several books in this area and the details of specific systems can be found in the manufacturers' manuals.) While data processing techniques for large complicated files are still being developed and research in this area continues, the subject is so important that existing systems, which are quite good, should be studied.

10-10 SUMMARY

This chapter introduced the concept of a *file*. Files play an important role in data processing. Maintaining files is an important function, and many programs are written to update files, search files, and so on. The concepts of record, item, sorting, merging, and searching were all introduced.

Programs were developed to sort, search, and merge data. These operations play an important large role in data processing. The efficiency of algorithms used in processing large files are important factors and the efficiency of several sort and search algorithms was analyzed using the number of passes made through loops in the program as a criterion for algorithm comparison. Because of computer costs, using efficient programs is especially important in large data processing operations where programs are used many times on large quantities of data. As a result, considerable time and money are spent improving the efficiency of the programs and algorithms used in larger operations because efficient programs will cost less in the long run. In smaller systems, where programs are not used so much and data files are not so large, programming costs become a major factor and an emphasis is often placed on producing correct programs that can be modified and updated as effectively as possible instead of minimizing run times.

The algorithms used in sorting and searching are interrelated in that the most efficient search procedure, the binary search, requires that the data be ordered or sorted. As a result, when many searches of a file are to be made it is generally kept sorted. However, when a file can only be read in a sequential manner, a search can only be made using the linear search procedure that was presented. There are other reasons for keeping a sequential file sorted, however. For instance, updating a sorted file is generally more efficient because the file can be updated in order.

BASIC systems often include a file processing feature. Most systems offer a sequential access mode of operation and a few offer a random access mode. The ideas behind these file systems along with an example were presented.

Questions

1. Explain the terms *record*, *file*, and *key*, and give examples.
2. Make up a small file of auto parts giving each part a part number, name, number in stock, and cost. What would you pick for the key in this file?
3. Explain how you would sort the file in Question 2 on the key you chose.
4. The file in Table 9-1 is sorted on license number. Explain problems that might arise if the car owner's names were chosen for the key.
5. Explain how character strings are ordered in BASIC and the meaning of the term *collating sequence*.
6. Show the steps in sorting the numbers 16, 8, 9, 5 into ascending order using the replacement sort.
7. Show the steps in sorting the numbers 25, 15, 4, 17 using the bubble sort approach.
8. Large files are sometimes sorted by breaking them into sections, sorting the sections, and then merging the sorted sections. Show how sorting a list of 200,000 numbers requires far more steps than sorting 5 files of 40,000 numbers each.
9. Identify the outer and inner loop in the sorting program in Figure 10-2. (Give statement numbers.)
10. Modify the program in Figure 10-2 so that duplicated values are removed from the list being sorted.
11. Modify the program in Figure 10-4 so it sorts character strings instead of numbers.
12. Explain how a program which sorts a list of numbers or character strings must be supplemented by more statements to sort a file consisting of records with more than one item per record.
13. Comment on the efficiency of the merge program in Figure 10-7. Can you see any way to make this program more efficient?
14. Can you think of any reason to use a linear search on a list of names that has been sorted instead of a binary search?
15. Write a program to find all numbers greater than a given input number in a list

of numbers in a data statement. If the list is sorted, will this make the program more efficient?

16. Modify the program in Figure 10-8 so it searches a list of sorted numbers in a data statement and test your program.
17. How many passes through the loop are required to search 2014 names using the program in Figure 10-11?
18. How many passes through the loops are required to search 24,619 names using the program in Figure 10-11?
19. How many passes through the loops are required to sort an array of 51 names using a bubble sort algorithm?
20. In maintaining a file in sorted form when the file must be updated daily (as in books), the following strategy is used. The updates (changes, additions, and deletions) are first sorted and then the file is gone through in order and changes are made in order also. Explain how this keeps the file sorted after the updates are made.
21. When files and programs are kept separately and named, the same program can be run against several files. Discuss the advantages of this.
22. When files and programs are kept separately in memory and named, separate programs can be written to sort, search, update, and perform statistical lists on the files. These programs can be tested using test files before usage. Discuss the advantages of this strategy.
23. Pick a program in the book which performs a statistical test (finding the standard deviation, for example) and explain how this program might be modified to process data in a file instead of a data statement.
24. Explain how the program in Figure 10-13(a) processed the data in Figure 10-13(b).
25. Add the name BOB WILLIAMS, student number 80, with grades of 79, 84, and 91, to the file in Figure 10-13(b) and show how the printout in Figure 10-13(c) would be changed by this addition.
26. If the file in Figure 10-13(b) was sorted on names instead of student number, what would the order be?
27. An organization has a number of employees and the employees' names and salaries are kept in a file in record format. The organization wishes to increase salaries by 7 percent and wants to know how much this will increase the total payroll. Write a program to find and print this value.
28. Modify the program written in Question 27 so that employees making $10,000–$15,000 get an 8 percent raise; employees making $15,000–$20,000 get a 7.5 percent raise, and employees making more than $20,000 get a 7 percent raise. Print the total of all raises and the total raise in each category.
29. We want to generate a sales report for top management. Sales data are placed in DATA statements as follows:

```
DATA _______, ____________, _____
      CITY    TOTAL SALES   AREA    East Coast   Midwest

                                    Pacific      South
```

Write a program to read the DATA statements and input a report as follows; however, list the cities in alphabetic order under their area name. The figures to the right of each city are the total sales from old DATA statements read relating to the city.

EAST COAST	
Philadelphia	45,699.00
New York	59,765.00
MIDWEST	
St. Louis	49,457.00
Chicago	96,457.00
SOUTHERN STATES	
Atlanta	74,694.00
Miami	69,476.00
PACIFIC COAST	
Los Angeles	60,744.00
San Francisco	73,699.00

Answers to Selected Questions

Chapter 1

3. (a) Applications
   (b) Systems
   (c) Applications
   (d) Systems
7. (a) Software
   (b) Hardware
   (c) Software
   (d) Software
   (e) Hardware

Chapter 2

5. The program in work space is operated.
7. In the order of their line numbers.

Chapter 3

3. A is given the value 7
5. (a) JACK
   BILL

(b) JAMES SUE

9. 2 4

2 4

Chapter 4

3. A + B, A*B, A + B*C + 4
15. (a) $X = (A/B) \times (C + D)$
    (b) $X = (A \times B)/D$
    (c) $X = \frac{B^3}{4}$
    (d) $D = (A/B)/C$
    (e) $K = (A - B) \times (C - D)$
    (f) $H = ((A \times B) \times C) + D$
17. NO; AB is illegal.
24. (A + 2)/X   12*X^2   + 1.3*A

Chapter 5

11.
```
10 INPUT N
20 IF N = 10 THEN 60
30 IF N = 20 THEN 80
40 PRINT "IT IS NEITHER TEN NOR TWENTY"
50 GO TO 90
60 PRINT "IT IS TEN"
70 GO TO 90
80 PRINT "IT IS TWENTY"
90 END
```
(No comments are used to conserve space.)

19.
```
40 IF A > = 6 THEN 200
```
21.
```
  2
  6
  8
  .
  .
  .
200
```
31.
```
10 LET N = 0
20 PRINT "YOUR NAME"
30 LET N = N + 1
40 IF N < = 5 THEN 20
50 END
```

Chapter 6

1. 2 4 6 8 10
4. 10 9.5 9 8.5 8 7.5 7 6.5 6 5.5 5
11.
```
 10 FOR I = 1 TO 20 STEP 5
 20 PRINT I,
 30 NEXT I
 40 FOR I = 25 TO 45 STEP 5
 50 PRINT I,
 60 NEXT I
 70 FOR I = 180 TO 200 STEP 5
 80 PRINT I,
 90 NEXT I
100 END
```
28.
```
10 READ A, B, C
20 LET X = (A + B + C)/3
30 PRINT "THE AVERAGE OF"; A; ","; B; "AND"; C;
40 PRINT "IS"; X
50 DATA 15, 39, 75
60 END
```

Chapter 7

1. (a) 7
   (b) 8
   (c) 9
3. LET B = INT(X + 0.5)
5. 80 LET P = INT(G*1000 + 0.5)/10
7. LET X = INT(57*P + 0.5)/100

Chapter 8

1. 10 LET A = INT(11*RND + 10) or INT(11*RND) + 10
3. (a) 10 LET B = INT(11*RND + 5)
   (b) 10 LET B = INT(− 5*RND − 5)
   (c) 10 LET B = INT(11*RND − 5)
   (d) 10 LET G = INT(49*RND − 16)
7. 610 PRINT "TO CONTINUE, TYPE PLAY. IF NOT, TYPE QUIT."
   630 IF V$ = "PLAY" THEN 110
15. 10 DEF FNC = 0.24639
17. 10 DEF FNX(Y) = INT(Y↑2 + 0.5)
21. 190 DATA 0, 10, 30, 0, 100

35.
```
10 PRINT "BOUNCE", "HEIGHT"
20 LET X = 10
30 FOR N = 1 TO 20
40 LET X = X*(2/3)
50 PRINT N, X
60 NEXT N
70 END
```

37.
```
10 PRINT "FRACTION", "DECIMAL"
20 DEF FNF(X) = 1/X
30 FOR N = 2 TO 20
40 PRINT "1/"; N, FNF(N)
50 NEXT N
60 END
```

Chapter 9

1.
```
10 LET S = 0
20 FOR N = 1 TO 3
30 READ A(N)
40 LET S = S + A(N)
50 NEXT N
60 DATA 4, 6, 9
```

3.
```
60 LET S = 0
70 FOR N = 1 TO 20
80 LET S = S + C(N)
90 NEXT N
```

5. Only integers may be used in DIM statements. Therefore the expression B(N) is illegal.

13.
```
10 FOR N = 1 TO 4
20 FOR X = 1 TO 3
30 READ D(N, X)
40 NEXT X
50 NEXT N
60 DATA 6, 4, 3, 5, 2, 1, 7, 3, 9, 6, 6, 2
```

17. The STOP statement causes a jump to the END statement of a program. It is usually used just before a subroutine to stop program operation before the subroutine is reached. The STOP statement in Figure 9-5 could be replaced with the following GO TO statement:

```
240 GO TO 350
```

21. Change statement 80 to:

```
80 IF ABS(Y - INT(Y)) < 0.001 THEN 120
```

Chapter 10

1. A *record* is a collection of all the items in a file relating to the same object or individual. A *file* is a collection of related records. To sort a file, usually a particular item in each record is chosen and the file is sorted by arranging the records in the file so that the selected items are in order; the selected item is called a *key*.
17. 11 (because $2'' \geqslant 2014$)
19. 1275 (because $51(51 - 50)/2 = 1275$)

References

Aho, A. V., Hopcroft, J. E., and Ullman, J. D., *The Design and Analysis of Computer Algorithms*, Addison-Wesley, Reading, Mass., 1974.

Alagic, S. and Arbib, M. A., *The Design of Well Structured and Current Programs*, Springer-Verlag, New York, 1978.

American National Standards Institute, *American National Standard for Minimal BASIC*, American National Standards Institute, 1403 Broadway, New York, N.Y., 1978.

Auerbach, I. L., Editor, *1979 Best Computer Papers*, North-Holland, New York, 1979, See Structured Programming in particular.

Baker, F. T., "System Quality Through Structured Programming," Proceedings 1972, Fall Joint Computer Conference, pp. 339–342.

Baker, F. T., "Chief Programmer Team Management of Production Programming," *IBM Systems Journal*, January 1972, pp. 56–73.

Baker, F. T., "Chief Programmer Teams: Principles and Procedures," Report No. FSC71-5108, IBM, Federal Systems Division, Gaithersburg, Md. 20760.

Baker, F. T. and Mills, H. D., "Chief Programmer Teams," *Datamation*, December 1973, pp. 62–68.

Bohm, C. and Jacopini, G., "Flow Diagrams, Turing Machines and Languages with Only Two Formulation Rules," *Communications of the ACM*, May 1966, pp. 366–371.

Brady, J. M., *The Theory of Computer Science*, Chapman and Holt, London, 1977.

Conte, S. D. and DeBoor, C., *Elementary Numerical Analysis*, McGraw-Hill, New York, 1980.

Dahl, O.J., Dijkstra, E. W., and Hoare, C. A. R., *Structured Programming*, Academic Press, New York, 1972.

Denning, P. J., Dennis, J. B., and Quality, J. E., *Machines, Languages and Computation*, Prentice-Hall, Englewood Cliffs, N.J., 1978.

Dijkstra, E. W., "Programming Considered as a Human Activity," *Proceedings of IFIP Congress 65*, Spartan Books, Washington, D.C., 1965.

Dijkstra, E. W., "GO-TO Statement Considered Harmful," Letter to the Editor, *Communications of the ACM*, March 1968.

Dijkstra, E. W., "The Structure of THE-Multiprogramming System," *Communications of the ACM*, May 1968, pp. 341–346. (Copyright 1968, Association for Computing Machinery, Inc., reprinted by permission.)

Dijkstra, E. W., "Structured Programming," Software Engineering Techniques, NATO Scientific Affairs Division, Brussels 39, Belgium, pp. 84–88.

Dock, V. T. and Essik, E., *Principles of Business Data Processing*, Science Research Associates, Chicago, Ill., 1978.

Gane, C. and Sarson, T., *Structured Systems Analysis*, Prentice-Hall, Englewood Cliffs, N.J., 1979.

Glass, R. L., *Software Reliability Guidebook*, Prentice-Hall, Englewood Cliffs, N.J., 1979.

Hopkins, M. E., "A Case for the GO TO," *Proceedings of the 25th ACM National Conference*, Vol. 2, 1972, pp. 787–790. (Copyright 1972, Association for Computing Machinery, Inc., reprinted by permission.)

Jensen, R. W. and Tomies, C. C., *Software Engineering*, Prentice-Hall, Englewood Cliffs, N.J., 1979.

Katzan, H., *Introduction to Computers and Data Processing*, D. Van Nostrand, New York, 1979.

Kemeny, J. G. and Kurtz, T. E., *BASIC Programming*, John Wiley, New York, 1971.

Kernighan, B. W. and Plauger, P. J., "Programming Style: Examples and Counterexamples," *ACM Computing Surveys*, December 1974, pp. 303–319.

Kernighan, B. W. and Plauger, P. J., *The Elements of Programming Style*, McGraw-Hill, New York, 1974.

Knuth, D. E., "Structured Programming with GO TO Statements," *ACM Computing Surveys*, December 1974, pp. 261–302.

Knuth, D. E., *The Art of Computer Programming*, Vol. 1, "Fundamental Algorithms," Addison-Wesley, Reading, Mass., 1968.

________, Vol. 2, "Seminumerical Algorithms," 1970.

________, Vol. 3, "Sorting and Searching," 1972.

Lien, D. A., *The Basic Handbook*, Compusoft Publishing, San Diego, Calif., 1978.

Linger, R. C., Mills, H. D. and Witt, B. I., *Structured Programming, Theory and Practice*, Addison-Wesley, Reading, Mass., 1979.

McGowan, C. L., and Kelley, J. R., *Top-Down Structured Programming*, Mason and Lipscomb, Chicago, Ill., 1975.

Mills, H., *Mathematical Foundations for Structured Programming*, Report FSC72-6012, IBM Corporation, Gaithersburg, Md., 1972.

Myers, G. J., *The Art of Software Testing*, John Wiley, New York, 1979.

Nevison, J. M., *The Little Book of Basic Style*, Addison-Wesley, Reading, Mass., 1978.

Parnas, D. L., "On the Problem of Producing Well Structured Programs," *Computer Science Research Review*, Carnegie-Mellon University, Pittsburgh, Pa., 1972.

Poole, L., and Borchers, M., *Some Common Basic Programs*, Osborne McGraw-Hill Book Company, Berkeley, Calif., 1977.

Rich, R. P., *Internal Sorting Methods Illustrated with PL/1 Programs*. Prentice-Hall, Englewood Cliffs, N.J., 1972.

Tansworth, R. C., *Standardized Development of Computer Software*, Prentice-Hall, Englewood Cliffs, N.J., 1979.

Tucker, A. B., *Text Processing*, Academic Press, London, 1979.

Wirth, N., "Program Development by Stepwise Refinement," *Communications of the ACM*, April 1971.

Wirth, N., *Systematic Programming*, Prentice-Hall, Englewood Cliffs, N.J., 1973.

Wirth, N., *Algorithms + Data Structure = Programs*, Prentice-Hall, Englewood Cliffs, N.J., 1976.

Wulf, W. A., "A Case Against the GOTO," Proceedings of the 25th ACM National Conference, Vol. 2, 1972, pp. 791–797. (Copyright 1972, Association for Computing Machinery, Inc., reprinted by permission.)

Yohe, J. M., "An Overview of Programming Practices," ACM Computing Surveys, December 1974, pp. 221–246.

Yourdon, E., *Techniques of Program Structure and Design*, Prentice-Hall, Englewood Cliffs, N.J., 1975.

Index

82 83 84 9 8 7 6 5 4 3 2